Backpacker
to
Nomad

Travel tales of adventure, discovery & despair!

Amit Vaidya

(Forever roaming the world)

Chapters

From the Author

Thank you so much for choosing to read and laugh about the birth of my crazy nomadic life – I hope you enjoy the read. These travel stories take you into the inner workings of my brain, deep thoughts, feelings, and perceptions, and shows the influence certain people had on this life-altering journey.

Disclaimer

All stories included are true, conversations are as true as memory serves. The travel companions are all real people, although some names and appearances have been changed to protect identities. All opinions included are my own.

Final note

It would mean the world to me if you could leave a review of the book once you have finished reading about my many misfortunes. As an independent author, I rely on reviews to get noticed, so it would be most appreciated.

To those who influenced this never-ending journey

Backpacker to Nomad

Travel tales of adventure, discovery & despair!

Amit Vaidya

(Forever roaming the world)

Plans? Sure, They Work!

The rustles coming from the thick foliage beneath the iron spiked fence would normally have scared the living daylights of me. However, tonight, the potential of snakes, giant spiders, lizards, baby dinosaurs, and who-knows-what-else lurking didn't matter. All that mattered was that my feet were firmly on the concrete ledge with my hands gripped tight around the fence's rusty spikes. My ear-to-ear smile was evidence that he came through—it was the perfect spot.

Anticipation, which had grown throughout the day, was reaching the climax, so much so the electric energy buzzing through the air almost felt physical. The source emanated from the dome of lights and noise around Sydney Harbour way down in the distance.

Although daylight had disappeared hours ago, the atmosphere only grew stronger by the minute. And apparently, so did the dampness on my body. Since arriving in Australia two weeks ago, not a day had gone by without leaking like a pierced hosepipe. It was the dead of the night and still warmer than most English summers. But the heat was nothing compared to the scolding giant ball of fire that made its presence known during the day. It loved playing a sickening game to torment us Brits. The game was hide and seek, not a friendly one, but a seek-and-destroy, "I'm-going-to-burn-you-to-death" type of game. Relentless in its sadistic pursuit. I may have been born with brown skin, but did the sun not realise I was from a part of the world where it only showed up for a couple of weeks a year? It had already turned me into a burnt chicken wing.

"Hey, Amit, you glad you stuck around and didn't lose your bottle like the other newbies did? Told you I knew where the best spot was," a southern English accent bragged.

His voice floated across the handful of other backpackers clinging onto the iron fence. It belonged to the entertainments manager from my hostel. His job was to simply take us out on pub crawls, get everybody wasted, and repeat again the next night, all week long. However, tonight was different, and he had stated all day that it was under control. Most newbies had lost faith throughout the day as the party in the hostel got wilder. Up until ten minutes ago, I was convinced this lifelong dream had slipped through my fingers. Will power, or more accurately, a lack of it, and drinking all day had overruled the numerous thoughts of leaving. There were times I cursed myself for not being more strong-minded. But here I was on this ledge, with just a couple of other newbies and a handful who had been in the hostel and in Sydney for months. While I was still settling in, Sydney and the hostel was home for them.

All of a sudden, strobe lights shot high into the night sky like laser beams, and instantly, goosebumps popped like popcorn from head to toe, blocking the leaking sweat ducts. The Opera House started to flash as did the equally iconic Sydney Harbour Bridge. A roar came from the thousands of people gathered around the harbour. Their voices travelled towards us, passing the dark void of the Royal Botanic Gardens, the naval base, up the hill, through the overlapping thick foliage—and whatever was hiding in it—to this secret viewpoint in Woolloomooloo.

How this main road below the notorious suburb of the Kings Cross remained empty of others was a mystery, but who cared. Voices perked up, not from those lined up along the fence but from within.

Are you kidding me? This is actually about to happen? Wake me up, this shit doesn't happen to people like me, professed one of them.

Yeah, sure, ok, it's not real, just imagining it, just like everything else in the last couple of weeks. Of course it's real, dumbass! All of it has been, so get used to it. This is the new life, the other one beamed back.

There were two of them, living rent free in my mind. While most people had one inner voice or an identifiable angel and demon on each shoulder, I was stuck with these two idiots. They constantly switched sides and bickered. Both popped up whenever they felt like it, said what they wanted, and disappeared again. It was a nightmare at times, but they had manifested throughout my life.

So, who am I?

I'm nobody, just an English guy from a life of sob stories (we all have them) who never had a sense of belonging and who sees life differently to most. I've felt more at home as a stranger in a strange country on the other side of the world than I ever have in my hometown. I don't know what it is, maybe because of how life growing up was back home, but I just couldn't fathom what society deemed as normal. That monotonous life of schooling, university, a secure career, a house, a car, a family life is not for me. I'm that guy who always questioned it but was deemed a disruption for wanting an actual logical answer. Personally, it made no sense to go through life checking those usual tick boxes. I craved escape from these shackles my whole life and felt like a free spirit trapped in a system with no way out.

Where I'm from, people like me take to the bottle or stick needles in their veins for escape, then there are those who simply just exist through life but don't live it.

As much as I hated that life, for twenty-six years, that's what I did—just floated through life, simply existing.

Forget about that, it's in the past, you don't need to think of it again—look at this, dreamt of this moment my entire life—shut up and enjoy it.

"This is actually happening!" the words escaped without my knowledge, but a giddiness started to flush through once again.

"It's a grand life, huh?" replied the soft voice next to me.

The familiar Irish accent belonged to Fiona. I had almost forgotten she was on the fence next to me since we arrived. She had also used those same words as we floated under the Harbour Bridge during the sunset boat party a week ago. Fiona was one of the residents in the hostel, she had been here for months and was someone I was becoming friends with. Before I could reply, the plug was pulled. Complete darkness blanketed the sky, the lights creating the bright dome disappeared. Thousands of gasps filled the air, along with whistles and cheers before silence descended.

Everything fell still, even the rustles below, as if they were waiting for this moment too. It lasted just a few seconds but felt like minutes. In an instant, the whole bridge shimmered momentarily in a blinding white before turning to complete darkness for a few more seconds. A wall of noise lifted as the number **ten** flashed up on the centre of the iconic bridge. Rust started to embed itself onto my palms from tightening the grip as the ten was replaced by a **nine** a second later. Goosebumps were forming on top of each other.

Eight… seven… six… five… four… three… two…

Every single voice from the harbour to the iron fence counted down in unison, my heart was about to explode—this was it, the moment I'd waited a lifetime to experience.

One!

A pause…

Darkness once more…

As one, all the voices roared and exploded just like the bridge did in a blaze of glory. The skyline erupted into a symphony of blinding colours, dancing in the night sky. Every colour of the spectrum bounced across the dark canvas, followed by glittery bombs. Roars and cheers lifted over the pounding music, the only words escaping mouths were overjoyed screams of "Happy new year!"

The Opera House, the tiny islands in front, the city skyscrapers, the theme park, and the other side of the bridge sent my senses into overload. Wave after wave of fireworks kept descending higher, louder, and brighter. There were more explosions than any Bonfire Night I'd ever experienced. The sky was on fire. Years of watching through a TV screen paled so much in comparison. The visual cacophony of vivid colours relentlessly exploding like atomic bombs and missiles was spellbinding with no sign of letting up.

I was utterly hypnotised by the dancing colours almost frozen to the rails. All the roars in the surrounding area turned into muffled noises and disappeared—it was as if I was there alone and deaf to the noise. My body was glued to the iron fence but not from fear of falling into the potentially snake-infested foliage below, but from feeling like a helium balloon. An emotion that I'd never felt before arriving in Australia but had become prominent here was back. It overtook everything, so light, warm, and fuzzy. It was addictive, and I was becoming hooked on it.

Is this what happiness actually feels like? asked an inner voice in a whisper.

Although my smile was permanently plastered wide, a wet slither started to trace a trail down the crevices between my nose and cheek. It rolled faster as it gained momentum, then another quickly followed as my knees nearly gave way as the realisation of this moment sank in.

To others, this might not be anything too special, but for me, there was no bigger accomplishment. For twenty-six years, life was a prison in a reality I wanted no part of, but these past couple of weeks, I'd felt alive, free, and dare I say it... genuinely happy. Finally living life, not just existing in it. A new year and the real start of this new reality.

More explosions erupted from above and behind the infamous Kings Cross, where my hostel was located, and joined in with the harbour and the rest of the city. It was a wake-up from my thoughts. As if the volume had been turned back up; music, chatter, screams of joy, and laughter filled every inch of the surrounding area. My eyebrows nearly ran back up into my jet-black short mohawk—dancing, bouncing bodies... hundreds, maybe thousands of them crammed into the street. The secret viewpoint was not so secret anymore. Residents and other backpackers covered every inch of road and footpath. There was so much energy in the air, bouncing from one person to the other. As cliché as it sounds, it was magical. The potential snakes, giant spiders, lizards, and who-knows-what-else were probably partying in the foliage behind too.

Finally, there was separation from the rusty fence as my feet landed back on the footpath, the impromptu street party begged for me to join in. The invitation was instantly accepted by embracing every stranger in arm's reach, wishing them a happy new year.

Euphoria had taken over and it coursed through every vein. Alcohol was being passed around freely and a lot rained down from above. A bushy-haired southern English beanstalk appeared through the crowd, along with a few others from the hostel, my arms were spread out as wide as the smile on my face.

"HAPPY NEW YEAR! BEST NIGHT OF MY FUCKING LIFE!" I bellowed.

As a group, a ball of hugs formed, bouncing and jumping together. From the very first day, it was clear to see those who had been here for months were a tight-knit group, almost like family. These long-termers, as they're known, had taken to a few of us newbies and started to become friends. It felt good to finally be around people on the same wavelength, who thought the same and saw life the same way. In a way, it was like we were all the oddballs or outcasts in our friend circles and even families back home. We didn't really belong there, but here we all came together no matter where in the world we were from.

Slowly, the group started to open up, dancing away, swigging alcohol as much as we could. My gaze swung back towards the harbour.

It's New Year's Eve and I'm in fucking Sydney! No matter how messy tonight gets, this will be burnt into the memory bank. Sydney, fucking Sydney—another dream come true.

There wasn't much I could claim to be an expert at in life, with no real skillset, but partying and getting wasted was definitely my forte. It was another reason why I seamlessly slipped into hostel life so easily. Before long, two beers were in hand and were chugged down to a dancing crowd and quickly replaced by more.

The dominant red Coca-Cola billboard shone like a beacon on the hill to signal the beginning of the Golden Mile that was Darlinghurst Road. Even in drunken states, it was unmissable, and for us newbies, it was the north star—a guide on how to get back to the hostel which was nestled in the heart of vice city as the Kings Cross was also known as. This famous stretch down Darlinghurst Road was referred to as vice city because of its notorious history. The seedy underbelly of Sydney's crime world had often ran through this road with biker gangs and gangsters running it. There was a history of bloodshed and gang wars dating back nearly a century. Now it was party central, a tourist attraction, and one of Sydney's main backpacker hubs, although crime was still present.

As most nights, it teemed with party revellers, hopping from one bar to another. Neon lights flashed and beamed out from the many strip clubs enticing would-be customers like flies. Security got heavy-handed with those who didn't adhere to the self-policing rules they set themselves. There was a different feel tonight though, more carnival like. Everybody was in a celebratory mood, and strangers flung their arms around each other instead of punches. We slithered through the dancing human sardines along the road and past the usual bars. It was a beeline straight towards the hostel, but my eyes were on the lookout.

It had been one of the first lessons learnt, taught by the long-termers—to keep my eyes peeled, no matter what drunken state I got in. Tonight would be a prime feeding frenzy for the local inhabitants of the Kings Cross. The homeless, drug addicts, and pickpockets were on the prowl, so much fresh meat for them. The street hookers who lined up outside bars and strip clubs were being overly friendly too, no doubt getting in on the act. But my pockets were secure.

Duck, bob, weave, don't make eye contact, cover pockets—that was the trick when any approached.

After what seemed like hours, we were free of the crowd, safely past McDonald's, and the Sugar Mill bar. The 'Funkhouse Backpacker Hostel' came into view once we ducked into the wide side street. It was an unfamiliar feeling having the corners of my lips constantly turned up, they naturally formed downwards, and smiling this much actually hurt. My cheek muscles were not used to it.

Guests, old and new, had grouped together outside, mingling and dancing like it was their last day on Earth. Drunk and high as a kite—some from drugs, some from pure euphoria of the night and welcoming in the new year. The reception area on the ground floor of the hostel had turned into a makeshift bar, the staircase and first-floor corridor were packed full of happy backpackers chatting away, and some hooking up.

The TV room had turned into a nightclub. I didn't even realise there were so many guests staying in the hostel. During the days, it was just the long-termers hanging around as most other guests were out 'exploring' the city and surrounding areas—something I should have been doing. But becoming friends with the long-termers meant one thing—partying, nursing hangovers, and partying again, not that I was complaining. One long-termer even had a go at me on my third day for going out to explore the city once, stating, "That's not what we do here."

Music pounded from the rooftop terrace like an open invitation, as it did every day and night. The party had started in the morning and was still going strong. The fairy lights surrounding the rooftop gave it just enough light to see the dancing bodies bouncing over every inch of the orange rooftop tiles.

The sea of bouncing bodies, waving arms, kisses, and embraces added warmth to the atmosphere. Without a single care in the world, nobody was doing anything but enjoying themselves. It felt so good to feel and be part of such a positive vibe and having that feeling of belonging. I belonged here, with these people. I finally knew how feeling like being home was like. But I couldn't get used to it too much—other plans were on the horizon

"Happy new year!" I could barely hear her words as Fiona leapt and wrapped her arms around me.

"Happy new year! This is crazy! Fucking insane. I love it. I love this city! I love this new life!" My arms clung to her as my head popped up, taking in and soaking up the brightly coloured sky.

"And ye still wanna leave all this already? Ye just got here, ye don't even know the city yet. This is just a taster. Just stay with us!"

"I'd love to, you guys are awesome, but no chance. All the partying has been great but I'm here to travel, got an iron-clad plan, and day after tomorrow, I'm off to Adelaide."

* * *

As if a shark violently erupted and crashed through a calm ocean surface, my body leapt, narrowly missing the frame of the bunkbed from the bottom bed.

"Fuck! I need to go. I NEED to leave like NOW!"

The abrupt announcement only prompted the slightest murmur from under a mountain of duvets as a pale, skinny, freckled arm slid out through the top bunk rail.

"Shh, too early… go back to bed will ye."

The arm belonged to Fiona, who had become my roommate in the hostel for the past six months now.

"No. I can't. I need get out of here. It's August, I've been here eight months! I ain't going back to England or my old life! I've royally fucked this up. I need to find farm work and I need to go now!"

So many clothes, bags, and rubbish covered most of the floor, I had no idea where to start collecting or even finding my own stuff. It wasn't long before tectonic plates shifted, the mountain of duvets rumbled and caused a volcanic eruption. Her small freckly face emerged with a growl.

"Wha' are ye on about? It's too early, I'm still drunk. Go back to bed," she huffed.

Her plea was ignored as my toes danced around the mess, the Xbox, the controllers, trying not to knock over the wireless heater. Why did we have a wireless heater? Because Sydney got stupidly cold in the winter—who knew? Our dorm room was a long-termers' room, and that is what I had become. Short-term guests were not allowed to stay in long-termers' rooms in this hostel, mainly because these rooms had turned into our mini homes. I had turned from newbie to long-termer months ago when my iron-clad plan went up in smoke, mostly due to sinking deep into hostel party life, a comfort zone, and also running out of money so many times. Our third roommate hadn't been seen for a few days. But he was the reason we had a widescreen TV, Xbox, wireless heater, and electric blankets. Let's just say he was the go-to guy for certain things in the hostel.

Where the fuck is all my stuff and where's my backpack? fumed an inner voice, while checking the fourth ownerless top bunk, which housed the spare TV and more clothes—mainly Fiona's.

"You realise I was meant to leave in the new year… the new year, and I'm still stuck here! I need to find farm work. Plus, everything that's happened recently with… well, you know… I'm NOT going back to England, fuck that!"

"Amit, that's grand and, yeah, I know what, but it's ye own doing. Are ye seriously doing this now? I hate ye. Pretend to sort ye life out later. We both know ye ain't going anywhere."

She was right, there had been so many pitiful attempts to leave to go travelling before, only to find myself utterly unmotivated to leave or with a lack of funds to go.

Truth be known, most of the time it was because of having too much fun with friends who had turned into family. Anytime the thought of moving on appeared, it was overruled. There had been times I even forgot the reason I came to Australia—to travel. That was until a few weeks ago when old demons started to rear their ugly heads. It turned out I didn't leave them behind in England, they had just been lurking in the shadows, waiting for the opportune moment to strike.

And strike they did, plunging their hooks deep, bringing out a side of me I thought I'd left behind in England. One that derailed my teenage years and early twenties. They had started to ruin the amazing time I'd been having. The freedom in this new reality was closing in, feeling trapped again. Finding farm work was priority to stay another year, but escape was needed before the dream really turned into a nightmare. I guess those days I spent feeling sorry for myself—when things weren't going well, when I didn't have a penny to rub, or knew where the next meal was coming from—opened the door for them to find me. The reality of backpacking, or more accurately, hostel life was much different to what was advertised. Well, for me it was.

"I need to think, I need a coffee, a smoke. How do I get out? Fuck, I don't have that much money. Doesn't matter, got to get out of here, soon."

A pillow wrapped around my face and momentarily blinded me. Apparently, I hadn't used my inside voice.

"Get out!" she shrieked. Then her voice softened, "Can I have me pillow back please?"

I returned her pillow before taking my leave. Just as the door opened, I was greeted by the wry smile of the hostel owner, Marcus.

"Good, Amit, you're awake. My office, now."

Bollocks, he fucking knows. Quick, think of excuses or I'll be leaving one way or another.

I knew what was coming and so did the knot in my stomach. Forget being a twenty-seven-year-old on the other side of the world—this felt like being a seven-year-old summoned to the head teacher's office for being naughty, something I had been accustomed to in my school days.

"Can we talk outside? I need a smoke," I asked as the prickles of my freshly shaved head were felt by my palms.

"No. My office now." His voice was stern.

'Yup he knows, I'm fucked!'

The Funkhouse Hostel was aptly named. A vibrant, bright party hostel, and as each famous cartoon character painted on the doors passed, the only door without a mural got closer—his office. He had a reputation for being a hardhead, but that was normally just with guests who passed through. With most of us long-termers, he relaxed a little, mainly because we did odd jobs around the hostel for him. However, judging by his tone, this was not a friendly chat.

"You know what this is about, don't you?" he asked as he stepped around his meticulously tidy desk. I didn't have a chance to reply as he carried on while I sat down. "Before you start giving me excuses, watch this."

The CCTV video came on from a few nights ago on the rooftop. It showed me and a friend sitting up there alone, drinking from a six-pack of beer. One of the newer hostel guests appeared. We didn't know him, nor care to know him, but he said something I didn't like. I was hungover and my fuse had been getting shorter in recent weeks as the inner demons got stronger. He started to wind me up, and then reached for a beer without asking. Before his hand could touch the bottle, his body bounced back, slamming against the table he sat on, bounced up, and was flattened again, courtesy of my forehead—twice. There was no need for it but it happened and it wasn't the first time either. The violent outbursts had started to become a regular occurrence, which is another reason I needed to leave.

The video was paused, Marcus's saucepan eyes glared a hole through me, nostrils flared like a bull, "What the fuck was that about, Amit? I give you guys so much leeway with things that happen here, but violence I will not tolerate!"

Again, he didn't let me explain and carried on as I sat there on the opposite side of the desk just nodding.

"Where did that come from? I know you, apart from running your mouth too much, you're not violent. What happened?"

Shows how much you really know me then, I've always been angry and violent, just hid it here until the last couple of weeks. Right now, I'm considering flying over the desk to head-butt you for no reason whatsoever.

Shut the fuck up, idiot, replied the other inner voice. Thankfully, those words did not come out.

"I'm sorry. I know I shouldn't have reacted like that, but he provoked me. He just kept pushing and I reacted. I shouldn't have. I should know better," is what I actually said.

His demeanour changed, the anger resided, but was replaced with a look he didn't want to wear.

"Was it race related?" he asked, clearing his throat and shuffling papers from the side.

There's our way out, use it. YES, say, "yes, it was". It's our get-out-of-jail-free card. Use it!

"No, it wasn't. Nothing like that. The guy was just a dick, he pissed me off, I was hungover, and I reacted without thinking." I shook my head, overruling my inner voice's plea.

Idiot! Should have used it, fucks sake!

It's not the way I was raised nor how I see myself. Using the race card was never an option.

Relief swept over his face and the normal stern look was back. He wasn't going to admit it, but it was clear he did not want to deal with a race issue in his hostel.

"Luckily for you, he checked out this morning so we're just going to leave it there. But if there are any more incidents, then I'm sorry but you're out."

OK, I definitely need to leave now; he doesn't know about the other two incidents. I need to leave before he does find out.

I agreed with him and the inner voice. In recent weeks, I had become hot-headed, temperamental, and a violent pressure cooker, blowing up for no reason and to people who didn't deserve it. It used to happen a lot in England, but back then, there was a reason for it. Here, there were no excuses.

As soon as the conversation was over, my legs bolted down to the ground floor, asking the receptionist for the rural farm work book. It listed all the places I could get work to obtain a second-year visa. In other words, places I could do slave-labour for three months to not get shipped back to England. As she looked for it, I stepped out the front door with a cigarette primed to be lit.

My feet had already started to walk towards Darlinghurst Road. Although it was a dreary day as usual, tourists of all nationalities, some in scores of tour groups, scoured the main road. Most relentlessly took pictures as tour guides filled them in on the bloody history of the Kings Cross. Some of them clung on tight to cameras hanging around their necks after spotting the homeless and drug addicts wandering around like zombies. It always bought a smile to my face to see the reactions of people the first time they came onto the Kings Cross, it wasn't too dis-similar to mine. That first day driving up this road, I wondered what type of hell-hole I had arrived in. I wanted to check out before I even checked in, thinking it was a huge mistake. But even with the predicament I've found myself in, I'm glad not to have left—but now I definitely needed to.

My hood lifted just a little, spotting a baby dinosaur hoovering up the floor in competition with the overweight pigeons as I passed McDonald's—even those freakishly long beaks and dinosaur claws belonging to Ibis didn't bother me anymore and I carried on to the coffee shop.

With a coffee in hand and the Coca-Cola billboard in sight, which sometimes felt like the signal for the edge of the world because the rest of city was not like this mini eco-system, I turned back towards the hostel but stopped for a second to take it all in. This could potentially be the last time I walk through the Golden Mile.

But how the fuck am I going to find farm work just like that? It needed to be planned months ago, moaned an inner voice.

I have four months left on the working holiday visa, I need to find it in the next couple of weeks or it's going to be too late, replied the other one who was much calmer.

Ok, go back, get the book, start looking, and just get ready to leave, anywhere, somewhere, by the end of the week at the latest.

A scraping noise felt like it was getting louder from behind before I could reach the hostel. The noise had become a familiar one over the past few months. I turned back, nodding my head towards the goon warrior. He was a local homeless guy who always carried a half-empty bag of goon, hence the name. Goon was the cheapest, nastiest Australian wine which came in a foil bag—better for a pillow than drinking, but because it was so cheap, it was a backpacker's go-to drink.

"Giz a dolla."

"Nah, not got a dollar to give. Here, have a smoke," I replied calmly.

Our interactions now were so different to when I first fearfully stepped out of the shuttle bus onto this street. Back then, the sight of him made me clutch onto my backpack and avoid him like he had the plague. It was the same for most of the homeless, but over time, they became familiar, like everything else here. These past eight months, I've got to see how certain dynamics work with the locals, tourists, and backpackers too. How the interactions change, how shop owners charge different prices, where to go for cheaper items, and tourists getting ripped off. The eco-system of the Kings Cross has been quite the education.

As soon as I headed back inside, the book was grabbed off the reception desk, and with a coffee in hand, I shot up to the sanctuary of the rooftop terrace. I jumped under the veranda which covered the bench running the full length of the back wall. Much to my surprise, Fiona was already sitting there hiding under a hoodie and a blanket.

"What you doing up here?" I asked.

"Some dickhead woke me up—made a commotion, going on about leaving. And I couldn't fall back to sleep. So, I came up here."

"What a twat, how rude of him."

"Exactly, he's so selfish. He should know by now to deal with his problems later in the day and not when people are trying to sleep off a hangover."

"What are you going to do? Can't win with some people."

I joined her on the bench, sliding into my usual spot as heavy balls of water started to explode on the orange floor tiles like water balloons.

"What am I going to do?" My brain felt like it was in a tumble dryer.

"Well, first of all, say, 'sorry, Fiona, for waking you up,' then what are ye options?"

I shrugged, and instead of concentrating on the problem at hand, as my back sank into the bench, my mind went in a different direction, recalling a memory.

"I just remembered the first time I ever came up here. It was my very first day, so spun out, seeing all the weird shit along the Kings Cross."

"Did the newbie thing no doubt?" she sniggered.

"Yup, walked out there, felt the full force of the sun, was about to walk off, but saw Thompson sitting right here playing DJ and drinking alone—he handed me a beer and that was that."

"Yeah, I remember ye sitting here that evening, and we were all like, 'Who is this guy, why's he not sitting with the other newbies?'" She laughed.

"I arrived in Australia as a solo traveller, and eight months later, I'm still fucking here like an idiot and haven't solo travelled yet."

"Maybe just think it through a little more. When do ye need to get it done by?"

"Need it in the next few weeks and need it done by Christmas or I get shipped back to England. I do not want to go back. You know, people thought I'd be back after a couple of weeks," I replied as my eyes turned back to the exploding droplets.

"But ye didn't, and ye've had the time of ye life and made amazing friends like me."

My hand wrapped around the hot coffee, but the hood of my jumper slipped over my head as I nodded back.

"OK, I didn't go home, but I ran out of money so many times. I've had to literally sweep up shit for a bed before."

"Oh, yeah, I forgot all about that... ye stank of sewage for days. I can't believe he made ye do that. What, for a week's rent?"

She burst out laughing like one of the raindrops hitting the orange floor tiles while waving her hands in front of her nose.

"I should have checked out on the 2nd of January like I was meant to." I huffed.

Things had not gone to plan since New Year's Eve, it had been problem after problem. Much of it was my own fault, but weirdly, at the same time, I was having the time of my life. It made no sense.

"Well, ye did only arrive with £600. What did ye expect? Especially the way we party. Ye remember we had a twenty-four-hour party cycle?"

"Yeah, I know. Of course I remember, I was in it most of the time. There have been some amazing times, that's for sure." I laughed, pulling out a smoke. "But then there were times I couldn't even afford smokes, how the fuck have I survived this long?"

"By picking up all those odd jobs. Ye told us before ye enjoyed them, not what ye would do back home and yer learnt new skills. Anyway, why is going back to England so bad? Ye never talk about yer past or home life."

"Yup, that's how it's gonna stay. My past is my past. That life, that old reality, doesn't exist and there's no way I can go back to it. And that's why I need farm work."

"Well, best get looking then, ain't ye?" She pushed the book closer to me and opened it up.

My eyes dropped to the book. She was right, I did need to start looking.

Me, Myself, and I

Sweet, bitter, fruity, and chocolatey aromas floated in the air, getting stronger with each step. The clatter of glasses, cups, and mugs joined the symphony of whistles and hisses from all the different types of coffee machines and presses from the hole-in-the-wall coffee shops all squashed together. The smells wafted from every direction and orders were screamed out to waiting customers who filled the tight laneway as I tried to squeeze through.

Every time a hiss of steam blew, it was like a calling to stop for a coffee—I needed to but there was just no space. All the stumpy wooden stools and tables outside seemed like they were made for children, but were full of adults either savouring large bowls of unusual coffees or snapping back espressos like a shot of alcohol. This was coffee heaven and, having been in Melbourne for only a few hours after my first overnight bus experience, I was desperate for one. However, whatever was written on the chalkboard menus seemed unrecognisable—none sounded like coffees I knew.

What in the blue hell is an affogato? Or a ristretto? A cortado? Where's the normal stuff like flat white?

My fancy coffee knowledge was limited to latte, cappuccino, mocha, or Frappuccino. Every menu was a head-scratch; did this just show how uncultured I actually was?

One of the holes-in-the-wall had some space, but as I tried to decipher the menu, the space in front of me filled and turned into the Wall Street trading floor. The bigger the crowd grew, the further I was pushed back and inadvertently into the human train of customers for the opposite hole-in-the-wall. One after the other, ordering, waiting to the side, picking up the drink, and leaving. The glistening pastries on the counter caught my attention as I waited for my turn to be served. But I needed to focus on the menu on the wall behind them.

"What canna get ya?" asked the soft Australian voice behind the counter.

It was a simple question, but for some reason, internal panic buttons were smashed, the white chalked words on the blackboard behind her turned into a blur.

Think, idiot. Quick, think quick. Just get a coffee, don't try and look clever in front of all these people.

"Just a coffee please."

"Yeah, what type?" Her eyes rolled as if to say, *No shit, idiot.*

"Err, a cappuccino—no, actually, an affogato please. Yup, an affogato."

"Take out or sittin' in?'

"Yeah, err, sitting in."

It was like I'd never ordered a coffee in my life. She still didn't look impressed and pointed to the little wooden table and stool outside pressed to the wall.

Wait… what? What did I just order? asked one of my inner voices as there was a bigger drop to the small seat than I had anticipated.

No bloody clue, but why did I panic like that? Like I've never been in a coffee shop before? That was weird. Ahh, fuck it, when in Rome and all that. Let's see what I've ordered. Solo travel life, right? Opening the mind, experiencing and trying new things, experimenting with the unknown and discovery. Time to get cultured up.

The laneway was manic, like a herd of buffalo crushing through a valley, but stopping for a fancy coffee along the way. It wasn't a place to be if claustrophobia was an issue.

The clanging and banging of plates and cups seemed louder from the small table. My back pressed against the wall, trying to get comfortable while taking it all in. This was Melbourne, coffee capital of Australia, and I was a solo traveller—finally.

Yeah, about that. Just a little question… how do we actually solo travel? Like what exactly are we thinking of doing here?

It was a valid point, I had arrived in Australia by myself, it was the first time in my life I'd been anywhere alone, let alone the other side of the world. Back then, I was prepared to travel solo, but from the moment I arrived, there hadn't been a single day spent alone—until today. Eight months on and it was the first of not knowing a single soul in a brand-new city and ordering who knows what.

So, solo traveling in a new city. Guess we do touristy stuff? Find activities, book some tours, wander around, explore. That's what people do, right?

A much-needed cigarette was lit and pursed between my lips as my thoughts drifted to the way I left Sydney, and how it was only a few days ago realisation hit to find farm work and I got away before the owner found out about the other head-butting incidents. Sydney, though, along with the Kings Cross and the Funkhouse Hostel, was in the past. This was a reset of sorts. and this was my chance for a fresh start.

Yeah, no more random head-butting incidents, no more getting angry and frustrated... get rid of that shit, those inner demons, they can fuck right off too.

There was a reason I had chosen to stay in a cheap budget motel and not jump straight into a new hostel—to spend a few days alone. I needed to remove myself from people for a while, not be social, just look internally to why those inner demons came out... why did I become angry, violent, and frustrated like I used to in England?

"Enjoy. Ya can pay when ya done. Would ya like a croissant?" said the same voice from behind the counter, who bought the drink over.

My eyebrows tried to join together from the sight of what was meant to be a coffee sitting on the table.

What the fuck is this?

Idiot, you ordered a dessert, not a coffee.

It was a glass of vanilla ice cream with some black coffee poured over it. No doubt it would be refreshing in the summer, but this was winter. It was no wonder she gave me such a weird look when I ordered. In the panic, trying to look like I knew what I was doing, it proved just how clueless I was. I nodded at her request for a croissant but also ordered a cappuccino too.

What a waste of money. This is gonna cost a bomb.

My eyes averted from the ice cream to the map of Melbourne the motel had provided. Not only did I not know what to do and see, but I had no idea where I actually was in the city. This first day was going swimmingly well.

A croissant sitting on a white plastic plate and a welcome cappuccino joined the party as the waitress asked if there was anything else I needed.

Yeah, can I get a refund because I'm an idiot and had no idea I ordered a dessert and not a coffee?

I shook my head as she hurried away and my eyes returned to the map, while ripping into the flakiest croissant in the world.

Yup, that's the one, make a mess everywhere, show people I have no etiquette along with not having a clue.

Forget that I need to make a plan, not wasting days doing nothing. And I need to find farm work. Remember, that is the main reason I'm here.

The train of humans slamming down shots of espresso slowed down just a little, but unlike normal coffee shops, nobody else was just hanging around or relaxing. Once their shot was done, they were gone, and all the clattering and hissing made it hard to concentrate. The simplest thing to do was ask the waitress for help, to get some local knowledge on what was worthwhile doing in Melbourne, but ego—well, embarrassment—was stopping me. To save face, I wolfed down the ice cream, freezing my interior. Crumbs and flakes from the croissant offered an open invitation to pigeons that flocked to the café, nipping away—some venturing in before being shooed back out.

I could feel it, I was going to be asked to leave for being so messy. It made no sense why there was such a mess being made nor why I was feeling so jittery. The little map was open with a list of suggestions for things to see and do, such as, 'Graffiti around the city; visit the Aquarium; explore St Kilda, go to gigs in Fitzroy and Collingwood, visit the Yarra River; head to South Bank; have a flutter at the Casino; watch an Aussie Rules football game at the MCG; travel down Great Ocean Road; see the Twelve Apostles.

It just lists touristy stuff.

But that's what I was, and tourists do touristy things.

Before I arrived in Australia, I was tempted to buy an Australia travel guide, but having seen the size of them, it was a good decision not to add another brick to my already bursting-at-the-seams backpack. I had forgotten just how much I packed—this was first time since arriving in Australia that I even carried my backpack with me. With a few things circled and the coffee, dessert, and croissant finished, it was time to be a tourist for the day. First of all, though, it was time to see if my daily budget was blown.

It was!

Nearly $30 had slipped through my fingers on what was meant to be just a simple coffee. It might not be a lot for locals and tourists stopping at these coffee shops, but for a guy on a tight budget, it was like three days' worth of spending. That's a lie, I spent way more on alcohol in an afternoon in Sydney, but this was different. I wasn't working anymore, I wasn't based in familiar surroundings where running out of money didn't really matter much because it could replenish at any given moment. I was solo now as a budget traveller, so every penny counted, and I needed to learn to cut the spending down to a minimum. Money management, or rather lack thereof, had always been an issue throughout my life. I've always been broke, but never liked to show it and spent too much—sometimes without realising and other times out of stupidity. That needed to stop, especially away from the comfort zone of the Sydney hostel.

With the knife dug in and twisted, pain screamed from my wallet as I reluctantly paid the bill and it was back into the herd of coffee addicts while pigeons went to town on the mess I left behind. The easiest option was to follow the flow of the hordes of locals and camera-clad tourists through one laneway to the other. Some became extremely tight, where it turned into single file, while others widened. The hole-in-the-wall cafés became fewer and further between and were replaced by an explosion of vibrant colour. Every inch of concrete was hidden behind layers of street art and graffiti. Most of the amazing work looked like it belonged in a gallery, produced by extremely talented artists with such vivid imaginations. It definitely didn't look like the crappy tags and amateur graffiti on walls back in my home town.

As the cafés disappeared into the distance, so did the clanging of mugs, plates, and glasses. Coffee machine hisses turned into melodic soft music as buskers strummed their guitars and softly sang out—some better than others. A mellowness drifted through the air, it was hard not to be captivated by it while drifting through the graffiti-covered spaghetti maze. Cameras clicked relentlessly, capturing the amazing and vivid artwork, from bamboozling patterns to lifelike portraits of famous celebrities to cartoon characters.

A crowd had assembled around one piece towards the end of a tight laneway, it wasn't obvious why until a man carrying an orange flag mentioned it was by Banksy—the most famous anonymous street artist in the world. He said it was a fresh piece, it wasn't there yesterday. That meant Banksy was in Melbourne at the same time as all of us. He could have been in the crowd and nobody would even know, which stirred a little excitement. The crowd moved on, following the orange flag-bearer, who kept pointing out buildings, their history, what they were and are now, as well as providing information on more street art. It became clear he was leading a tour.

Should I get involved? It's the thing solo travellers and tourists do, right?

I was slightly curious about the walking tour, having never done one in Sydney and lingered behind to see what he said. It didn't last long, my interest waned quickly; in all honestly, it was like he just memorised a script. These tours were meant to be free, but at the end, the tour guides force people to tip them. That's how they earn their money.

Give me a couple of weeks, I could do the job. Just point, carry a flag, and read a script.

Before he realised there was a tag-along, I peeled away into another alleyway.

Hours had passed by as I just wandered around the city, hopping from one place to another. It felt good though. In fact, it was quite liberating; calming and something I could get used to, even if it was only a few hours into my solo travel life.

Melbourne felt like it had a much calmer vibe than Sydney, a slower pace, and that helped me feel at ease in a strange new city. A familiar baked smell wafted through my nostrils and it didn't take long for my eyes to lock on. The traditional Australian eatery, that was Pie Face.

No, not today, I want a proper meal tonight. If I'm going to be solo travelling, I need to learn to eat and go into bars alone, especially if I want to see live gigs.

I had never sat and eaten a proper meal or drank in a bar alone before, it was just something never done where I'm from. In Sydney, I cooked in the hostel most of the time, but if I ate out, it was with other people or I would bring a take-away back to the hostel. It was definitely never something I had done in England.

Darkness had replaced daylight and, for now, it remained dry, but temperatures had plummeted. Apparently, according to the stunning black-and-white graffiti mural on the wall, this was Fitzroy. With the streetlights pointed towards it, the mural stood out more than it would have during the day. Friends in Sydney had raved about this place… well, those who fell in love with this city. Melbourne and Sydney divided a lot of opinions—there were staunch, almost tribal supporters for both. Those that loved Sydney hated Melbourne, and vice-versa. After just a day, Sydney was still home, but the appeal of Melbourne was evident, especially with its calming vibes, which did wonders from the way I felt in Sydney towards the end.

Here I was, a stranger in a new city, gliding through the mellow atmosphere that spread a calmness through me. It's amazing how just being taken out of an environment can change a mood so drastically in such a short space of time. I didn't know a single soul and was wandering the streets all day, getting lost from one alleyway to another, it felt so freeing. Fitzroy turned it up a little from the city centre. A cocktail of musicians and street performers filled the streets in front of quirky shops and odd art, from bright-yellow painted bicycles to unusual sculptures. People floated down the street with a smile, the atmosphere was infectious, and even I wore a natural grin. Another crowd had formed on the corner, but this time, there wasn't a guy holding up an orange flag. Music pounded out as a solo guitarist sang famous cover songs. He was very talented.

Before I knew it, my body was in sync with the music, moving to the strums like the rest of the crowd. I was falling for Melbourne's charms—its courtship was intoxicating. It was as if people just let go of their inhibitions, very bohemian-like. This was exactly what I needed after how I had felt over the past few months, either my demons *were* left behind in Sydney or Melbourne was soothing them.

Time had slipped by, but the music got louder down the main street. People poured out on to the street from the many bars lining one side of the road. Live bands started to play, gigs were going on, adding a student element to the bohemian flair. Most of the little open-front bars, much like the cafés earlier, were filled with a mixture of locals, students, and backpackers, chatting and laughing away. A rock band played in one of them, the music was quite alluring.

But…

My body froze up as I tried to enter. I tried again but couldn't move. As if an invisible force field was stopping me. Others walked in and out, some looked over as I tried once again, but I couldn't do it. Not to embarrass myself too much, I just walked away.

What's going on?

Nope… not doing it. Not going into a busy bar alone looking like a loser with people staring at me.

Nobody was looking, and even if they are, who gives a fuck? We'll make friends inside, come on.

I do and nope. Try all you want—I'm not letting us go in.

I laughed it off and headed towards another bar. I wanted a beer and to listen to some live music after such a great day. Again, I forced myself, but my body was just not playing ball. My inner voice had taken control and wouldn't let me go in. I tried another quieter bar, but just carried on walking by like I wasn't interested. That was a lie, I was.

Come on. I need to do it. Dive in and get rid of the paranoia and fear.

Nope, not today. Not gonna happen.

Stubborn, insecure fuck. Tomorrow, though, I am going to a bar.

Sure.

It didn't sound convincing at all. The main street disappeared as I stepped on to a quieter one looking for a place to eat instead. One looked quite appealing, a Mexican street food place that was cheap enough. After studying the colourful menu almost forensically, I went to step inside but the same thing happened again.

No, don't like this either, just go back to the motel.

All my confidence had been drained. I didn't put up a fight—fear, anxiety, or paranoia had gripped hard, taking the loss for the night, I headed back to the metro station to go back to the motel.

* * *

Low-hanging dark clouds started to form, turning the wind bitter. I waited along with a number of winter-coat-clad people for the old traditional tram to St Kilda, across the road from the famous Flinders Street station. Melbourne had turned on the charm once more after whatever it was that happened last night. It didn't make any sense—I hadn't had an issue sitting in a café alone this morning having breakfast and fruitlessly trying to get in touch with farmers. There weren't any issues while I explored the city, winding through Melbourne's quirky and odd graffiti-clad buildings. It was a funky city, no doubt, from the old French and Italian architecture, European-style layout of the tight laneways to the funky modern buildings like the Federation Square building behind me. The shell of the building was like a 3D jigsaw piece stacked together, but it fitted with Melbourne's personality. As did this weather, the temperature felt like it was dropping by the second, it was a far cry from starting the day hiding behind sunglasses and wearing nothing but a t-shirt.

Those of us waiting for the tram started to bunch up a little closer, just like the penguins I'd seen in the aquarium earlier. It was the first time since being in Australia that I had actually seen sharks, stingrays, all kinds of tropical fish and penguins. Although the gloss was taken off a little as I was seeing them in an enclosed place, it was a better experience than my other attempt to entertain myself today.

It turns out it's always best to check when a sporting season is finished before strutting up to the ticket counter of one of the world's most famous stadiums or risk looking like a clueless idiot. As I did. Standing in awe of by far the biggest stadium I'd ever seen, I casually asked when the next Aussie Rules footy match would be played at the MCG, which was met by laughter from the lady behind the counter. The season had finished three weeks before. Other than a stadium tour, which was way out of my budget, there was no way of getting in. Speaking of budgets, it seemed like most things were out of my price range—the joys of being me. I had enquired about some tours and either they took one look at me and hiked the prices up or they were only meant for tourists with loaded pockets. It seemed like the aquarium and exploring the city myself were the only options. It's times like this I hated being in the financial situation I was always in. Broke! Life was testing me, it liked to fuck with me when it was bored, and it seemed like this was one of those occasions.

St Kilda was the main backpacker beach area and it was time to find a hostel. While it had been great having my own space and private room, the budget wouldn't allow for it much longer. This was another cost-cutting effort, learning to manage my money. Backpackers filled the streets, most of them hiding under hoodies as I was, but some carried surfboards, even in this weather they had spent the day out on the waves. Surfing was something I had zero desire to get into, mostly because I prefer admiring the sea from a distance and not getting in it—another fear of mine.

My mind quickly flashed back to the first night in Sydney, drunkenly talking about wanting to learn to surf, saying it to anybody who listened but having no intention of actually going through with it. I just wanted to sound fearless and up for anything, to sound cool and for people to like me. That was a huge insecurity, not being liked. It wasn't as if I liked everybody, in fact, I was quite brutal in telling people how I felt about them; but it was as if *I* needed to be liked by everyone.

My feet started to drag along the concrete slabs, watching as groups of backpackers laughed while passing by. It reminded me of the group I'd left behind in Sydney. Although I was enjoying being alone, there was a part of me that wished they were with me too. It was funny, I missed the friends from Sydney after just a couple of days, but didn't miss any from England. I'd barely spoken to any of them since arriving in Australia. It was like this was a completely new reality and the old one didn't exist—just a faint memory as if a fading dream.

*

I stopped outside a bar with a live gig going on, I wanted to try my luck again, and with it being a backpacker area, it should be easier to go in and make friends. There seemed to be a good vibe emanating from it and I lit another cigarette.

Come on, I can do this. It's not hard. I've seen people eating and drinking alone all day with confidence. Just walk in and pretend it's a café. There is no fear. There is nothing stopping me but myself. Come on, this is no big deal.

As soon as I had smoked the cigarette, I willed my feet towards the large blue double doors, opening one up, one foot lifted, that same feeling from last night was present, but I fought against it, pushing through.

No, you're not going to win, I'm doing this.

I was in, but beads of sweat dripped down my back and my body had turned into a quivering leaf against a hurricane.

Abort, abort, abort! Turn around, get out of here, people are looking at us.

Don't you dare abort. Quick, to the bar, order a beer, quick!

Nope—can't do it—too many people.

That defeats the object, idiot, keep fighting.

The back and forth from within was relentless, I needed every ounce of strength to push through. The voice grew louder, trying to dissuade me. Fear tried to grip tighter, paranoia tried to suffocate me while anxiety clung to my legs, trying to stop them getting closer to the bar. I pushed through and practically jumped to the bar before they could take over.

I did it, my arms felt the bar top, eyes instantly scanned around the small, open, but dark, floor. Nobody was watching, nor were they concerned that I was alone. I ordered a beer and gulped it down as soon as the barman placed it in front of me.

Just calm down, there is nothing to be scared of. Nobody is watching. Nobody cares if I'm alone. Look, they're all just getting on with their night.

I care! They are watching, let's get the fuck out of here NOW!

No, I'm here now and staying for another.

NO!

My legs felt like I had guzzled ten pints. The force became too strong, my mouth was trying to order another beer, my eyes wanted to look around, but in a shot, I was back out into the open streets like a bat out of hell.

Fuck's sake, why are you so scared?

Don't like it, don't want to do it.

I walked past other bars, but the fight still wrangled on, wrestling and tussling internally. Just as the fear gripped at one point, determination took hold and forced me into another bar. This one was a little livelier—more people were scattered around, but the fear was out in full force once more. But determination stood strong. A live band had already started playing in the far corner, a crowd in front of them danced and sang along, the bar was empty and pushed against the force of a tsunami towards it. Words barely came out as I was once more strangled by paranoia, but I managed to order a beer.

Ha, fuck you! I am having this beer and taking my time to enjoy this music.

I had broken through, I needed to keep going until this bullshit was defeated.

All eyes in the bar were on the band and not in my direction—even the barman paid more attention to them. The bar top, however, was not enough to prop up my jelly legs, so I sat on the stool.

I'm doing it, I'm defeating this shit.

There was no reply. I had defeated the fear, anxiety, and paranoia. The beer was enjoyable, satisfying even, and went down like a treat. I was about to order another, but the band finished a song, eyes turned in my direction, and people started rushing towards the bar. It struck me once more. I slipped off the stool, bulldozed through the crowd, and back out onto the street.

My legs tried to go back inside but the fear had gripped tighter.

No fucking chance. Going back to the motel now. Not doing it again.

Yes, I am. Not going home until I get rid of the fear.

Nope, not happening.

I tried to walk into another bar on the corner of the street, but fear seemed to overpower determination—

there was no getting through. The fight was almost over, I tried one last push, but the fear had grown too strong. Just when it seemed I was making progress, fear won the battle—again, for a second night. But this war wasn't over.

* * *

My face winced, just moving a millimetre caused the whole bunkbed to scream out in agony. It was on its last legs and threatened to collapse at any moment, while springs from the wafer-thin mattress stabbed into my back.

How the fuck am I going to sleep tonight? Maybe I should have picked the top bunk, at least if the frame falls apart, nothing will come crashing down on me.

That was the fear—the top bunk collapsing. There were only three of us in this oversized six-bed dorm; so much space, but with nothing to fill it except three wiry bunkbeds and wooden broken lockers pressed to the wall. The other two backpackers in the room hadn't moved all day—one glued to a book, the other to a laptop on the screaming bottom bunks of their bunkbeds. They had no interest in me whatsoever, even after I had tried to break the ice. And judging from the way they left their stuff scattered around their area with no concern, they were long-termers. I didn't even want to open my backpack or put it in the wooden locker, it was staying propped up against my bunk within arm's reach. I was so out of place here and hated being ignored.

Is this how short-termers felt when they arrived in the hostel in Sydney?

Being on the other side of the fence, firmly being the 'new guy' in the hostel, made me think of the way I had treated people in the Funkhouse. To many, I was an asshole. The cold shoulder I had received, not only from these two but the others lounging around in the common room, prompted Fiona's voice to pop into my mind. I could picture her standing there with her arms folded and head tilted, saying, "What goes around comes around. You should have treated short-termers better in Sydney This is Karma biting you in the ass." Karma, if I believed in it, would be a bitch to me, that's for sure.

The dorm led directly into the even larger and barer common room, each step along the dark hard wood floor was followed by an ache emanating from the boards. It was in desperate need of some TLC, but the fact that a stained sheet was used as a curtain said all there was to say about how well this place was maintained. They didn't have anything to make a guest's arrival feel comfortable. No cheerful welcome, no TV, no music, not even any couches, just a few overused and dirty bean bags that had lost their colour. It was a surprise there weren't any cockroaches or rats scurrying over the counters in the kitchenette. Or was it that this place was too dirty for them?

This was my first experience of a bottom-feeder hostel, where fresh air was replaced by the pungent stench of stale damp clothes fused with body odour, it was just for one night but I hated being in it. Every other hostel in the area was fully booked and this was the absolute last resort. I couldn't afford to stay any longer in the motel as my money was running out. The joys of being a budget backpacker. I'd arrived in Melbourne four days ago and felt liberated for finally travelling solo. But things had taken such a dive since then.

At any point during the day where I was able to relax, the voices piped up at the failure to find any farm work. I could feel my inner demons scratching to be loose again, they hadn't been left behind in Sydney, they had just been hiding. The nightly battles of eating and drinking alone had also taken their toll. It was exhausting trying to fight so hard against myself. It really made no sense. During the day, there was no issue, but as soon as it got dark, bars and restaurants were a no-go. What made it worse was seeing other people able to sit alone seemingly enjoying themselves—why I couldn't do it was beyond me. This hostel… well, it was just the rotten cherry on the crap cake. It looked like solo traveling wasn't for me. Sure, some parts were enjoyable, but for the most part, it wasn't for me, I liked being alone for a while but I couldn't be by myself for too long.

Night had fallen once more, the rain that kept me imprisoned in this sorry excuse for a hostel had stopped, allowing for escape and some actual fresh air. Hiding under a hoodie and wrapped in a coat, I stepped out onto the dimly lit street, which was a fair reflection of my mood. A friend from Sydney had suggested checking out the pier. Apparently, penguins could be seen there. I had never seen any before my trip to the aquarium here. It may have stopped raining, but the winds howled out, helping waves to violently crash against the large rocks along the pier. The bitter air cut against my cheeks like tiny knives, while spray rained down like a heavy arsenal—it might as well have been raining. There was no sight of any penguins though, but my feet kept dragging me towards the old wooden café at the end of the pier.

Salt in the air got stronger the closer I got to the end of the pier. The winds had chilled through my bones and my nose was so bright red, I could see it. There was no feeling left in my toes or feet, but I kept going until I reached the rails. A wild angry choppy ocean churned in front of me, only lit up by the moon above.

What the fuck am I going to do now?

Jump in?

Shut up, idiot! I'm being serious—what are the options now?

Go back to Sydney—fuck it, at least my friends are there, replied the other inner voice.

No, I'm not doing that. There was a reason I left, going back now defeats the object.

Yeah, but you won't be lonely there. Doesn't matter how chilled it is here if I feel lonely… I can't even eat alone.

Both were valid options, but in that moment, it felt like I had jumped off the pier with a cinder block, drowning, getting darker as the little light from the moon disappeared until there was complete darkness.

Realisation hit!

This was the beginning of the end. In a few months, I'd be back in England having accomplished nothing but getting drunk on a rooftop in Sydney and not being able to eat or drink alone at night. I fucking sucked! And just like people thought back in England, I was a failure. They were right, somebody like me had no business trying to travel. They all knew I'd fuck it up somehow while I was in denial and kidding myself to think I could backpack alone with barely any money or willpower.

I had arrived in Australia with all these grand plans, full of excitement, feeling free of the shackles I'd yearned to break free of, yet had wasted all my time and not a single thing had gone to plan because of my weak mind.

There had been no great adventure from Adelaide to Melbourne, there hadn't been any experiences of spectacular beaches from Melbourne to Sydney, no Whitsundays, no Fraser Island, no Great Barrier Reef. Just my shit willpower and weakness for partying but not by myself.

That's what I'm good at, so I might as well go back and finish how I started.

Yeah, fuck it, I give up too. Let's just go back to Sydney. The sooner, the better.

Go and do it now, fuck staying in that hostel, see if there's a night bus back tonight.

It was done, the decision was made, I finally turned from the angry ocean, heading back down the pier, blasted by the assault of salt-filled drops bouncing off the rocks.

The spray had soaked me through from head to toe, and to make it worse, there was no heating in the hostel so it was going to be a sodden night on a shitty mattress or on the night bus back to Sydney.

Yup, all the luck in the world.

There was a late-night internet café on the way back to the hostel, but walking past a few bars, one of my voices perked up.

How about this… try to have a beer, if I can't do it, then go back to Sydney, if I can, then it proves I can't get through it and stay in Melbourne—just need to find a better hostel.

Deal!

After the deepest of deep breaths, I put one foot in front of the other and pushed the doors open; another step was taken before the sonic boom of paranoia hit, but I pushed through… nearly. In a moment of weakness, I gave up, letting it take over. Defeated without any real fight.

Nah, fuck it, I'm going back to Sydney then back to England, so no point in even trying. Bollocks to it.

Just like that, retreating was the command that followed. Weak with no fight and straight to the internet café.

The old Chinese man pointed to one of the computers in a room that looked like a call centre minus the phones. He must have known I was coming—the screen was already on the Greyhound bus webpage.

Definitely set on going back to Sydney. No final change of heart? No staying here, find a better hostel and a job?

Nope. Sydney, that's it.

OK, then, guess I'm going home.

ORIGIN:

Melbourne

DESTINATION:

I started to type in the words: Syd...

The table started to buzz and my eyes looked down at my phone—an unknown number was ringing. I was tempted to just leave it, I didn't like picking up unknown numbers, but for some reason, I accepted the call.

"Alright, mate, it's Nick, I've been trying to find your number all week, but I lost my phone. Are you still looking for farm work?" he practically sang down the phone.

"WHAT? Wait, serious? Are you fucking with me? Don't take the piss, mate."

This can't be happening!

"I'm being serious, I talked to my boss, I'm with him right now… told him you were desperate, he agreed but I couldn't get in touch with you. Fiona literally texted over your number right now," he sang back.

"YES, FUCK, YES, YES, FUCK, YES!"

All control of my voice volume was lost and the words jumped back, my eyes popped open, my spare fist punching the air as a wave of relief flushed through my body.

"OK, OK, calm down."

"No, you don't understand, mate. I'm in the internet café right now. I was literally booking a ticket back to Sydney. I've typed it all in, just about to confirm and you called. That's madness."

"Good job I got you when I did. I'm gonna pass you over to my boss. He just needs a quick chat."

"G'day, mate. A-mit, is it? Nick has vouched for ya, but I know ya Pommes are fairies so I needed to talk to ya. I don't normally take on workers this late, I'm squeezing ya in a favour for manual labour work. Are ya hard-working and are ya gonna give me any shit?"

No, I hate manual labour and hate hard work even more, depends what mood I'm in if I give you any trouble

or not. Oh yeah, I hate authority, but I'm fucking
desperate.

That's what I thought, but I replied with:

"Yes, 100% hard-working, doesn't matter what the work is, I'll do it, just thankful and grateful for the work."

"Alrigh' then, if ya can get down here by the morning, you have got yourself a job, and 90 days guaranteed work."

"Awesome, yes, that's no problem. Wait where is here? And where am I staying?"

He passed the phone back to Nick.

"Don't worry about that, I'll get you booked into my hostel, we live in the house next to the main hostel, there's a spare bunk in my room. You are coming to Mildura."

Instantly, I smashed the delete button on the destination, retyping with Mildura. Waiting for it to load, imploring it to go quicker. It popped up.

"Yes, there's a bus tonight, 12.30 am, arrives tomorrow at 7.45 am—I'm on it."

"Brilliant, the bus stops in town, we'll pick you up in the morning."

As soon as the phone fell to the table, it was as if a winning goal had been scored by my favourite football in the cup final. I leapt up high from the seat, sent it crashing into the desk behind and nearly punching the low-hanging lights, which even I could nearly reach.

"FUCK, YES! WHOOO, YES! FUCK!"

My roar prompted the Chinese man to stand and shout something in my direction and gesture for me to sit back down. My smile was so wide, it was hurting my cheeks as my hands ran over my shaven bristly head.

How the fuck has this just happened, like fucking seriously, how? Wait… Mildura? Where the fuck is Mildura?

I dropped back to the screen, pulling up Google Maps, it was somewhere inland north of Victoria and west of New South Wales. It seemed like it was the arse-end of Australia right out in the middle of nowhere. But it didn't matter, I was going to stay in Australia for another year! More importantly, I wasn't going to be shipped back to England!

Clenched Skin

Holy fuck, what are you doing, you crazy lunatic? You're going to kill us!

No actual words could come out while my skin clenched as tight as my teeth, and my fingers dug into the pleather seat. All my excitement had evaporated—a noise that shouldn't come out of a twenty-eight-year-old man escaped again as my eyes bulged, nearly popping out of their sockets. Not just my guts, but all internal organs slammed against my throat. The voices within were screaming, even inner demons were hanging on for dear life.

What the hell did I do to deserve this? cried one.

The other wept, *I don't wanna die like this, please don't kill me!*

A highlight reel of my life started to flash by as the ocean lifted to swallow the plummeting plane. My body didn't need any help from the vibrating plane to shake uncontrollably—fear was doing that all by itself. I braced for impact, with my heart ready to explode, this was how it would all end. It was all over…

Goodbye, world!

…Two hours earlier

"This one's still fresh, check it out, guts and everything," called out Tom.

He flipped his red baseball cap backwards, jumping and leaning over the carcass. Flies and bugs were already feasting on it as I joined, leaning over, but the stench was too foul. We were no vets, but it didn't look more than a few hours dead. My sunglasses slid back on as I jumped away. The grassy ditch along this side of the never-ending main road was like a kangaroo graveyard. The mystery was where they came from—there were no live kangaroos jumping around through the tree lines or in the fields either side of the road.

"Do you reckon I can get to its teeth?" asked Tom innocently.

"Yeah, sure, just like the dead shark on Fraser Island," I mocked from a distance.

"That was covered in maggots, I would have got it out if there weren't so many people watching." His head snapped back, shaking a little.

"Sure you would."

He gave up investigating the kangaroo and trying to extract a tooth. Both of us scanned the tree line once more; if there were any kangaroos, they were doing a good job of hiding. Dead wild animals had become a theme on this journey up Australia's east coast. Dead kangaroos were the latest, from a decomposing humpback whale, a dead tiger shark, giant spiders, mono-lizards, and a couple of dead snakes. We had also been lucky enough to see live sharks, stingrays, snakes, copious variants of lizards, and my personal highlight—a humpback dive out of the water in the Whitsundays right in front of us. The death-to-live ratio was quite balanced.

"Will you two stop messing around? We're going to be late. You don't have to stop at every animal you see."

Vicky's dark bobbed hair bounced back as she maintained a distance between us. Four of us, friends from the Funkhouse Hostel in Sydney, were on this trip up the east coast together. Our latest stop was the small coastal town of Agnes Water. Tom caught up to Vicky, swinging his arm around and pointing back towards the kangaroo carcass, but she wasn't interested. Both were English, Tom was a very boyish typical Brit abroad from the coastal town of Ipswich or somewhere in Essex—it was hard to tell at times. Vicky was from the north of England. They, like me, were on working holiday visas, but this was their first year while I was on my second-year visa. We had all become good friends in the Funkhouse Hostel after I had returned, following a short stint back in England.

That giant ball of fire was flexing its might high in the sky. After feeling deadly scorching temperatures in the arse-end of Australia, also known as Mildura, anything less was manageable. However, shade was still needed and the high tree line on this side of the road provided the perfect cover.

Since completing my farm with the scrape of my teeth towards the end of last year, so much had changed but yet remained the same. New backpackers had become long-termers in the Funkhouse Hostel, yet a handful from my first stay remained. There had been the impromptu return to England, which was only meant to be a couple of weeks but turned into a few months. If it wasn't for somebody who was turning into a good friend pulling me out of my darkness, I'd still be there, back to my old ways. However, I returned to Sydney with a new focus and a promise that couldn't be broken. Once this trip was over, it was back to that laser focus, nothing else mattered… well, except for trying to deal with the momentous fuckery that was going on but was out of my hands.

As usual, nothing was straightforward. Life loved to fuck with me, and over these past few months, it had turned sadistic. It's like it opens its arms up, provides amazing experiences and moments, lets me touch and taste happiness, then wraps a baseball bat around my head. It even tried to mess with me while returning to Australia, making me sweat. If it wasn't for proof in the form of pictures that I did, in fact, in complete my farm work, I'd be back in England again. Permanently. That, it seemed, was just for its own amusement. It was the far more serious issue that had started to plague this trip.

There wasn't a cloud in the perfectly blue sky except for the one above my head, which grew darker and heavier by the day. My friends back in Sydney and those here with me had tried their best to help it from playing on my mind, but it was right there festering in my brain any time I was alone. It's nearly ruined this trip on more than one occasion and have been close to just going back to Sydney to get answers, but as I've been informed so many times, there is nothing I can do right now.

"Shit, he's thinking about it again. No, no, no, get it out of your head," implored Tom as he spun on his heels, waiting for me to catch up. Shaking his head, he continued, "Mate, you're not allowed to walk alone, we're not having a repeat of Nusa Dua."

"Can't help it, how can I just let it go? Until it gets sorted, it's always gonna linger." My shoulder lifted and dropped instantly while catching up to their concerned faces.

"Yeah, I get that, but you can't do anything about it. You know the score, geeza, you know what they said. Just let them do what they need to. We all know even if you went back, you will just get angry and start throwing head-butts around and make it worse."

From the moment I heard the news while in Brisbane, I couldn't stop thinking about it. Something like this could only happen to me, only I had this type of luck. But all my friends were right—there was nothing I could physically do about it.

"Come on, you're about to go on an incredible adventure, remember how excited you were about it when we booked it? Try not to think about that, think of what we're about to experience. Even I'm excited about the next few days." Vicky's skinny tanned arm flung around my shoulder.

"Will you lot hurry up? I'm tired, we're the only ones walking. Why couldn't we get a taxi like everybody else? You idiots making me walk."

A screech broke through the air from blondie in the distance—the fourth friend. It was a long walk, the receptionist in the hostel said it was only a short walk into town. In Australian terms, it might have been short, but in English terms, it was fucking miles. Tom shook his head, laughing, but held his hands up to acknowledge.

All four of us planned to travel up the east coast and a friend of ours worked in 'Peter Pans'—a backpacker tour operator opposite the Funkhouse Hostel. With my insecure disaster of solo travelling in Melbourne, it made sense to get things pre-booked—everything, all activities, excursions, routes, and hostels had been organised, booked, and paid for before the trip even began.

Although still out of sight, the sea could be heard as we walked through the short-stacked square buildings with one wide road running through them like an American-style small town. The streets were scattered with locals who probably knew everything about each other's entire lives. As the bottom of the road drew closer, Tom tried to figure out the address of the unit we needed to find, leading us down a sandy side road before we found it. The small sign above confirmed it was the right place, but it was closed.

Fuck, prepare for these two to erupt!

But they didn't, instead, they laughed at the note stuck to the wall: "Back by 2 pm… if not, I'm late or dead, up to ya if you wanna wait."

Both nearly jumped out of their skin when, like a jack-in-a-box, an older man, who seemed like an over-exuberant second-hand car salesman, jumped out from the side of the unit.

"Ahh, G'day! My next victims, I presume. And who might ya be?"

Neither had climbed back into their skin yet, but clung on to each other for dear life as Tom interjected, pulling out the paper receipts with the reference number on.

"Fair dinkum, Pommeys, 'n four of ya… its ganna be a tight squeeze."

His white hairy hand slid into the window, grabbing four clipboards and handing them out to us without moving his eyes from the girls.

"OK, I need ya all to sign this form, just to make sure none of ya are crook, or if ya get crook, it's defo not on me. It's a corka this arvo, ey?"

It was like being around my old boss in Mildura again, making complete sense to himself, but not to anybody else.

"Got ya goon, your stubys, your slabs? All ready? Who wants to go on the ride of their lives first?" He threw the forms back through the window while grabbing a pilot's hat. "I'm your amazing pilot, this is my company. Anything goes wrong, you've signed the forms so you can't sue me. The dunny is in the office—anybody with a weak bladder, you need to go now. I'll take the two Sheilas first, then come back for you lads."

Wait, what? You're actually the pilot? Oh, fuck my life, we're gonna die! And what does he mean if anything goes wrong?
"That's cool, we're OK to wait here?" is what I actually said.

"Ahh, yeah, no drama. You boys looking forward to heading out there? It's a real treat," he sniggered.

Both the girls hurried inside to use the bathroom as he suggested.

"Yeah, been looking forward to it since we booked it. Out in the wild, in nature, on a deserted island, gonna be feared." Tom bounced forward, nodding like a dog about to get a treat.

"Feared? Nah, it's ganna be gnarly, trust me. I've neva had anybody leave disappointed."

Both girls sheepishly walked back out like they were about to be sent to slaughter, with neither saying a word. He did his final checks, making sure they had everything and took most of the alcohol. He even did a little skip, making one of his sandals fly off as they walked off down the wooden side path.

"Ah shi', let's hope my flyin' is better than my skippin', hey?"

With a quick shuffle, my shoulder satchel dropped to the sandy pavement as I fell into the deck chair outside the unit.

"What are you doing?" Tom pulled his head back, looking directly at me.

"Gonna chill, have a nap while we wait."

"Forget the nap, let's go explore, head on to the beach, this tan needs topping up." He couldn't stand still and was looking back down the sandy road.

"You need to be in the shade as much as me, you're the same colour as your hat. That's not a tan, that's a problem."

"You're just jealous of my awesome tan."

"Yeah, sure. Because everybody wants to look like a boiled lobster."

"You're just feared, bro." He laughed it off, already taking a couple of steps.

"That fucking word—it makes no sense," I fumed.

My eyes were already closed under my shades, but I flung my arms above my shaved head.

"Just embrace it and admit you're feared."

There was no point in replying. It was his little saying, he used it for everything, and it made no sense. If we were drunk, found something new, adventures, discovery, something exciting, sad, miserable, happy—it didn't matter, he used that word.

"Come on, you're not allowed to be alone right now, we all know what will happen and where your mind will go. I'm not coming back to depressed Amit when we're about to have the adventure of our lives."

"Yeah, if we make it there... did you see how fucking crazy that guy seemed? And I'll be alright, not gonna think about it, just want a nap, you go do your thing," I assured him, shifting back up in the seat to look back at him.

He didn't look very convinced, but shrugging his shoulders, he bounced away. The crunch of his footsteps against the sandy footpath became fainter, allowing my mind to start drifting off while safely under enough shade. It was a lie...

Of course I'm going to think of it, it's pretty much all I've thought about since Brisbane. It's easy for them to tell me not to think about it, it's not them going through it. This is the most serious disaster that's happened to me; I can't access my own money, I can't prove anything even though I have my original documents, proof of everything, it fucking sucks!

My mind switched gears, it wandered to the sound of the soft waves behind the unit drifting in and out. The promise I made to my grandad came to the fore—he was the reason I went back to England, for his funeral. I had promised to make a life out here in Australia and nothing was going to get in the way of achieving that goal. The sounds of the waves along with the soft breeze drifting through the palm trees surrounding the unit were strong enough to take my mind further away, into a dream state.

"Well, that was rubbish, there's nothing to do in this town." Tom's voice caused my eyes to spring open.

"What the fuck, you back already?"

"Geeza, I've been gone for over an hour, I can't wait to get over to the island."

"About that, how are we going to survive the next couple of nights? I'm telling you, if I see polar bears, a forgotten tribe, or black smoke, I'm swimming back." I was referring to the TV series, *Lost*.

"You, swim? Bollocks will you. I've never even seen you get into water." He cackled while flipping his red hat backwards. But our conversation was interrupted.

"Serious question, are ya two scared little Sheilas too or do ya have a pair of cahoonas because ya two friends screamed so much. One nearly deafened me." Like a kangaroo in khaki shorts and sandals, the pilot jumped out in front of us.

Both of us nodded without saying a word, grabbed our bags, and followed towards the little sea plane. It didn't even occur to me to ask him what the island was like. I think we wanted it to be a surprise—the tingle of fear of the unknown felt exciting. After some pushing and shoving, Tom jumped in the back before I slid into the passenger side next to the pilot. All other thoughts disappeared, and the dark cloud momentarily vanished too as he handed over a headset.

"Ready, co-pilot?" he asked.

My heart skipped a beat hearing his words, it was the first time since Fraser Island that there was a genuine cheesy grin plastered across my face. Just as the propellers started to spin and the engine turned, vibrations shot through the seat and adrenaline shot through my body as if being hit by a lightning bolt. I could feel it coursing through my veins. All the dials on the wooden dashboard started to move—nerves, excitement, fear, and adrenaline mixed together like a cocktail as the plane moved. As big as my grin was, the pilot's was even bigger as he looked across.

"Gnarly, hey?" His words came through my headset.

I nodded back, my eyes fixed on the rattling plastic window as we skimmed over the calm waters. It was another first experience to tick off the bucket list. For the first time since meeting him, the pilot was calm and acted like an actual pilot. Up until now, it seemed like he had taken too much acid in his life. Something dropped in the pit of my stomach as the plane lifted, turning back to see Tom beaming as he looked out of his window.

We slowly rose high into the cloudless sky. The plane reached altitude but was still low enough that we could see the pristine coastline and foamy waves lapping on to the golden beach. As the plane went further out, the sea started to change colour, the foamy white replaced by tranquil emerald, the waves gently rolling over the calm surface. It is moments like this that are made to savour and pushes all the bullshit away. Even with the engine roaring and propellers buzzing through the headset, my mind felt as peaceful for the first time in weeks and as calm as the sea below.

"This is amazing. See, you would have missed this if you went back to Sydney," roared Tom as his hand pushed against my shoulder, but I couldn't peel my eyes away from the view outside, almost hypnotised in it.

"Lemme know if ya spot any dolphins, there are always pods around. I'll take us down to them," the pilot's words came through the headset once more.

He opened up his window, letting in a blast of warm air that caused Tom to sit back.

As soon as I heard those words, my eyes turned into sniper scopes on the hunt. It had been a good twenty minutes since take-off and nothing had interrupted the ocean yet.

Without warning, my hands instantly grabbed hold of the pleather seat, gripping tight. The plane started to shake unnaturally, bouncing in the sky like a speed boat over choppy water, climbing, dropping, climbing, dropping, bowing left to right. That feeling in the pit of my stomach was going again, but I was trying not to show any emotion.

Oh, momma, what the fuck is happening?

"Not scared of a little turbulence, are ya? If you need to throw up, just open the windows and let loose. It's chowder for the fish," teased the pilot through the headset.

It's a clear sky, no clouds in sight or any wind, where's this turbulence coming from? I looked at his hands on the steering wheel. *He's doing it on purpose, the lunatic!*

"Ahh, just testing ya out, boys, any dolphins yet?" He laughed back.

There was nothing but vivid blue ocean. I don't know what noise leapt from my mouth, but it wasn't mine—it was that of a five-year-old girl. My guts filled my throat as he flipped the plane on its side and nosedived straight for the sea.

Holy fuck! What're you doing, you crazy bastard? You're gonna kill us!

At the last possible second, the plane pulled up, levelling out. That was worse than being on a rollercoaster. My heart was ready to explode, my body couldn't stop shaking.

Don't ever fucking do that again, you crazy fuck!

"Whoo, yeah boi! Feared! That was awesome," Tom roared out from behind.

Awesome? Are you mad? No, it fucking wasn't, this crazy lunatic nearly plunged us into death. Don't ever do that again!

"No, sorry, I got the wrong side. They're over this side," laughed the pilot.

What? Nooo!

My inner voice screamed as he straightened the plane and flipped ninety degrees in the opposite direction with the other wing now hovering off the ocean. We were so close, waves splashed into the plane. My guts had taken permanent residency in my throat. My head spun like a merry-go-round on speed. Once more, the plane was straightened up and my guts fell back into place as we rose high into the sky.

"Ah ha, there they are!" he joyfully cried out.

I couldn't open my mouth for fear of lunch and breakfast coming back up.

No, they're not stop it, you lunatic! cried out one of my inner voices.

The plane started to lift once more, but this co-pilot was now a frozen statue, zoned out, head spinning, and zero clue what was really going on. Instantly, I sniffed around like a dog just to make sure there was no point where I shit myself. The pilot's laughter filtered through the headset in between his conversation with Tom. It took another few seconds to register… his body and head had twizzled around and he flicked his hazel eyes towards mine.

"Enjoying the ride? Gnarly rush, right?"

"Yeah, for sure, fucking awesome," I replied.

Bollocks was it! I'm hating this ride, you mad bastard! Wait a minute, where the fuck are your hands… why are they not attached to the steering wheel?

"What are you doing? Why are you not steering?" With that realisation, my eyes pushed against their sockets.

"I got tired of flying, been doing it all day, ya fly it for a bit, you're not the co-pilot for no reason."

Not for a second did it occur to me that the plane was on autopilot—and out of instinct, the steering wheel was in my grip.

"Have ya ever flown a plane before?' he asked.

"Yeah, all the time, it's my hobby. No, of course I've not!"

"Ya got this, too easy, mate. Just keep it steady, just make sure ya keep watching these dials, I'll take it off autopilot now."

"What… wait… what?"

He was messing around, surely he was. Who would really trust a clueless passenger to fly a plane, but on the other hand, he was a lunatic. The dials were steady as was the steering wheel, although it shook a little and felt heavier than expected.

"Doing good, want to take it up a little?" asked the lunatic pilot.

Adrenaline had taken over and pushed the fear out. A warm, fuzzy, slightly electric charge ran through my body, nodding back in glee. He instructed me to pull back on the heavy wheel, push it down but keep within the dials. The plane actually started to lift and he wasn't controlling anything.

"Holy fuck, I'm doing this. Tom, are you seeing this? I'm fucking flying a plane, this is fucking awesome! YEAH, BOI!"

I'm flying a freaking plane, like for reals in the sky, actually flying this thing. I'm a pilot!

"You can let go now; you guys want to see the gnarliest trick?" he asked while taking back control.

"Not really, I want to keep flying, but yeah, sure. What's next?" My adrenaline spoke and words just flew out without a thought.

What the fuck did you say that for? yelled one of my inner voices.

The pilot pulled back on the wheel, lifting higher, the nose raised up high. My back melted into the seat—my organs were on the move again the higher the vertical plane lifted towards the heavens. He asked us for a camera as the plane levelled up.

Does he want to take pictures of us shitting ourselves for whatever he has planned?

Tom handed his over.

"Have you boys ever felt zero gravity?" asked the pilot. "Watch the camera."

All my organs braced themselves, my body had already started to shake in anticipation as he turned off the engine, sat back, waved, and smiled at us like he was just waiting for our reaction.

We were miles in the sky and this fuck just turned off the engine—I'm definitely going to die!

In an instant, my organs shifted to my throat, my eyeballs popped, and blood rushed to my head. The pleather of the seat was gripped harder than ever before. Like a rock, we started to silently tumble through the air. The metal tin can plummeted, gathering speed by the second. But I didn't scream. In fact, there was no panic or fear.

Everything was in slow motion, the camera floated off the dashboard like it was in space, my body tried to detach from the seat, only held in by the seatbelt. Anything that was loose started to float in the air. It was the most surreal thing I had ever experienced. Weird tingles rushed through my body, but at a snail's pace. My smile took forever to grow; time and space changed; reality felt suspended. I tried to reach for the floating objects, but my coordination didn't match—it was like a trippy dream.

This is mad trippy! Is this what astronauts feel in space?

My brain and body were not in sync, it forgot to even remember the plane was actually freefalling. Tom's arm came through between us in slow motion trying to grab the camera, but it eluded his hand. This was zero gravity, and it was awesome.

The pilot straightened the plane back up and everything fell to the floor instantly as gravity returned. That was the weirdest feeling I had ever felt in my life, but it was incredible. He hadn't switched the engine back on, we were just gliding through the sky like birds. My eyes were back outside, taking in the views once more. A golden sandy causeway alternated with clear blue streams joining to the sea.

"Whoa, WOW. That was awesome, now that's feared, bro!" Tom exuberated from behind.

No words could come out—none of it felt real. My hands tried to touch and feel anything in sight, from the grainy dashboard to the smooth wood on top, even touching my legs it was back to normal speed. My grin didn't feel like it could get any wider, but it did.

"Fucking hell, what the fuck was that? That was... wow, just wow!"

"I thought ya would like that one. Real gnarly, right? Ya friends didn't like it at all, they just kept screaming."

He started to inform us of other tricks he used to do, including doughnuts in the air and flipping the plane 360 degrees, but he wasn't allowed to anymore because of complaints and too many people throwing up. Apart from nearly killing us with the first trick, the rest—especially zero gravity—were unforgettable experiences.

A tropical island started to reveal itself, with golden sand around the rim of the hilly luscious vegetation. The plane climbed higher to get a better view. Cliffs and boulders on one side opened up to the causeways, while heavily vegetated by forest on the other with a long stretch of beach. This was home for the next few nights. The Bear Grylls out-in-the-wild experience, fending for ourselves, living wild, hunting and feeding ourselves, or whatever snacks the girls had bought. The plane flew over the outer rim of the island before it went over the forestry centre.

"Now, where did I leave the girls? When I get low enough, get ready to jump, boys."

It sounded like he was joking, but it was hard to tell— he could have been serious. He aimed for the trees in the middle of the island, soaring through towards them—the canopy becoming more detailed—and pulled up just before crashing into it.

I thought you were done with the tricks. Just get us on the ground now.

What are you on about? This is fucking insane! Can we just do this all day? laughed the other inner voice, drunk on adrenaline.

Clearly, one of my inner voices was enjoying this ride. The plane circled around the island, showing us the only other humans on the island were an old couple living in the cottage next to the lighthouse we had just passed. They were the caretakers of the island.

Oh, that doesn't sound at all like a horror movie couple ready to slash up and eat anybody that arrives on their island. We all know who goes first in horror movies.

"Here we go, boys, are ya ready to survive this island?"

He came down with precision, a soft landing, and it was a relief to feel solid ground once more. As soon as the plane stopped, I sprang open the buckle and reached for the door, but apparently, my legs had turned to jelly and my body scrambled. The girls' laughter could be heard as both Tom and I flopped to the ground. It took a few minutes for some stability and strength to return before we got up. The camp was a few short steps away from the plane but we both stopped to see the girls sitting on chairs on the beach. The pilot introduced us to the caretaker of the camp.

How many caretakers does this island need?

He took us over to where the girls sat. Two more guys were putting logs together for the night fire pit. The caretaker disappeared into the bush, but it was actually a makeshift kitchen with a plastic tarp over it. He returned with a couple of beers.

"Here you go, lads, the stew will not be long."

It was confusing—everything had been set up, this wasn't how it was sold to us. He explained he was here just in case anything went wrong, to make sure we behaved and—in his words—to make sure we didn't set the island on fire, but he wasn't here to babysit us.

Tom was not pleased as he took a seat next to Vicky. I didn't know what to make of it. In a way, I was looking forward to fending for myself in the wild, but the reality was, if that was the case, we would probably starve. The ice-cold beer tasted like it was sent from heaven, well-deserved for surviving the lunatic pilot. The two lads building the fire were also English. This was their last night, having been there for two days already. They started to share their experience, letting us know what there was to do and where was best to explore. Tom already wanted to go exploring the near-deserted tropical island, but the caretaker who was also English had warned us not to stray out too far as darkness would fall soon. This whole camp on a deserted island in Australia, and only English people were here.

It was nearly time for the giant ball of fire to disappear for another day; we all kicked back on the beach watching it in all its glory as it started to fall into the ocean like it was getting put out. It shot out a beam of orange across the horizon, leaving a stunning pattern of layers from bright to dark in the sky. A white shimmer took over the sea as the sun was gone and darkness took its place, but lit up by the shining torch of the moon.

A cold beer while watching the sunset on a deserted tropical island, now is this not living the dream? So what if we can't hunt for our own food. Look at this place, look at where I came from. I'm on a fucking deserted Island in Australia. I could never have imagined this a couple of years ago.

My inner voice was right, and with another beer in my hand, I moved away from the group.

"Dude, where are you going?" Tom asked.

"Nowhere, just give me a minute, I'm just over here. I'll be back as soon as I finish this beer."

"Don't go sinking into any holes in the head."

Soft cool grains of sand rolled between my toes, feeling each gritty grain tickle the soles of my bare feet. Just a few feet away from them all, close enough for their conversation to be heard, but far away enough not to be involved. My thumb covered the beer bottle as I dropped to the sand, my satchel followed, resting to the side. Stars started to appear in the unpolluted night sky, shimmering and sparkling down over the dark but calm ocean. The slight breeze was enough to keep the air cool, and the long rolls of waves were therapeutic. My fingers stretched into the satchel, pulling out a picture I had bought back from England and kept on my person every day since. The picture was of me as a child lying next to the most important person in my life—my grandad.

He had been my wall and support all my life, no matter how much I fucked up, trouble I got into, or life fucked me up, he was there for me. He practically raised me like a son, but now he wasn't around. No matter what I did in life, there would be one regret—not being in England when he needed me to be his wall. Instead, I was getting drunk in the Kings Cross in Sydney, being selfish, thinking about only me. That night, I returned from partying and got told to ring home just to hear his final breaths because he couldn't speak. It was a moment that will stick with me more than any experience I'll ever have.

By the time I returned to England, he had already passed. My wall was gone and the darkness I'd felt in the past was there waiting to greet and take me back. It was only when a friend from Sydney threw a rope and pulled me back out that I could breathe again. Funny thing is, at that point, she wasn't even a friend, just somebody I knew, but for some reason, she took it upon herself to pull me out. It was then the promise was made.

There's no letting him down. Remember how proud he was when we told him we were actually going to Australia in the first place? He didn't believe it until he saw the ticket and he fucking cried. The man that never showed an emotional side cried out of happiness. Can't let him down. Can't break my promise to him.

My eyes drifted out along the swaying shimmering waves as I thought about how the plan was in place, and what it required once I was back in Sydney. But, like a freight train carrying nothing but lead, it smashed through my thoughts, sending my head into a spin. The dark cloud was back, filling my brain with only one thought. The thing my friends have tried to help me not think about. The thing that just will not leave, but the same thing I was powerless to do anything about until the first part of the investigation had been conducted.

The identity theft!

"FUCCKKKK!!! WHY THE FUCK DOES THIS SHIT HAVE TO HAPPEN TO ME? FUCK YOU, LIFE. JUST LEAVE ME ALONE, JUST FUCK OFF!!!"

***

Smoke rose from the embers of the ashy logs from last night's campfire, which was still warm, while the giant ball of fire had risen to take its place high in the cloudless morning sky. The calm sea shimmered from the rays bouncing off it; all was calm—except in my head. I sat alone, thinking about the identity theft. It wasn't just that, but the reality of sleeping in a tent on a near-deserted tropical island didn't match the expectation. It was uncomfortable, I was attacked by sandflies and mosquitoes all night, the unrecognisable weird nocturnal noises didn't help, and that's not to mention something was out there making its presence known. As soon as sunlight hit, I was out on the beach in the open. It felt safer.

Although my eyes were hidden behind sunglasses, when the smoke blew in my direction, I didn't even think about moving—it was like I was vacant, thinking about this momentous fuckery of identity theft. It all started with my tax return. Being on a working holiday visa, at the end of the tax year, whatever was paid in tax was meant to be reimbursed. In essence, it was a savings account. My tax rebate would fund this trip up the east coast, but it wasn't released when it was due. The tax office just said there was a delay.

It was only after we arrived in Brisbane and was advised to go into the tax office with my proof-of-identity documents that all was revealed. There was somebody else in Australia claiming to be me. My first reaction was anger, but that was quickly followed by, *who the fuck would want to steal my identity*? It's not like I'm flushed with money or have anything of worth to take. Nevertheless, whoever it was had somehow obtained my bank details, tax number, employment number, and had applied for my tax rebate just as I did. It was only because of the two identical tax claims this came to light and was flagged. Since Brisbane, there had been a block on my bank account. My documents were all with the fraud/identity theft investigation team, but there was nothing I could do until they were satisfied I was me and not the imposter. That was my biggest gripe, I had all the original documents, I could prove I was who I said I was, but they needed to carry out their investigation.

Who else could sit on a deserted tropical beach watching a majestic sunrise and it not be the most perfect moment of their life? This shit can only happen to me.

Yup, only to me. Amazing experience on one hand, slapped in the face by the other.

My skin started to feel the burn, the giant ball of fire's rays had locked on, hell-bent on destruction, the game of seek and destroy was back on, though the light sea breeze did help a little. But I did move, skirting across the soft grains of warming sand, away from the campfire and into the shade of a hammock under the safety of an overhanging palm tree. Before my thoughts were able to drift away again, a welcome boisterous voice echoed through the camp.

"Yeah, buddy. This is the life—me, nature, and this island, living the dream. It's perfect paradise—so feared."

My head popped up from the hammock to see Tom, like an excited child, investigating the sandy ground and looking up every tree trunk for anything that moved as he made his way from the camp area. He was truly in his element. Vicky followed behind trying to be as enthusiastic as he was. Both spotted me.

"Here you are, geeza, got worried you got eaten or something when I saw you weren't in your tent."

"Yeah, been out here since the sun came up—couldn't sleep in that tent, it was well uncomfortable."

"Ah, it was sweet. Get used to it, got another couple of nights yet. I bet you've not been out there for an early morning swim though?"

I shrugged, sinking back into the hammock, but it didn't take long for him to start shaking it.

"Get out of there, out of your thoughts and the hammock, we're going exploring. Got this whole island to explore—let's go, come on."

"Alight, dickhead, I'm getting out. Chill, I need to get my bag."

My flip-flops kicked up sand as I moved slowly behind the makeshift kitchen and into the bush. Low-hanging wiry tree branches were the perfect hiding spot for any of the wild animals out here. The tent came into view—it was unzipped.

I made sure it was zipped up.

Tom, he left it open, the idiot.

Approach with caution.

Which was exactly what I was doing… slow footsteps, edging closer to the tent, eyes bulging, scanning with intent.

Fuck me, there better not be anything in there.

My satchel, which I used as a pillow, was lying just inside the tent, but it looked like it was open. Gingerly, I approached, trying to peek into the tent. Shivers shot down my spine, every hair popped up and stood to attention. I was frozen again. Half a scaly body, dinosaur claws, and a long tail were all that were visible. I felt like

I was trying to step into a bar in Melbourne all over again—I couldn't move.

What the fuck, is that a…?

Yeah, it is…

A fucking mono-lizard is rummaging through my bag. What do I do?

My heart was ready to explode, but then another thought came over me—a stupid one.

Get the caretaker—that's his job, to take care of me or grab its tail, pull it out.

No, idiot, don't do that.

"Geeza, what's taking you so long?" Tom's voice bellowed from behind.

I snapped my head around and shouted in a whisper, "Shut the fuck up. You didn't zip my tent up, there's a fucking giant lizard in my bag."

He burst out laughing but ran over, nearly knocking me into the tent.

"I have got to see this. You lucky fucker, ah damn, I don't have my camera."

This was not lucky. Both of us watched as this giant mono-lizard had its head in my bag.

There's no food in the bag, what's it doing?

Tom tried to step into the tent, reaching out towards its tail.

"What the fuck you doing?"

"Wanna see what it feels like," he responded, doing his best Steve Irwin impression.

As Tom got closer, he must have disturbed the lizard as, all of a sudden, its long head popped out from my bag with a warning hiss. Looking us both dead in the eyes, its tongue slid out like we were breakfast, I jumped out of my skin and back out into the open. Tom, however, didn't follow. There was a rustle and the tent shook like it was going to fall down.

What's he doing in there? Wrestling it?

A few seconds later, he emerged again holding it up. Not the lizard, but my satchel.

"What the fuck were you doing?"

"Nothing, I just grabbed your bag. It got scared and tried to get out the bottom through the back, I think that's how it got in."

I grabbed my bag off him, searching through it. For some reason, I was expecting it to be slimy and covered in lizard drool, but it was dry and nothing was missing.

"Zip the tent up properly this time!" I fumed.

"What a start to the day, I wonder what else we're gonna come across on this island—it's gonna be amazing!"

My only thought was to let the caretaker know to batten down and fortify my tent. As much as I loved seeing wild animals, my excitement levels were nowhere near Tom's. The caretaker had some eggs and bacon cooking, it was enticing enough for us to eat before heading off to explore the island.

Thor's Ragdoll

There haven't been many times in life where I have felt emasculated, but having Thor, the god of thunder, manhandle me like a ragdoll… yup, this was definitely one of those occasions. His tree-trunk-like tattoo-covered arm slid in front of me, the watch on his wrist read 12,000ft, which prompted a thud from within like a giant Chinese gong. It was the first time my nerves had jangled. Regret of this decision started to grow, and my senses started to heighten to the point where my ears sharpened over the sound of the roaring engine.

In the space of a few weeks, I had gone from never setting foot in a small plane to sitting in two. Although this one didn't have a lunatic pilot doing tricks and there wasn't any co-piloting, just sitting on a wooden beam attached a man who resembled the god of thunder, Thor. The small tin can soared through the sky—anything that wasn't strapped down was clanging and banging, metal on metal, with nuts and bolts trying to dislodge.

Whatever was hanging in the netted straps tried to break free, forming this unusual orchestra of noise. Yet none of that took my attention more than the lead solo singer, right towards the far end of the plane—the roll-down hatch that wanted to burst open, desperate to shed its little locks. I was lucky to be right at the back, it was Tom who was sitting directly in front of the hatch cutting a ghostly figure, even though he was attached to another human. Vicky was straddled on the beam in front of me with her human backpack, while the other three faces were a blur.

Vicky had got over the panic attack she suffered that morning, wanting to back out, but once we arrived, a calmness flushed through her. It was Tom who became the panicked one, although where he was sitting might have had something to do with it. What we were about to do was probably seen as more dangerous than the flight over to the island, although it felt much safer. Thor kindly stuck out his tree-trunk arm once more, his watch revealing 13,000ft. It was the wrong time for my thoughts to drift, but they did. Unwillingly, that big cloud of identity theft re-appeared.

Well, if shit goes wrong today, whoever stole my identity can have it, right?

The thoughts disappeared as high-pressured air blasted through, rocking the plane. The hatch had been opened. My knee started to rock, and my right foot bounced rapidly.

Whose great idea was this? I want to go back down now.

It was too late, there was no backing down. I was fully committed and with the god of thunder showing 13,500ft, it was nearly time. He yanked on the straps, making sure I was glued to his chest. His hips bulked once more, causing a whimper to escape my mouth. My body was not on the bench anymore and I didn't I have control of my own body. It was like he was carrying a light backpack on his chest. His bushy beard pierced through the back of my hoodie through to my neck, his heavy breath brushed over my ears. In that moment, I had turned into a cowering little child, especially as his thick heavy voice penetrated my ears.

"Remember, hook your feet under the rail. It's very important that you do it."

Instantly, my inner voice started to repeat the instructions on a loop.

Feet under rail—hook feet under rail—feet under rails, don't forget. Fuck, what are we about to do, why was this a good idea?

The other one jumped in, pushing away any negativity.

It's gonna amazing, deep breath, calm down, ultimate thrill. It's gonna be insane, woo yeah, just remember, foot under rail and I'll be all good. I got Thor with me; nothing will go wrong.

It was sound advice, I filled my lungs deeply before slowly releasing. My attention was directed back towards Tom, who was being edged forward by his human backpack. His hair seemed like it wanted to escape his head, he looked back in my direction, there was nothing but fear in his blue eyes. That look triggered a million Formula One cars to start zipping through my nervous system and veins. In a blink, he was gone, vanished from sight, leaving behind a howl or a scream of "Help". Whichever it was, the next three blank faces were next in line, shot out from the plane and maybe from existence.

Vicky was shuffled off the beam and into position, edging to the hatch, she too looked back, there was no fear, just utter calm and a smile before she was gone. It was just me, Thor, and the pilot left. There was no time to think. Thor had bulked once more, this time carrying me all the way to the hatch like I was weightless. The air blasted through—it was like sticking my head in a wind machine.

"Ready?" Thor's heavy voice carried over the deafening air.

No, fuck no… I don't want to do it! yelped one of my inner voices.

Yes, fuck yes… let's do it, feet under rails. Shit, did I tie my shoelaces? boomed the other one.

My eyes quickly averted to my Nike pumps—they were tied. I could only return a nod as my feet slid out the hatch. My cheeks were already full of air, the clear goggles tight over my eyes.

Jesus, take the wheel. It didn't matter if I was an atheist, if he was real, it was in his hands now.

My foot nearly flew off before I could even think about hooking it under the rail.

Quick, idiot, find the bottom of the rail.

Fighting the air, I put all my concentration into it, hooking my foot under...

MOTHHHERR FUCCKKKEERR YEEAAAHHHH!
The words didn't leave my mouth.

I had turned into a rock plummeting through the sky, nothing made any sense, up was down, down was up, left was right, inside was out, spinning uncontrollably. The millions of little Formula One cars inside my nerves had reached maximum speed, colours were a blur, whitewashed into each other, spinning at a million miles per hour. This is what a penny felt like in a washing machine, or even an egg getting scrambled.

Thor took control of my arms, spreading them wide. We stopped spinning but were still hurtling towards the ground.

Woooo, we're flying. Fuck, this is insane! Superman, baby.

Thor's hand came into view, giving me a thumbs-up, which I didn't care to respond to. My brain was too busy trying to comprehend, taking a million snapshots, but nothing computed; cheeks full of air, rattling like they were going to rip off. My skin felt like it was melting away against the G-force. I had never felt so alive nor scared at the same time in my life.

Thor tried to point out things below us, but I saw nothing but blue blur, my eyes and brain were not connected. Everything inside my body had gone haywire, nothing was working as it should, just that the world was getting bigger by the second but with no sign of land.

Without any warning, there was a sharp jerk and we instantly shot back up higher into the sky while it felt like the contents of my body carried on hurtling down. But then, complete serenity—everything fell silent.

"Whooaaaaa, fuccckkkk yes! What a rush, whooo!" I bellowed out in uncontrollable laugher.

Reality started to fall back into place, things slowly started to compute, the blue blurs started to form 3D images and Earth came alive. Little sandy islands of different shapes and sizes—which looked a lot like chicken nuggets floating in the ocean—came into view, before the golden coastline appeared. There was separation in the baby-blue sky and green and turquoise ocean, the Great Barrier Reef. Thor controlled the parachute, but my laughter hadn't stopped flowing with the realisation of what had just happened filling my entire being with a rarity—utter joy and bliss. It was like a warm fuzzy bubble had formed around me, floating through the sky, the coastline getting bigger and closer.

"Amazing, right?" asked Thor from over my shoulders.

"Fucking hell yeah, better than amazing. It's spectacular."

This was a new level, a new state of mind, serenity had taken over. It was yet another moment, another that will last forever. Vivid bright colours from corals under the ocean started to reveal themselves, shimmering out as the sun bounced off the ocean like a natural underwater light show.

"Phenomenal, never seen anything like it."

This was without a doubt the greatest natural high I had ever felt. Every inch of my body tingled, feeling like it was glowing. Blood rushed everywhere, and it was as though I was trapped in this euphoric feeling. In this moment, I was a feather floating through serenity. That feeling of complete freedom from everything ran rampant—excitement and adrenaline were off the charts.

But nothing lasts forever, and Thor had to take us down. Those few minutes of freefalling were the ultimate adrenaline rush. I chuckled, thinking how just a week ago, the lunatic pilot used a beach as a landing strip, but here I was about to land on one with my own feet. Thor didn't threaten to crash land into the trees behind the beach though, he lined us up perfectly along the beach. I still wasn't ready to go down, blood was still pumping, adrenaline was flowing harder. I wanted to go back up.

"Remember to lift your knees when we land," Thor's voice once more boomed through like an announcement.

It was like Heathrow Airport down there as the others came into land and we circled a little longer, waiting for permission to come in. Finally, one of the guys gave us the signal. The white sandy beach took over my vision, bodies turned from ants back into humans. We were coming in nice and smooth, past the tree line, my knees rose up high as Thor touched us down, running along the beach. I felt like a baby in his possession until we came to a standstill and the parachute caused a little drag. As soon as soft sandy beach came to a standstill, like an impatient child, I couldn't wait for him to unclasp and free me from his clutches. Feeling the last one click, my feet had already started moving, while looking around for my friends to share this incredible feeling with. Both were laughing and hugging while I jumped in front of them, hurling my arms around and pointing my fingers to the sky.

"Holy fuck! That was immense!"

Every fibre of my being was on fire. It felt like if I flapped my arms, I could fly back up. I tried but it didn't work.

"We just fell out of the fucking sky... what the fuck! Out of the sky, flying like Superman, like a bird and that view! The Great Barrier Reef, are you kidding me? I want to do it again!"

"Yeah, boi! That was awesome. Amit is back and is totally feared!" laughed Tom.

"You're damn right I am. That was insane. We need to get fucked up tonight, I wanna go on a mad one, like I have never felt this type of rush before, buzzing like mad! Let's get fucked up."

My feet couldn't stop bouncing around, dancing and bouncing again, full of so much energy, it was pouring out, I wanted to do everything all at once, right now, anything, everything.

I turned back to look for Thor, his huge frame was bent over, wrapping up the parachute. I headed back to him to thank him once more.

I started quizzing him, my adrenaline had taken over and I was shooting questions like an inquisitive child having discovered something for the first time. My two friends joined as they heard I was intrigued; it was the job I wanted. They laughed it off, but I was serious, this is what I wanted, I could fall out of the sky all day long and feel that rush over and over again. They laughed about how I wouldn't meet the height requirements to become an instructor—they were probably right.

* * *

The giant ball of fire high in the sky reflected a fusion of turquoise and emerald off the swaying ocean all the way to the horizon. The soft lapping of the waves was all that could be heard. It had been an incredible couple of days, from jumping out of the plane over it to floating on the Great Barrier Reef.

My sense of smell was lost due to the sea salt filling every particle in the air, clinging on to my clothes, attached to my skin and every nose hair. Even the coffee fumes lifting from the mug smelt like salt by the time it reached my nose. There was no sign of land, there hadn't been for two days since we left the coast behind. We were in the middle of the Great Barrier Reef—everything should be perfect right now, but as is the case when there is a soaring high, there is the inevitable crash. What goes up, must come down.

While everybody else—including my friends—were sizzling like sausages desperate to tan on the front deck, the small upper area to the back was where I'd been hiding since morning, alone with nothing but the sound of the waves and my thoughts.

Why can't I just be like everybody else on this boat, just enjoying it without having that fucking dark cloud get darker by the minute? I hate feeling this shitty when I should be in a perfect state of serenity. I'm on the Great Barrier Reef for fuck's sake!

The identity theft was mentally eating away at me.

The boat rocked a little, spilling my remaining coffee into the sea. My free hand clutched the metal rail, which was all the protection there was from falling overboard. And with my luck, that wasn't as far-fetched as it seemed. As the boat settled back to just softly bobbing from side to side—and before my thoughts could start spinning once again—Tom's voice sprang up from behind.

'Geeza, here you are. Not seen you all morning; thought we'd lost you. What are you doing back here?"

"Nothing, mate, just taking in the view. What's up?"

"Lies! You're all in your feelings, aren't you? What happened to the guy from the other day, Mr I'm-not-going-to-think-about-it-any-more? Look where you are. Did you ever think in your life you would be floating around on the Great Barrier Reef?"

"Yeah, I know. I want to just enjoy it but I can't. It's just fucking there!"

"Because you're letting it. Geeza, sometimes it's like you enjoy feeling like crap. Come on, there are some islands that only appear at certain times of the day. We're heading out to them. Let's go, no more feeling sorry for yourself."

Finally, I detached myself from the rails, turning to see Tom standing on the ladder—his bright-red face matching his red cap.

"Seriously, mate, you need to get some shade. You're going to burn your face off."

"I'll get shade when you stop feeling sorry for yourself," he laughed back, disappearing from sight.

I left my thoughts behind on the back deck, joining back up with the other two and a number of strange faces and voices who were also on the boat. This wasn't a party boat like we opted for on the Whitsundays. Everybody on this one was here to dive, snorkel, and experience the majestic Great Barrier Reef sober.

Everybody lined up towards the back of the boat, getting into rubber dinghies in groups of six. The two girls instantly started to take pictures of nothing but ocean. Although the giant ball of fire was still high in the sky, at sea level, it was blustery enough for my hood to slide on without any assistance. But I was the only one in a hoodie—everybody else was in swimwear. One of the crew members stopped the motor as everybody looked around while bobbing up and down to the motion of the soft waves, wondering where the islands were—there was no sight of them.

Was this a trick? Are we about to be thrown into the middle of the ocean as shark food? Where is this island? asked an inner voice.

Why? Why even think that? replied the other.

Just saying. It's like a scene from a gangster movie— taken out, murdered, and dropped in the ocean as shark food.

All of a sudden, a collective gasp rose. A small golden mound of sand peeked from the ocean to reveal itself. It wasn't even big enough for one person to stand on, and the dinghy was quite far away, but it kept growing, revealing more sandy mass.

"That's pretty fucking cool." I nodded in appreciation.

"Yeah, pretty gnarly, hey? The reef is full of magic like this," beamed the crew member.

The cloud was gone, all my thoughts cleared while I marvelled at the sight of the island, which was growing bigger by the second. The crew member explained it was due to the time of day and the sun. When the sea levels dropped, lots of these little sand islands revealed themselves.

Once the all-clear was given, everybody jumped off the dinghies into the clearest water imaginable. My feet planted in the wet sand. The water was only knee-high, but instantly, a scream flew out of my mouth. It was like standing in a bucket of ice. They all laughed as I tried to high-tail it on to the sandy mound, but once the initial bolts of shivers had run through me, it felt quite pleasant. My feet stopped running, feeling every grain of wet sand rolling and tickling the soles of my feet like a soft grainy massage while moulding around them. Clumps of sand stuck to my feet as I finally got out of the water and on to the dry mound. Although it had just risen from the ocean, the sand was already dry.

My friends were all busy taking countless pictures. Following a rave in the middle of the sand dunes back in Mildura, I was camera-less. Turns out, using a large plastic container lid as a sledge to sandboard is not a good idea. That night, I lost a phone and a camera, along with a wallet and a little dignity.

"Fucking hell, Amit's actually smiling. Not seen that since you landed back on Earth from jumping out a plane." Tom laughed.

"Are you kidding me? How could I not be smiling? Look at this, we're standing in the middle of the freaking Great Barrier Reef. Like, fucking literally standing in the middle of the ocean."

"Yeah, boi! Walking on water now and we'll be inside it later on… feared, bro!" He burst out laughing, stepping to the side where waves started to roll in.

"And you had to go and ruin it."

"Nah, bro, so feared. You know you love it!"

In what world would a guy, who had repeatedly been told there was no hope in life and wouldn't succeed at anything, be standing on a mound of sand in the middle of the Great Barrier Reef while somebody was trying to steal his identity? My life is ridiculous.

Attention shifted to a swarm of chip-stealing seagulls appearing from nowhere, interrupting the laughter and calm waves with their defeating chirps.

Where did they come from? Did they spot breakfast while flying past or are they keeping distance from becoming something else's breakfast? Sharks... are there sharks close by?

The Great Barrier Reef was teeming with all kinds of tropical sea life, which was another reason why people came out here—to see and experience the corals and the marine life. We would also be finding Nemo later on in the day and an opportunity to confront a huge fear of mine.

The ocean lapped around, although we had been on the boat for a couple of days with no sight of land, this was a completely surreal feeling. The ocean had started to reclaim the mound, which was our signal to leave after a quick flurry of pictures.

*

It had been too hot to be out on the deck with the rest of them. Since returning from the sand mound, sitting inside had been the best option to hide from the afternoon sun. Another battle had started within, concerning more immediate and pressing matters than the identity theft. It had been a constant back and forth about the scuba dive. One minute, looking for excuses not to do it, then feeling excited about what was down there—the corals and different types of marine life.

A force I hadn't felt since Melbourne was making its presence known. It was on another level compared with the slight fear and anxiety I felt jumping out of a plane. This could become crippling, but I was determined not to let that be the case. Tom's matching bright-red face and body appeared through the varnished wooden doors of the main cabin area, taking slow steps inside as the boat rocked left, bouncing back down on the wave—the currents had decided to wake up a little.

"Just checking up on you, you've not disappeared into a hole, have you? Not coming up with excuses?"

"Nope, just relaxing, let's go for a smoke."

While most were on the front deck, we headed towards the back deck. I kept my hood up as protection from the sun but slipped on sunglasses as Tom followed. Even the cigarette tasted of salt. As amazing as it was out here, I for one would be glad to be on solid ground, not just on a temporary sand mound and away from salt. The two of us leant over the rail, there were already a few people out floating on the turquoise calm sea snorkelling, including our other two friends.

My attention, though, went to the handful on the lower deck directly below. They were getting their final instructions while putting on scuba gear and oxygen tanks. It was while watching the first few jump into the ocean that a boulder plummeted in the pit of my stomach. That force from Melbourne was back tenfold, nearly physically pushing me back from the rail. The cigarette couldn't find my lips as my hands trembled from just the thought, my whole body was vibrating, fear was taking control.

"I don't want to do it, I can't."

"Boorrrinnnggg!" Tom sniggered while shaking his head, and continued, "I was waiting for this. Do you really want to be the guy who went out on the Great Barrier Reef and didn't dive?"

He was right, there was no way I couldn't. This was a fear I had to conquer today, I wasn't going to let it win like it did in Melbourne. Both of my inner voices had done a runner right when I needed a pep talk—typical of them. Tom was called down by one of the girls who needed some help. I took another long pull and smoke filled my lungs once more—probably not the best idea before a scuba dive. Affirmations were needed in the absence of the inner voices. I could do this by myself.

Fear isn't real, just a state of mind that can become debilitating but can—and will—be conquered. I'm going to do this, fear is just a lack of understanding.

It was working, my confidence started to grow, but then instantly evaporated when my name was called out from below, leaving my whole body to shake. The boulder had got bigger, falling harder, my throat clammed up so much, I couldn't reply back. I wanted to shake my head and go and hide, but I nodded. Somehow, I needed to get down there, but it felt as if my legs would fail if I let go of the rail.

In all the years of doing dumb shit, jumping off walls, trees, breaking bones, doing dangerous jumps off bikes, the fear was never there. So, why was it making its presence known now? Was it because of age and being more conscious, or because of the unknown? Fear feeds from a lack of understanding, the sea was that for me. I just needed to understand the sea to get over the fear. And I could only do that by getting in it. A scattering of bodies was out in the calm blue water snorkelling, while Tom sat waiting for me.

"I take it this is your friend who's scared to dive?" asked the instructor.

She stood with a clipboard and a high-vis jacket like she was on a construction site.

"Not scared, no, not at all—I'm shitting myself. No idea why, I can swim, never had a drowning experience or anything bad happen. It's just something in my head blocking me."

"It's OK, you're in good hands, and with your friend's ear and regulatory problems, you'll have an instructor between you both. There's nothing to worry about." She nodded back, while pointing for me to sit next to Tom.

She was doing all she could to calm my nerves, but the more words that came out, the more I zoned out, missing most of the instructions. We hadn't even had any training—no PADI or any training in a swimming pool. The instructions that did not compute were all the training I was going to get. As she carried on talking, flippers appeared on the floor as did a wetsuit, goggles, and the tank. The sight of them made my heart want to escape and run back to the coastline, wherever that was. The others leapt up, sliding into their gear, while I struggled to get into the tight rubbery suit—much to the delight of the other two. However, it was the flippers that were the hardest to adjust to.

How the fuck do penguins walk? one of my inner voices piped up.

Now it decided to appear; where was it when I needed a pep talk?

I had never put flippers on before and could barely lift a foot. Once the oxygen tank was placed on my back, it felt like an anchor, nearly falling back like a tree being chopped. Balancing was not fun, and it didn't help that my nerves were jangling like bells on Christmas Day.

There were a few more instructions about hand signals—the most important one being the signal to come back up to the surface. Soon, it was just Tom and me with our instructor; my heart hadn't calmed in the slightest. I could see my wet suit thumping.

Are we seriously doing this? I think I feel sick. ABORT, ABORT, ABORT!

Every fibre in my body wanted to back away the closer I waddled like a drunk penguin to the edge.

Fuck, come on, we can do this, deep breath, fuck fear, remember the time you jumped off the school building, remember the countless trees and rope swings you jumped off into lakes. It's the same thing... just do it! No more thinking about it—just do it.

A countdown started in my mind.

1... 2... 3... Go!

I braced for the impact of the freezing cold water... but my feet were still on the deck, they didn't get the memo to jump. More encouragement came, which prompted a look to the sky. More deep breaths followed. The instructor was clearly getting frustrated, especially after I tried to jump again but failed. There was ladder that seemed like the better choice. One foot submerged, breaking the surface.

"Fuck! It's FREEZING!" I wept.

The shock rose, seeping through the wetsuit and freezing my organs, making it hard to breathe. As the other foot followed, it slid on the ladder and the shock from the freezing cold water shot through my body, hitting my brain. My diaphragm squeezed tight like a bear was squeezing the life out of me, barely able to breathe.

Breathe out, idiot, I need to breathe out—and put the goggles on—now breathe in!

The commands were getting lost somewhere and my mind was spinning like I was having a panic attack in the water. The instructor came over before it registered that I should start climbing out. He tried to get me to relax, but the water was too cold—it was an ice bath of shock.

The others kept encouraging me, and against all my wishes, I climbed lower with the goggles over my eyes. Neither fear nor panic were going to win—not this time.

Once in the water, there was a little cheer, my arms instantly wrapped around the rail under the back deck as I tried so hard to remember how to breathe.

The rail acted like a safety blanket, but my body felt like it was getting sucked under, holding tighter, trying to frantically push away, the current felt so strong. Even though I was wet from the ocean, I could feel sweat pouring out; this felt like the hardest workout I'd done in years. The instructor must have seen me struggle as he came over and helped to pull me away towards where Tom was wading around.

"You don't want to do that. The boat's propellers are down there, you could have got sucked in."

My eyes were as wide as saucers under the goggles. This was not going well so far—all I could do was nod.

You what now? Propellers! Like I could have got sucked in and become mincemeat for sharks. Fucking hell, I wanna get outta here. I don't like it.

But I didn't, we were going under, taking the mouthpiece of the oxygen tank, making sure it was covered like the instructor advised. My mouth clamped down like a vice, almost biting into it. Fear had fully gripped me from the panic and shock, but I was learning to breathe with the aid of the oxygen. It took a few minutes to get used to, and either I was getting used to the temperature or my body had just become so numb to it. Who knew the Great Barrier Reef would be so like the Arctic. The instructor slid in between us, ready to submerge. In an instant, my breath became shorter and quicker; I bit down harder on the mouthpiece as the sky and open air slowly disappeared. The surface became the ceiling as a new lucid world came into sight. One that was apparently terrifying for no reason.

Breathe, Amit, just fucking breathe… slow, deep breaths, regulate it, nice and slow.

Instantly there was a sense of accomplishment for being under the surface for more than a few seconds. My hand raised to give the OK sign to the instructor, as did Tom's. I was happy to submerge a little more. I had started to control my breathing, long deep breaths helped to calm me down. The further we dropped, hitting the first metre below the surface, little fish started to come into view. Most were smaller than my hand, but the bright colours shone through as did the rays from the giant ball of fire in the sky.

There were no corals in sight just yet. I could feel a smile trying to grow, but my mouth remained tightly wrapped around the mouthpiece, breathing nice and slow. This new liquid world started to open up, and the fear, it seemed, was disappearing. It still remained a mystery why the fear took over so much. I had seen so many underwater documentaries in the past, wishing I could explore like the divers did. And here I was, doing exactly that in one of the most famous spots in the world, but I nearly chickened out of it.

The instructor made another signal to go further down. It felt like time had stopped in this alien world. A few curious fish approached to see what these giants were doing intruding on their world, while others just carried on with their lives. Some were in a hurry, zipping by, while others took their time, gliding, almost dancing, across the ocean. There was one type of small fish my eyes were on the hunt for—clownfish. All of a sudden, my eyes started to shoot around like a radar on the hunt for Nemo; all kinds of fish, from tropical vivid colours to dull colourless ones swam around, but there was no sign of Nemo. So far, there hadn't been any sign of any bigger fish either—namely reef sharks, hammerheads, and stingrays—which was probably what was keeping me calm.

Again, the instructor took us down further, I could feel my body ease up the further down we went, almost to a relaxed state. There was no issue with pressure, my breathing had calmed right down, to slow, long breaths, bubbles floated out and up to the surface with every exhale. As more inquisitive fish approached, my bravery had appeared. My hand even reached out to touch the slithery scaly fish. Some felt so smooth, while others' scales were rough.

Another thing to tick off the bucket list, sky dive over the Great Barrier Reef—check; standing on the Great Barrier Reef—check; scuba-diving under the Great

Barrier Reef—check. I'm fucking doing it. Fear of the ocean demolished—fucking check!

Vivid bright colours started to dance around us as corals came into view like rubbery tentacles. It was an underwater light show. The rays from the sun pierced through the water to provide spotlights and the corals' bright colours were so inviting. It was amazing to watch how the fish were attracted to them. Some headed to specific spots to feed, to rest, some just rubbed up against them before moving on to the next. This was their ecosystem and they knew exactly what they were doing. However, along with the vivid ones, there were some colourless ghostly white corals.

From documentaries, I knew they were dead corals—it meant the algae living in their tissues had left, this was caused by a number of things, but mostly climate change. The instructor didn't want to stick around those corals for long and headed further down. It was the first time the water felt denser, causing me to take deeper breaths as the water appeared to tighten. It was the first time Tom stopped the instructor. His ears were not regulating as they should, he took us up just a little, letting Tom get sorted before slowly descending. It felt like we had been down there for hours, I had no idea just how far down we had gone but it felt deep.

The water tightened again, but with Tom OK, we descended to what felt like the depth of the Great Barrier Reef but there was still no sign of nemo.

There was nothing to be afraid of, the fishes got on with their lives, dancing around, although they did start to get larger the further down we descended. The water felt tighter, the pressure was getting to Tom's ears, he was struggling just as I was ready to keep going further. His single hand gesture to the instructor set alarm bells firing. Internal sirens went off everywhere, fear latched on, pushing all my confidence and bravery out of the way to take over. It hadn't been demolished, after all.

ABORT, ABORT MISSION, ABORT.

Panic shot through me as Tom started to ascend. There was no rationale behind it, just blind panic. The instructor slowly led us back to the ever-lighter surface, my breathing became uncontrollable, desperate to get out of the water, quickly breaking through the ocean ceiling. A breeze slid past, signalling the return of air; I spat out the mouthpiece, gasping for fresh air.

The bleach-blonde instructor tried to persuade me to stay in the water, claiming I was doing so well, but that was it for me.

Fear controlled all my thoughts and actions, shaking my head against my own will. My inner voices implored me to stay and go back in. I wanted to go back in and go further down but my body was already on its way out of the water, saying no—it was Melbourne all over again. There was no listening to reason or to my own inner voices. That was it… it was over for the day.

Once out of the sea, out of the wetsuit, and dry, it was back to my little spot. This time, Tom joined me in staring out at the ocean we were under a few moments ago. It was another world under the surface, and although I stayed as long as I should have, just getting in and being submerged was a victory. Everything else was a welcome bonus. I just needed to learn to not let the fear take over like that.

"Going to give it another go?" Tom asked with his feet dangled over the ledge.

"I want to give it a go, yeah. Didn't think I would say that, did you?" I responded, staring out at the ocean.

"Bro, you should have stayed in longer, gone further down. I would have. Anyway, what's the plan when you get back to Sydney?"

"Alex is sorting out the apartment for a few of us, so I will finally be out of the hostel. Go back to work, no more backpacker life. It will be head down, working, hardly any parties. I'm not gonna break the promise," I responded.

"Good luck on that, we'll catch you at Christmas after our farm work."

"You got anything sorted for it? Trust me, don't leave it to the last minute. I was lucky Nick got me a place, otherwise, I would have been fucked."

"Yeah, we started looking before the trip, we've got a few places lined up. Will check more in Cairns and get it sorted before we go to Cape Tribulation. That's gonna be sick—in the Daintree Rainforest. Monkeys boys!"

"Fuck it, I might just disappear in the rainforest and become Tarzan. Fuck all the bullshit, the bad luck, let the other guy have my identity, he can deal with my bad luck. I'll live in the rainforest."

"I'll join you if I can't get any farm work."

Both of us burst out laughing at the prospect. This trip up the coast had been so incredible—full of so much discovery and wonder. From venturing around the rocks on Byron Bay, the experience on Nimbin, the mini road trips, experiencing pure silicon sand, the wildlife, canoeing through Nusa Dua's everglades, people we had met, to life on Fraser Island. It would have been even more incredible if the other side of my life wasn't so fucked up. But once this trip was over, that and the promise of getting my sponsorship was all that mattered, along with getting the identity theft sorted.

Nah, We're Not Lost!

"You are such a dickhead, Amit—not again!"

It wasn't the usual soft southern German accent floating across from the driver's seat to the passenger side of the campervan. It was stern, and a good job Alex was still driving. The tarmac on the road outside had turned to loose white stone, like an old dry dirt road not used in years as the bushes grew thicker and taller either side of it. There hadn't been a single vehicle pass us in hours. Although my finger traced along the map resting on my lap, it didn't feel right. It had been hours since we left the wide-open sprawling highway. In our—well, in my—infinite wisdom, I suggested to come off the highway and follow what I thought would be a scenic route to the campsite. I may have been wrong, the highway provided the view of rolling green hills and this route provided bushes closing up on us. But I couldn't admit that.

"What do you mean 'not again'?" I asked, knowing what the response would be.

"We are lost again. All the time getting lost!"

There was no need to look to know her nostrils were flaring—her tone said it all.

Yup, we are 100% lost, not a clue where we are, probably should have just stuck to the main highway. This map doesn't look right either.

"No, we're not lost… look, the map says we're going the right way. It's OK, just keep going."

"How can I look, dickhead? I am driving, but I do not believe. I know you too well. And, of course, I keep going. I'm not just going to stop in the middle of nothingness. Dickhead!"

Since getting lost on the very first night heading up to the most north tip of the country, it had become our thing, getting lost was a regular occurrence, the only difference was that this time, it was in the heartlands of the North Island. Before the coast was always reachable, tonight, having left behind the rotten-egg-smelling, sulphur-fuelled Rotorua, we were heading further inland. Rotorua, along with the Coromandel and abseiling into the Waitomo Caves just outside Hamilton, had been the highlights so far. The sulphur park, the natural hot springs, geysers erupting, the Mauri experience, learning the Haka, eating food cooked under the ground—all had been amazing experiences. But the foul eggy stench of sulphur would not be missed.

I couldn't take all the blame for getting lost... we had both decided not to plan anything except for a general idea of direction—from Auckland to Christchurch, touring both islands. We wanted to freestyle it because of both our experiences travelling Australia with everything planned and organised. This trip was unplanned, discovering and finding things as we go, so technically, we had never got lost—just discovered, like the true explorers we were.

Along with the map, a book listing all the campsites in New Zealand also lay open. We bought the book after we had got lost on that first night, massively failing to find a campsite. However, since acquiring the book, it hadn't stopped us from getting lost, but we had found some amazing places. Wild camping in New Zealand was quite popular and there had been some incredible locations with the most breath-taking scenery. Hopefully, tonight, we would stumble on another or I was going to be in trouble.

"According to the book, there should be a campsite close by, in about a mile—sorry, kilometre. There will be another road to turn off, we just follow that down and the campsite should be right there. See, I know what I'm doing. We're just discovering, that's all."

Tall thick trees replaced the bushes on either side of the road started to close up like they were swallowing the van up. Branches from both sides enveloped us and intertwined over each other, keeping the sunlight out to create a natural tunnel. Loose gravel churned against the rubber tyres, kicking up against the white van, causing Alex to slow right down.

"Wow, looks like an enchanted forest, where are the fairies?" Her face lit up. Her smile was back as she took it in.

"See, if we stuck to the highway and main roads, you wouldn't have got to see this," I said with a smug grin.

"Yes, that is true. OK, I do not mind. Amit did good."

Alex was a Black Forest girl, growing up in a village in the foothills of the forest a few hours from Munich. She had arrived in Australia as a backpacker, barely able to speak English, but in two years had picked it up to speak it fluently. A girl with an infectious personality, which people just gravitated towards. She was the person who not only pulled me out of the hole in England and helped me return to Australia, but she was the one person who balanced me.

When I lost my compass, my way, she centred me. Without her help, who knows where I would be. It was testament to her how she put up with my petulant bullshit at times. And she would never stay angry—she didn't see the point in it. That was something I was trying to learn from her.

The campervan started to bounce around, potholes who knows how old started to get deeper, but it was the perfect condition for one thing. A new skill I was forced to learn in New Zealand was to roll my own cigarettes rather than buy readymade, simply because it was too expensive. The only issue was, I sucked at rolling unless it was on a bumpy road. The road became only slightly smoother as the branches above unlaced a little, letting beams of sunlight through like punctured holes in a box, but the campervan came to a stop. Alex's dainty fingers slid over the map, following the route, murmuring something in Bavarian before starting back up. It wasn't long before a gorge started to reveal itself as the treeline grew thinner; the gravelled road ran alongside a fading river, it might have been raging in its glory years, but it was nothing more than a shallow wide stream now.

We're, like, proper lost, there aren't even any birds flying around. She is gonna be pissed big time.

The stream disappeared as the vegetation got thicker. This was the heartland of the North Island. The further we drove, the further we sank into thicker vegetation, but then… reprieve.

"Look, there's a sign to a campsite in two kilometres. See, I knew we were going the right way."

Woo. Thank fuck for that.

The rusty sign didn't exactly fill me with confidence, in fact, it looked more at home in the opening scene of a horror movie the way it hung on by a lonely nail on a broken post.

"Amit, this does not look right. I do not like. I have the… how do you say, creepy crawly."

"The heebie-jeebies?"

"Yes, this. What is it? Heeby-jeeb? This not real, you make these words up. Amit language?"

She turned off on to a tighter gravel road than the previous one.

"No, they're real words. But, yeah, it does look a little sketchy... I think we might need to update the book. Not my fault."

My words were cut short as everything started to get tossed around, the maps went flying as did the backpacks and bedding in the back and anything else that wasn't fastened down. The kettle, bottles of water, our snacks were all jumping around like the campervan was possessed. If I hadn't had my seatbelt on, I would have joined the splattered mosquitoes on the grey ceiling. A 4x4 was required to get down this road—not this old ex-rental campervan that we'd picked up for cheap. There was no way campervans came down here on a regular basis. Alex had to manoeuvre off the road and on to the long grass for fear of snapping the chassis underneath. As had been proven with previous breakdowns of this campervan, neither of us were mechanics—well, we were clueless. However, the old girl was proving she still could dance.

A huge huff from Alex flew in my direction like a spear—I was in the doghouse, that was for sure, especially as she hadn't called me a dickhead in a while. Slowly rolling along the grass, her sighs and grunts were saying everything. To make it worse, the bushes either side of us started to close in, scraping up against the van from either side, forcing us back on to the potholed death trap of a dry muddy track. My eyes flicked over to her as she wrestled with the steering wheel.

"We are so lost, it's not even funny now!" she snarled.

"Actually, I do know where we're meant to be, the Matahina forest."

Why? Why try and be a smart ass right now—just stay quiet!

"Oh, fuck off, Amit!"

No dickhead, she is pissed! Don't say anything else.

"Oh, come on, you're always telling me not to be so angry, let go of it. Where's your sense of adventure? We're exploring nature, discovering places off the beaten track. And we've been in worse places."

Stop talking. Shut the fuck up!

Finally, everything in the van settled, but it was like a tornado had just passed through. The bushes started to open back up, just enough for us to roll down the dry muddy track to the welcome sign, which was covered in moss and pinned to a tree. There was a very eerie and still feel to the place, but there was another vehicle with a tent next to it in the small field.

"No, I think this one is the worst one. I do not like it at all. If Hannibals come to eat us, I push you in front."

"Oh yeah, thanks. But I think you mean cannibals. Hannibal is a character who is a cannibal."

"Yes, this, but you still get eaten first."

She rolled the van into the field. Normally, she would have parked it up against the bushes to shield us from the wind, but with the 4x4 already there, she parked opposite next to the little stream. We didn't know if the person in the 4x4 was a traveller who had got lost like us or a mass murderer waiting for his next victim. It took a few minutes of sitting in the van, surveying the damage inside and looking out at the dead stream outside before finally stepping out on to uncut grass to check the area out as normal. There was nothing but near silence. No birds chirped, no noises from the surrounding woodland. Just the slight trickle from the sorry excuse of a stream beneath the bank. It didn't feel right at all, there was something in the air and the place felt abandoned. Even the old wooden bridge towards the far end looked like it could fall to pieces and nobody would care.

Alex was right, this did seem like the worst of all the times we had got lost and found random off-the-grid campsites. There were no facilities, not even basic ones within eyeshot, and while normally we would go off to explore the area, we thought better of it this time.

"We should cook, get the van sorted, we leave early in the morning if we are still alive," she fumed.

She really didn't like this place—usually, her sense of adventure came out once she got out of the van, but not today.

"Yeah, I agree, but not like stupid o'clock in the morning."

"When it is light, we leave. OK, you cook, I will tidy the wan." Alex opened up the back of the van, it was like a tsunami had hit it not a tornado.

It wasn't the right time, but a chuckle escaped my mouth, her not being able to say 'van' properly never got old.

"Wait, what food have we got left? We didn't do any shopping," I said.

"We have lots of pasta and I think some sauce too."

Oh, great… another night of pasta, moaned one of my inner voices.

I'd eaten more pasta through these few weeks in the campervan than in two years in Australia. A hatred of pasta was growing by the day.

The minivan was equipped with a little campfire stove on one of the back corners. It was lit and the pasta put on to boil. Alex dove in from the sliding side door, humming away while tidying what was our bedroom, living room, and dining room rolled into one tiny space.

"Alex, we have a little bit of a problem," I said while looking through from the back of the van.

The pasta hadn't cooked even in the slightest. I hoped she didn't have a heavy or sharp object in her hand. There had been many occasions over the past year where I had royally pissed her off, but for some reason, she put up with my shit. I could tell today was testing her patience.

"Oh, Amit, don't… the gas?"

"Yeah, we didn't top the canister up, completely out. The pasta is not cooked at all."

Her eyes shot daggers in my direction.

"This is…"

"Yeah, yeah, I know, all my fault. I fucked up again. I know, I know. Always Amit's fault."

"Yes, you are correct, but I was going to say this is why I have the emergency food bag." She grabbed a bag, smiling at me.

"The what now? When did this happen?"

"Always, since we begin, I top up for emergency like this. Some bread roll, fruits, and potato chips." Her smile widened as she started to rustle through it.

I jumped into the van as she sourced that night's dinner, while she tucked straight into the fruit. She could live off fruit, but I couldn't.

Just do what we used to do when there was no food in the house growing up.

She watched curiously as I cut open the bread roll, or cob as it's called where I'm from, and stuffed it with the potato chips.

"What are you doing?" She looked horrified.

"Crisp cob," I tried to say with my mouth stuffed.

"Oh, you are so, so, so weird at times!" She burst out laughing.

"I'm weird? Says the girl who eats pickles on an open slice of bread."

"Oh, so good, I would love now if there was pickles." She leant back, rubbing her tummy and licking her lips, salivating over the idea.

Laughter filled the van, not so much about our different tastes in food, but more about the latest predicament we had found ourselves in. Since she arrived over from Australia, instantly, my mind had been at ease. All the thoughts swimming around had gone, my own situation, the way I've felt over the past month since having to leave Australia because my sponsorship fell through—it all just vanished. She was the one who took it upon herself to pull me out of the darkness in England and help get me back to Australia. The weird thing was, before I left, we barely knew each other. We were different in many ways—completely opposite upbringings, different outlooks on life, different tastes in practically everything, but somehow, we just gelled together. From the moment we became friends, she balanced me out, the positivity to my negativity… whatever it was, it just worked. There was a comfort level, trust, and ease with her I'd never had before. She had seen all sides of me, including my demons and had laughed in their faces. She pulled the map from the passenger side on to her lap, but looked up at me laughing.

"What, why you laughing?"

"Nothing."

"There's obviously something. Go on."

"Just that you now have your tax money finally after all this time today, but we are stuck here and you are eating this. You were so happy this afternoon, wanting to eat everything in a restaurant tonight."

"Yeah, but tomorrow in Gisborne we can. It's such a relief I finally got it. All that bullshit for no reason, just because they fucked up," with my final mouthful done, I nodded back, trying not to laugh and spit my food back out.

It turned out there wasn't any identity theft after all, it was the tax office that created a duplicate identity and then claimed it was identity theft. They put me through hell, the stress levels were through the roof—and it took a lot of back and forth with the tax office to get to the bottom of it, and then it took so long for it all to get processed. It was due back a week after we returned from our east coast trip, but it only took nine months from them acknowledging it was their fault to landing in my account that day when leaving Rotorua. So much stress but for no reason.

"But what did I tell you before? It will work out at the right time because it always does for Amit. When you need it the most. If you had it in Australia when you were supposed to, you would have spent it all before leaving. If it came when you arrived in Auckland, you would have spent it before I came. But now you have it for the rest of this trip and to help you when I go back to Australia."

She was right, it would have been all spent. There are times I think she knows me better than I know myself. In fact, she is the only person outside my immediate family who knows everything about me. Even my pre-travelling past, which I don't talk to anybody else about.

Just as I finished rolling a crooked cigarette, her face changed from smiling to scowling, with her eyebrows pushed together in a frown.

"Dickhead!"

"What? What have I done now?"

The map was pushed in my direction, along with the map on the book.

"Look, you said no other roads. Look like you need my glasses. There is another road, compare on both, there is an old road and new road and look at the campsite."

"Oh."

"Yes, oh… dickhead. We are on the wrong road, the new road is where the campsite now is."

That made a lot of sense—the old bridge, how hard it was to get to, the sign about falling off. I tried to laugh it off.

"Another Amit and Alex adventure."

"No, another Amit mess-up."

That was my cue to slip outside for a smoke. Day had turned to night in the time we'd been in the van and we hadn't even noticed, but the eerie levels had edged up. There was silence, no nocturnal noises interrupted it, no hoots from owls we had become accustomed to in and around wooded campsites—nothing but the sliver of water from the stream. It was instinct to look around to the 4x4, but there was no light from the car nor the tent.

Whoever is in the tent is either asleep or just sitting in the dark. What if he is a murderer or on the run for something? This is the perfect hideout, no way anybody would come out to look for him here. What if he skins us alive tonight and assumes our identities?

He's fucked if he takes mine and has to deal with all the shit that goes with me.

My inner voices needed to be reeled in, they were running away with my imagination. Something else started to take my attention, it wasn't actually that dark. It felt like spotlights were shining down on the campsite, so much so, the bridge was in clear view.

It's an alien hotspot. We're gonna get abducted!

It wasn't aliens at all, it was the stars, they were shimmering down so brightly and hanging so low, almost touchable and very hypnotic. The more I focused on them, the more of them appeared. The stars were not just sprinkled in the night sky as usual, it was covered in them, like millions of diamonds illuminating, some sparkling, others glowing green and red.

This wasn't ordinary. To see this many stars should require a telescope, but these were all seen with my naked eye—the silence made sense. Sitting on the grass looking up at them, my hand reached up as I tried to touch them, they felt so close. Layers upon layers flickered and shimmered down to the point it felt like there was more light than dark sky. It was like being up there in the cosmos.

I had never seen anything like it from a night sky, not even back in Mildura or on the castaway trip. This was something else, especially seeing the fumes, smears, or space clouds behind them.

Is that the Milky Way? Are we looking at this for real?

It needed to be asked, it was like being in a lucid dream, it just didn't feel real, I felt lost in them. Things that had happened over the past few months started to float in front of my eyes—it was like seeing it all on a highlight reel.

"I'm sorry. I broke the promise. I tried my hardest, I did everything I could, but it didn't work out. I let you down."

A lonesome tear trickled into the crease between my cheek and nose, like the stream below leaving a slithering trail. Another quickly followed behind. Not since the night I had heard the news of my grandad's passing had I shed a tear like this. England was hell for me, and it was made even worse laying him to rest. The thought of his final few days eat away at me because I wasn't there. And now the promise I made him to make a life for myself in Australia had been broken.

Just as everything was falling into place and it was looking like I would finally live that 'normal life', life said no. It wanted to fuck with me and snatched it away right at the last minute. My world imploded even more because I couldn't keep the promise and I've felt lost ever since. It was also the reason why I was in New Zealand on a new working holiday visa. My sponsorship had been pulled by a jumped-up twat. There wasn't any time to try for another and there was no way I would return to England. Whatever it took, I never wanted to go back. It was a new start, a new beginning, a new mission to keep away from England for as long as I possibly could.

More than the sponsorship, I would have given anything to hear my grandad's voice again. To be able to sit with him and share a whisky, tell him of my adventures in Australia and so far in New Zealand. The funny thing is, I know his response would be to shout at me about it first. He would tell me off because I'd not settled down yet. He would tell me to stop fucking around, calling me an idiot for travelling in a campervan, but then want to hear all my stories. I wish I could hear him shout at me, I'd just smile and hug him. I hadn't taken my eyes off the stars once—time and space felt like it had stopped. The stars were getting stronger, closer, the smoke behind them thicker. The trees, the grass, the van, everything else disappeared for a moment.

All of a sudden, my body nearly jumped out of its skin as I leapt up to my feet like a cat.

"Mother of Jesus! What the fuck was that? Who the fuck was it? Alex, was that you fucking around? Not fucking funny."

There was no response, the loudest noise now came from a thumping African drum—it was my heart and was showing no signs of calming down. Every hair on my body stood on high alert as mini lightning bolts shot through my spine on a constant loop.

What the fuck was that? That was real, I didn't just imagine that—it felt real.

Something pushed down on my shoulder like a hand. My eyes shot around the field trying to figure out what just happened or if somebody was hiding out there, it wasn't clear what it was. The tent was still dark, as was the 4x4. With force, I flung open the side door of the van, thinking—hoping—it was Alex messing around.

I caught her, red-handed, but not for what I thought— she was doing something else. Her innocent green eyes turned into saucers.

"Whaaa?"

For a moment, the reason I had burst open the door was forgotten as I burst into laughter.

"Oh, look at you, caught you red-handed, never again can you say anything about my food habits."

"Wha? I was hungry, I tried it. It's OK. But I think because I'm hungry I like it."

She moved the crisp cob from her mouth, continuing to swallow down the rest.

"Where have you been? I thought you got taken or something," she said.

"And you didn't step outside once to check?"

"Nope, I not go outside. They take you, not me. Why do you look like this? Scared? What happened?" She was stuffing another cob with crisps, shaking her head.

I had jumped back in the van before any mosquitoes could follow me. They were probably already in there, laying low until the lights went out and they could start their feast like they did every single night.

Get back on track, forget about the mozzies.

I proceeded to explain what just happened outside, but she didn't laugh or mock, she just kept picking at the cob.

"Maybe you just have a moment and felt him. He wanted to show he is here with you always and knows how you are feeling and wanted to tell you not to feel sad. That it was OK that you were not there, or about the sponsorship."

I lay back on the long cushions and bedding on my side, shaking my head and staring up at the splattered mosquitoes. There were just as many as the stars in the sky outside.

"Come on, bollocks was it that. You know I don't believe in that mumbo-jumbo."

"What else could it be? It wasn't me and there is nobody else out there. Unless it was whoever is in the other car, but you scared them away."

Now she was mocking, but that was more believable than my grandad's afterlife spirit touching my shoulder. I had sunk so far into my thoughts, it was probably just my mind playing tricks, or it felt real because I was lucidly dreaming.

"I did fuck up, though, didn't I? I had the apartment with you guys, all of you are getting
sponsored now, just me who fucked up as usual."

She rolled on to her side to face me, shaking her head.

"Oh, come on, stop that. You know it wasn't your fault, it was your stupid new boss. It just wasn't meant to be. You have a new life now. When I go back to Australia, you will have your own adventures, and when the time is right, it will come to you."

"You know me, you know my past, why do you have so much faith in me when I don't even have it?"

"Because of this, I know you and you don't see it. You don't see how lucky you are."

"Yeah, so lucky, right? I wish people would stop saying that."

"It's all part of your journey. One day you will see it and you will call me to say, 'Alex, you're amazing, you were right.' But right now, Alex needs to sleep. Goodnight."

Before I could even reply, she was out cold. She had literally just finished eating. I didn't understand people who could fall asleep just like that. My mind needs to decompress before sleeping. It likes to go on a wild goose chase, think about something from when I was a child, then make something up before fading away. Falling asleep is a long process. I guess that's the difference between a clear-thinking mind and a tangled one like mine. I needed another smoke.

The stars hadn't budged, in fact, it felt like there was more. The night sky was barely visible against the bright shining and shimmering diamonds. This time, my back was not leaving the side of the van though.

* * *

"Amit, stop touching it."

"It's fucking right there on my lip, a fucking balloon! Why don't they ever come for you?"

"Because I'm sweet and nice and you are…"

"No, actually it's because my blood is sweet, they feast on me. So, I'm sweeter than you."

"If you believe this, OK, but you look like you got hit by a boxer and I don't. This is fine with me."

Her comment only warranted a growl, which was laughed off, but my tongue hadn't stopped rolling over it since I discovered it when I woke up, which had also provided Alex with her morning's entertainment. Apart from a mosquito biting my upper lip, we had survived the night and there had been no more imaginary interactions with my grandad. Alex even admitted the drive through the scenic backroads had been incredible—mountain ranges with the sun shining down through the low clouds, which had caused shadows to reflect off the ranges, had greeted us for most of the journey.

However, those clouds got thicker and darker along the way—and none were over my head but over Gisborne itself. Our welcome wasn't all sun rays, but the patter of rain bouncing off the roof—at least the van got a much-needed wash. The darkness overhead had seemingly sucked the colour out of the town. There was only one reason for coming all the way to the most easterly point of New Zealand, and that was to see the sunrise. With it being the most easterly point, it was the first place to see the sun rising in the world.

Alex drove the van right through the glum-looking town, through to the point where the sun rises on the coast, which was coincidentally also where the campsite was. At least there was no getting lost looking for this one. As she turned in to the stretch of grass for campervans, the sea and sky shared the grey tone—it was hard to tell where the sea ended and sky started.

"So, this is great, it's meant to rain all week. It's summer. It's been baking hot everywhere we've been and the one place we need it to be warm and with clear skies, the clouds want to cover it all up. Just bloody fantastic."

Laughter rang out in the front of the van as she parked up, switching the engine off.

"Because you say you have no luck." She was mocking once more.

"Yup, just adding this one to the long list. Let's have a look at the good luck list—oh, just three items."

Her eyes rolled as the rain started to batter the roof like an army of arrows barraging down on intruders. She knew I was about to say something and jumped in.

"Not everything is your fault. It's the weather. It can change. Stop being negative."

"I was just going to ask what you wanted for lunch since I have my tax money back. I want sushi."

A scrunched-up face looked in my direction—she knew I was going to moan but said the lunch thing to save face. She nodded back in agreement but tilted her seat back and closed her eyes.

"Sure you were, but, yes, let's have sushi. I have a nap until the rain stops a little. Wake me up when it stops."

The grey dullness was a stark contrast to the glittery shining stars of the previous night, but New Zealand was a country of stark contrasts. It had provided so much natural beauty and scenery, which had educated me about how travelling isn't just about the action-packed activities or checking off a list of famous spots. An adventure can come in many forms—the journey yesterday didn't feel like much but a wrong turn to begin with, but in a way, it ended up being an adventure. If we hadn't taken the wrong turn and followed through with the treacherous road, we wouldn't have ended up there and potentially wouldn't have seen those incredible stars. That was a unique experience, and feeling and travelling is about the moments, experiences, and feelings acquired—for me it was anyway. New Zealand had provided a few of those moments through getting lost, wrong turns, and finding natural beauty everywhere.

Blood, Sweat & Mordor

"Wake up, dickhead! We have to go soon!"

The words barely penetrated, they felt faint, almost like they weren't real, but another round volleyed through, this time louder but not strong enough to deter me from the juicy steak. However, the third time prompted a response.

"Fuck off, Alex, let me sleep," I pleaded.

The dream evaporated. The interaction also caused my senses to awaken. Cold air attacked from every direction. Any hope of slipping under the duvet and the dream returning was thwarted. Protection from the cold was pulled away. I was exposed to the frosty air filling the campervan and had only one response—to curl into a ball under any item of clothing in arm's reach. But they too were pulled away from me.

"No, no, no—wakey, wakey time," rang her floaty voice.

"What time is it?"

"The half past of the quarter to five."

No, it's too early for your riddles, just let me sleep, woman. Why are you so sadistic waking up so early?

"Come on, Amit, it's adventure day. You want this one, so wake up."

That tone was repulsive, so light, bouncy, and ugh—happy! I hated that about Alex, the early bird that she is. I hated it in Australia, and I hated it in this campsite, but my body rose from the dead.

"Alright, alright, I'm up."

"Open your eyes then."

"Can't we go later on?" My head shook in response, my eyelids refused to open.

"No, we have to go soon. Come on, Amit, the coffee will be ready in a minute."

A growl escaped from my mouth. It was what I like to refer to as 'stupid o'clock', and judging by the groans throughout the heavily wooded campsite, others being woken felt the same way. It was so early, even the birds were not chirping yet. Slowly, the heavy shutters over my eyes started to lift, but there was a malfunction and they slammed shut. The smell of sweet, almost creamy, cheap three-in-one coffee swimming in the brisk morning air got the attention of my nose. There was some internal communication in my brain that caused my eyelids to attempt to lift. This time, they got stuck halfway. My morning smile was out of commission, on strike it seemed, as a coffee was handed through to me from the back. Just the faintest moonlight shone down through the thick tall trees, giving enough light to make out a few other shadows moving in and out of tents and campervans outside.

"Good morning!" Alex beamed.

"I hate you." It was the only appropriate response and was followed by a growl and a curling top lip.

"No, you don't."

Stupid early morning adventure days. Whose stupid idea was it anyway?

*

Light started to fill the vast open dry landscape in the early morning half-light, the slow rising sun caused huge domineering sharp and jagged silhouettes to rise up from the earth to stand tall in the surrounding distance. It was as if an artist had made brushstrokes behind the shadowy silhouettes, painting the sky from a deep orange beam to blend into a light blue, leaving the moon high above. It was remarkable, one of the best daybreaks so far. New Zealand, on many occasions, felt like travelling through a masterpiece. The scenery—from black sand beaches to rolling green hills to dry rocky mountains—was simply stunning and this was no different.

Tour groups and individual hikers marched past on the raised wooden boardwalk towards the bottom of the silhouettes. All of them kitted out in full hiking gear, the correct type of footwear, cargo pants or shorts, aided by hiking poles and carrying backpacks. The tour groups followed flag bearers, while the individual hikers made sure their maps were in hand. It was like watching a well-drilled army unit march by. However, I decided to take another route, jumping off the boardwalk, dancing past the little spiky shrubs poking out of the dry dusty earth, making sure not to disturb them.

"See, happy Amit is here, dancing and chasing the waterfalls, glad that Alex woke him up early."

Alex's soft bouncy accent flowed as softly as the mini streams and baby waterfalls that held my attention. The baby waterfalls falling off the little rocks flowing downhill were away from the boardwalk, but there was enough footing and dry earth to dance around in my cream Nike pumps—not exactly hiking footwear, but they were comfortable and light.

"Nope, Amit is happy because of the adventure today and because I drank three cups of coffee before the sun could come up, not because Alex woke me up at stupid o'clock."

"Oh, come on, waking up early is not so bad. We have the whole day to adventure and explore it. How do you call this... Merder? Molder? Mondor?" she asked while also dancing around the bushes.

"Mordor, Alex, Mordor! We are in the setting for Mordor. We're in *The Lord of the Rings,* and today, I am Frodo going on a quest to Mount Doom."

"You are right, you do drink too much coffee today. You know I've never seen or read *The Lord of the Rings*. I do not know but my sister is huge fan, she has all the books and the DVD collection, so lots of pictures to make her jealous." She beamed, hiding under her windbreaker jacket.

How has she not seen The Lord of the Rings? Doesn't matter, I'm going on a quest wherever my imagination takes me. 'Bout as tall as Frodo anyway.'

Today wasn't the first time we were experiencing a setting from *The Lord of the Rings* movie. Through the North Island, we had abseiled into the Waitomo Caves, which was also used in the movies. The only place we had ignored was Hobbiton. Although I had never read the books, the movies had captured me, but it was the scenery I fell in love with the most, New Zealand for the most part felt like being in a fantasy movie setting, and today was another opportunity to be a part of that amazing setting. A few tuts could be heard across the boardwalk as more hikers marched by. They obviously were not impressed with our dancing over and around the shrubs. Or they just didn't approve of my hiking gear consisting of an England football jersey, hoodie, and shorts.

The dusty colourless dry earth started to turn to a rich, coppery red the closer and bigger the mountains became. They were emerging from the shadows to reveal their true domineering rock faces.

They're a lot higher than they seemed at the beginning of the boardwalk. I have to go up there?

Yeah, maybe we did come a little underprepared.

Alex had already jumped back on to the boardwalk and it didn't take long for me to follow as there was no other obvious route to take. There were more looks, shaking of heads, and tuts as more hikers streamed past. It seemed my attire screamed out 'clueless or typical backpacker'. One of the hikers in front was even carrying a rope.

Why does he have a rope? Do we need a rope? Nobody else has one, though, I guess he's just being cautious or he's a rock climber. We don't need a rope, we'll be fine.

"Alex, are we a little underprepared for this? Look at what everybody else is wearing. We look like we're just going for a leisurely walk."

"No, I'm fine, just no hiking stick. You are just you." Her green eyes dotted around and she shrugged.

"What do you mean, just me?"

She ignored the question as the boardwalk started to get swallowed up by the earth until it completely disappeared. All of a sudden, a coppery rusty smell took over the air. Loose charcoal had replaced the dry grey dusty ground and it almost felt like we were standing on a different planet. Wind swept up some of the finer loose charcoal grazing across my exposed legs like crushed glass. It only took another few steps before I was dwarfed under a sheer rock face that stretched up high to touch the sky.

So, yup, a lot bigger than it looked. Maybe we do need a rope. There probably should have been some planning and research done rather than just turning up.

Yeah, and where is everybody? Where did all the hikers go? Where's Alex? Is there a secret way through the mountains?

"This way, dickhead," Alex's German accent floated down from the side.

There was no secret door, but a rocky pathway was hiding behind a huge boulder. I could feel the corners of my lips widening, the adrenaline was just kick-starting into action.

Here we go, the quest is about to begin.

The first few metres were deceiving, luring me into a false sense of security—it was an easy climb for the first fifty metres, but then the incline suddenly become steeper. The ground loosened and little stones rolled around under my feet. Before I could think, tiny sharp stones were being embedded into my hands and knees,

Alex was laughing but pain shot through from the moment the ground gave way.

"Maybe you should have got better footwear?"

That was her response to seeing me hit the ground. Fifty metres in and blood had already been spilled. It took a little while to pick all the little stones out, but they left indents and burning sensations ran from my palms and knees.

"See, this is karma. You make fun of my hiking boots, always saying they just get in the way. This is what happens. I don't fall, but you do," Alex was taking great pleasure in my pain.

"No, not karma, I just slipped that's all. Come on, let's go."

The ground kept swapping from long stone slabs to flattened dirt, to loose stones, and caution was needed. The wind wasn't helping, little swirls passed by, picking up dirt, grazing as it drifted by. With each step up the incline, it was clear this wasn't a manufactured path. It would be much easier if there were wooden steps with a handrail. It made complete sense why others had hiking sticks. The higher the ascent, the smaller everything below seemed—the little shrubs were barely visible, but there wasn't much of a view from this side of the mountain face. It sounded like other hikers were struggling, but looking, there was nobody around. The heavy breathing was from my lungs—years of smoking was not helping the climb.

Dusty but crisp mountain air had started to fill my lungs, trying to break through the layers of tar from years of smoking, which made breathing a little difficult. At the same time, blood had started to pump through dormant muscles, which became tired in an instant from a lack of use. My body's engine was trying to kick into gear while climbing a mountain, but it was a strain. The pathway started to veer inwards for a few metres until it just stopped. Rocks arched over; jagged splints stood as obstacles to the other side. It was really starting to feel like an adventure. Alex had already made her way over.

"It's easy, just climb up and look on the side for footings." She stood on higher ground, looking back down.

My eyes followed her finger to see little stumpy rocks poking out of the side of the mountain, acting like foot holes. The stone slab was cold against my palms as I held on and pushed with my legs to climb over. My inner child had burst out of the adult suit, and monkey boy—just like my grandad used to call me—was climbing away. I would never claim to be a mountain climber, but from a young age, I would climb anything—walls, rocks, trees. But that's not to say there were never any mishaps.

One of my earliest childhood memories was trying to conquer a tree outside my grandad's house out next to the steam train tracks. It took a few attempts, but the first time I reached a high branch, it snapped, causing me to crash on to concrete, splitting the back of my head open. I must have only been four or five, but that was the start of my injury curse. Since then, visits to A&E (accident and emergency) became regular occurrences. The climbing and being a monkey boy continued and so did breaking practically every bone on the left side of my body. However, the older I got, and as my attitude to life changed, the less the injuries came from climbing and more from fighting and drunken mishaps. There was more than a chance today could end in broken bones.

Alex had already started to slip over the crevices, climbing up on to the next ledge as I followed.

"This is fucking awesome, we're climbing up a mountain in Mordor, just let that sink in for a second," I beamed.

"Yes, it's fun, no Black Forest, but fun." She smiled back.

Alex was also not one to shirk away from climbing adventures, in fact, there had been a few places she had got up trees and boulders quicker than I had. She was very much an up-for-any-adventure type of girl. But then what do you expect from someone who grew up exploring one of the most famous forests in the world and snowboarding since she was a child? There was a reason she thought driving around death-trap cliffs was a Sunday drive.

Sturdier ground greeted my feet, but the incline was much sharper. The wind picked up again, but my hoodie was doing a terrible job at protecting me from it. Alex's windbreaker was looking rather appealing right now. The flat, almost polished, slabs of the mountain wall started to be replaced with speckled jagged rocks sticking out of the side. Although some felt crumbly, they were strong enough to take the weight.

The charcoal dirt ground came to a halt. Giant boulders, seemingly fallen from higher up the mountain, had lodged into the ground, and sliced-open slabs lay in the way. Alex took long strides from one to another. I, on the other hand, had just turned into a hobbit and needed to climb up and over them, dragging myself across, lifting up, climbing, dragging, lifting… it was exhausting.

I could feel an enemy approaching, it was close to taking control of this adventurous spirit—this enemy was fatigue. The climbing had taking its toll, my internal engine was running out of gas; negativity was starting to creep in, especially when I didn't seem to be making any progress. My defences had gone up, mental barricades were in place to stop the negativity from seeping in, and fatigue would break through today. An army of positivity was ready to fight to the death.

Where does it end? was the first negative missile launched.

It doesn't matter, just keep going, was the shielded positive defence.

The battle was on, back and forth, volleying from one side to the other.

The enemy had one upper hand—my body. It knew I had spent a lifetime avoiding the gym. No matter how much positivity and determination remained strong, my body was their best way in and they attacked.

Firstly, by shooting pains through my calves, cramping them up and setting them on fire with each step. Muscles—ones I didn't know existed—started to scream out in torturous agony, but there was no quitting, not today. Negativity's next move was to release and open every sweat gland as if opening the valves to a dam. As it poured out, the ashy dust started to cling and stick to my face, arms, and any other exposed body part like I had been working in a coal mine. But, again, it wasn't enough. My defensive army was sticking together. The ashy dust continued to build, caking over my face, nestling into my nostrils; luckily, my sunglasses proved protection for my eyes, although that giant ball of fire still wasn't visible from this side of the mountain.

The next onslaught began along with burning muscles, as slashes started to appear across my bare legs from any little scrape with each step—but again, it was rebuffed with a strong,

No pain, no gain!

My body was being tested. It was built for drinking copious amounts of alcohol, but it was not well oiled and definitely was not a temple. It was not built for this strenuous type of physical exertion.

One rock after the next, rough to smooth, from slab to boulder, pulling and dragging, the climb continued. Ahead, Alex was happily stepping and jumping away, with the occasional glance back down, smiling as if it was a leisurely stroll. Her smile was the fuel and determination to keep going. There was a final onslaught to come though—the attack on the lungs. As the air thinned, altitude started to come into effect, and breathing became harder. But the blue sky started to broaden, heat pushed through, it became brighter, and the peak was close.

Just a few more steps, it will be worth it.

My body slumped to the ground, flat on my back, that giant ball of fire was there to greet me. It blasted down directly on to my already burning body, and breathing didn't get easier. I could only manage short breaths as my diaphragm felt like it was going into spasm.

"Oh, come on, it wasn't that bad," laughed Alex, standing over me and inadvertently providing shade.

"It was fucking awesome, but being short, and not healthy, not so easy, but I kicked negativity in the ass… I won!"

It took a few minutes for my body to calm down internally as she passed over a bottle of water. New Zealand never ceased to amaze me. At every turn, the countless times we've got lost, and this was no different. My jaw gaped open at the sight of countless jagged peaks poking through the sky far into the distance. We were in the middle of a range, and with the sun shining down on them, it felt otherworldly. But then the monster next to us stood taller, stronger, and more majestic, commanding my full attention.

"Is that Mount Doom…" The words barely came out as my heart hadn't stopped racing yet.

It looked demonic, helped by the thick chalky streaks running down the face of the volcano against the same coppery smear, which looked more like dried blood pouring from the crater.

'Holy fuck! I'm standing next to an actual volcano. OK, this climb was more than worth it… fuck—a volcano. I love my life!'

"Alex, you might want to take a few pictures of that monster and tell your sister you saw Mount Doom."

She was already taking pictures of it—and everything else in sight. The climb up was a workout, but my body had become light, and nothing could wipe the smile away.

"We have to go this way." Her constant clicking had her feet moving as she called out.

Alex didn't get the same feeling from being in front of Mount Doom, which was, in fact, called Mount Ngauruhoe, but the scenery and the climb had captured me. It took a few minutes of really soaking it in before my feet started to catch up with her. The volcano was going nowhere—it seemed like we were circling it. Although the ground beneath kicked up with every step, it was the first time since the boardwalk that it was flat, which was a welcome relief. In fact, not having to press against sharp rocks, it was comparable to walking on clouds. Other hikers, for the first time since the climb, started to come into view. I overheard one of the tour group leaders reveal to his group this was a volcano complex. The three major volcanoes, Mount Ngauruhoe, Mount Tongariro, and Mount Ruapehu were all active. The ground beneath us was, in fact, the collapsed crater of a dead volcano. As soon as those words hit my ears, my eyes nearly popped out.

"Alex, did you hear that? We just climbed up a volcano, not a mountain... holy fuck, I am actually standing in the collapsed crater of a volcano. What the fuck!" I ran my hands through my hair and span on my heels. "Like, seriously. What the actual fuck! WOW."

"I know, awesome, right? A volcano."

She stopped while pulling off the hood of her windbreaker now the sun was directly beating down, letting her short blond hair fall free, and nodded back. There wasn't the same enthusiasm in her voice, but she was beaming.

"So, you know at the beginning where you just jumped off the boardwalk chasing the streams? There is a sign with the route and also saying this is a volcano. I already knew this," she confessed.

"Alright, smart arse."

She her tong flew out like a lizard catching a fly, but flushed with a revitalised energy from this newfound information, I laughed it off before we had another little climb. This one was nothing compared with the first and we quickly made it over. Mount Doom was left in the background as the loose volcanic sandy ground felt a little like the top of a sand dune. Other hikers walked across the ridge and it didn't take long for my eyes to pop out once more.

What is this place? It's incredible.

The ridge was also a viewpoint to see the incredible scenery and the smaller peaks were filled with emerald, sparking blue, crystal clear, and lime green pools. They were like floating lakes in the sky. None of this was like anything I had ever seen in my life. The colours stood out vividly against the charcoal peaks. While Alex snapped away with her camera, my mind was relentlessly doing the same wherever my eyes pointed, storing it in the 'do not forget' file in my mind.

How fucking lucky am I to get to experience this. Who could have believed it, hey? Maybe leaving Australia was the best thing. All this I've experienced in New Zealand so far wouldn't have been possible if I had been sponsored. We've not even got to the South Island yet. I am the luckiest unlucky guy I know.

My jaw hadn't lifted from the ground yet. Soaking it all in, every jagged peak, every pool filling them, and the dark desert view on the right. Most of the hikers and tour groups were sat eating away while taking it all in. The scenery couldn't get old. There are some sights where witnessing them once is enough, but this view just kept growing and growing, becoming more incredible the more I looked at it. Suddenly, like a spring coil, I leapt to my feet.

"What's wrong?" asked Alex

"Down there… it's just clicked… Mordor. That's Mordor."

As if discovering a trove of treasure, I could feel my face lighting up as I pointed towards the dark desert area. A light bulb went off. Apart from the lack of a huge iron gate, the desert looked just like the setting from the movie from this height. Dark deadlands—a barren wasteland of nothing but emptiness.

Amit completes the quest to find the hidden magical and mysterious lakes in the sky, and as soon as he was refuelled, the quest continued on into the barren wastelands.

My imagination was going again, it didn't matter how old I really was right now—in my mind, I was ten. As Alex jumped, she too noticed something we had missed a little further away from the ridge and ran over to it, calling out to bring the camera.

She stood behind a red warning sign we had missed before reading:

WARNING, VOLCANIC FLYING ROCK—DO NOT STOP HERE!

Once she was done, I took her place to get a picture. That rebelliousness will never die—if there is a sign saying not to do something, most people will do it. But I instantly jumped back, the sign wasn't lying, a smouldering volcanic rock lay just a foot away from my shoe.

"Where the fuck did that come from?"

Both of us started to investigate, but it wasn't obvious which volcano around us had spewed it up. However, it was close enough to know it was time to move on. As we headed back down the ridge, we saw the majority of hikers, including all the tour groups, start to head back the way they had come. Both of us were a little confused and asked one of the hikers why they were going that way. They explained that most people only come to this point as it's the main viewpoint, then head back or do more of the smaller trails near the boardwalk. He went on to say only hardened and experienced hikers do the full hike as it becomes quite dangerous and getting down to the desert area is the hardest part. His eyes scanned me up and down, noticing my attire and subtly suggesting we might not be best equipped for it.

Fuck that, we came here to see Mount Doom and to trek through Mordor. We're not turning back. No chance. And this prick can stop looking at me like that or I'll head-butt him.

No, I won't, no need to get violent any more. Just calm down, still going down to Mordor… I can't believe I just said that!

Alex glanced over just to double-check. Neither of us said a word as I picked up the green daypack. There were less than half a dozen hikers left, including rope guy. We watched on as they walked further up the ridge, then just disappeared into thin air. It was only when we walked a little further that it became clear what that hiker had meant about danger.

"So, we want to go down or are you chicken?" asked Alex.

"I laugh in the face of danger—hoo ha ha!"

"Do you? When? OK then, we race?" Her faint eyebrows lifted up the blue stud piercing on her forehead as she chuckled back.

She was goading me, daring me to test me but I didn't back down. My feet had already started to sink into the loose ground, but she tried to push me to gain an advantage. It didn't work, I disregarded all safety and leapt. She was a snowboarder, had grown up playing in the Black Forest, and sliding down mountainsides came naturally. I, on the other hand, had knowledge of sliding down wet muddy hills with exposed branches and weeds in England. The race was on! There was no grace to it— the only aim was to make it to the bottom without breaking a bone.

Down we went, sliding, running, bouncing, jumping down the loose rocks side of the volcano, where Mordor awaited. All of a sudden, my foot sank in deeper than it should have. In an instant, I became a rock, tumbling, bouncing down, but avoiding the bigger rocks. My howls and groans were met by her laughter as I wailed out cries of pain, pleading and hoping not to break any bones. It seemed like she was gliding and skipping off the loose ground with the finesse of a gazelle. Eventually, my body came to a halt and I lay there with pain shooting in every direction from head to toe as a ball of dust floated above.

"Ow! That fucking hurt! Whose brilliant idea was it to race?"

A couple of other hikers must have seen the calamity tumble and rushed over to ask if I was OK—the only laughter came from Alex's mouth. A raised thumb and nod of the head confirmed I was OK, but I wasn't ready to drag myself off the ground yet. New scrapes, bruises, and cuts were added to the day's growing collection—it was all part of the adventure. As soon as the other hikers were out of sight, a thick deadly silence fell. Only the sound of lifting myself off the ground broke the silence. The giant ball of fire shot its rays down like Saruman's Eye, but there was nowhere to hide from it—no cover, no shade, just small, charred rocks, dead as the ground. It was lifeless, nothing at all moved except for Alex and me. An eerie feeling took over as the dead air lay still. Not even the slightest breeze kicked up any of the dark volcanic ashy ground.

The handful of hikers who had gone before must have just marched through like an army of orcs; footsteps in the charcoal sandy ground provided the route through the vast oblivion. Neither of us had said a word, we were just taking it all in with every slow step. It was summer in New Zealand, but the sun hadn't been anywhere near as strong as it was right now, it was no wonder everything here was dead or burnt. After a few more steps, my eyes began to dart around. Alex started laughing as a rush of energy hit me and my inner child burst out of its adult suit. All of a sudden, jumping around, hiding behind the small rocks, running around looking out for imaginary orcs and fantasy demons. I was fully aware I looked like an idiot, but I didn't care, my inner child was out to play.

*

It seemed this barren desert was going on forever. No other hikers had passed us for a few hours, either they were hanging back enjoying the experience or we were the last stragglers. It didn't matter, although some of my energy had been zapped because of the intense heat, it was incomparable. Alex stopped in her tracks and pointed over to one of the larger rocks.

"Look, doesn't that look like a knight kneeling over with a sword?"

"Yeah, it does, like it has a hood over his head, the sword is stuck in the ground. Maybe he was real but got turned to stone."

"Yes, maybe. Or he comes alive when somebody needs him or tries to take his sword."

The two of us started to make up stories using this volcanic barren land as the setting, laughing our way through. No matter what we did, no matter how different we were, we could always get on to the same page and laugh. We passed by more rocks and both tried to look for shapes and figures we could make up stories about. But then she changed the subject.

"After we finish travelling and I go back to Australia, what are you going to do? Go back to Auckland or something else?" she asked out of the blue.

"Not sure to be honest. I am free as a bird, nowhere to go, have no ties. Nothing. I might go back, might not. We still got ages left and the South Island to travel through," I answered while kicking a small rock around.

"Yes, I'm looking forward, Abel Tasman, skydiving, going through the glaciers, Arthur's Pass, Queenstown, Milford Sound, and fiords. So much to do in the South Island."

"Oh, somebody's been doing a little research—but, yeah, I'm loving the North Island, but heard the South Island is even better."

"Yes, I cannot wait. Afterwards, if you carry on travelling, you need to not be stupid with money. I know you do not like to work, but also, without me, you will spend too much."

"What do you mean without you?" I asked, still kicking the rock on the dry ground.

"You know what, same in Sydney, same here. You spend less money, if I wasn't here, how many times would you eat pasta in the van? Not many times, you would spend on food, on

drinks, on things you don't need."

She's got me there. Properly knows me inside out.

"Yeah, good point, I probably would. I've not really thought of what to do, depends on how much money is left after this trip. Maybe I'll find a spot we pass through that I like and make a base there. Or just travel and work when I need to like I was meant to in Australia."

"Are you going to look for sponsorship here?" she asked before she bit into her apple.

"Don't know, not planning anything or getting my hopes up like Aus. If it happens, it happens… if it doesn't, it doesn't. If not, just get a job when I need to. Let's see."

"Whatever it is, it will work out for you like always."

"Are we actually going the right way? We've been walking for hours and I swear it all looks familiar." My cigarette wasn't finished yet, but I leapt up, looking around, changing the subject.

"Yes, we're going the right way, just everything here looks like the same."

During that little break, tiredness had crept in; the mid-afternoon sun wasn't helping, and the novelty of walking on the same terrain, seeing the same dead barren land started to wear very thin. My feet dragged in the loose volcanic dirt, losing more energy with each step. My pumps had turned the same colour as the ground. The end was not in sight, just more dead land.

Why did I bounce around like an idiot at the beginning? I should have conserved energy, not hid from imaginary orcs. None of the actual hikers were doing that.

My legs had turned to lead, and knuckles practically dragged along the ground while my back was melting away. More than anything, it was the heat that sucked all the enjoyment and energy away.

Finally, though, there was a slight reprieve with a change in the terrain, the volcanic floor was replaced by hundreds if not thousands of loose rocks piled on top of each other. It only took a few steps and instant ankle rolls to wish for solid volcanic floor again. The rocks were on an incline, and it didn't take long for me to realise it was not ground level. Every step, every time a rock gave way underneath me, it was greeted by a scream of pain from the soles of my feet, ankles, and muscles. It had turned tortuous. My ankles were suffering the most, pressure from my heavy drained body and the loose ground below made them feel like watermelons carrying the weight of the world. Every muscle screamed in agony as my joints and bones stiffened.

When will this suffering end? This isn't fun anymore.

Thoughts of a long shower filled my mind to wash off the dirt clinging to my skin, the relief, and to get off my

feet. Alex hadn't said a word for ages, she too was
fading.

I wanted to quit. Both inner voices had joined in
unison, begging for this nightmare to be over. Negativity
had truly taken control.

*Call in the air ambulance or let me die out here. I
can't do this anymore*, begged one of the inner voices.

My muscles had started to cry and their tears poured
out of my dusty body, but then Alex provided hope.

"Look, Amit, the forest! It's close. We are nearly
done, we just have to go through to the other side of it,"
said Alex with optimism in her voice.

My boulder-like head could barely lift, but she was
right—in the distance, a tree line appeared, it was
motivation, all there was to do was get to the forest, get
out the other side, and it was over.

*Come on, we can do it. 'Eye of the Tiger' time. Push,
push, push.*

In that moment, a surge of energy shot through my body, but in taking my eyes off the rocks and stones below, two of them lodged my foot—one foot stepped, the other didn't, and before I knew it, my lips were kissing dry rocks. I bounced, slipping down a few metres.

"Fucckkk!"

Crimson covered the pale rocks like somebody had poured red paint over them. My hands frantically checked my head and the rest of the body—it was seeping out of my knee. Shooting pains screamed out, echoing through the vast emptiness.

"Oh my God, Amit, are you OK?" Alex rushed over to check, looking concerned.

"No, it fucking hurts! My ankle is fucked and my knee is busted open."

"Is something broken?"

I lay there writhing in pain, not just from the open wound or the ankle that felt like it had been shattered, but my whole body. The giant ball of fire was not sympathetic and carried on burning down.

"No, nothing broken… I don't think."

Get up, need to get up, the forest is close, it's just a scratch on the knee. Come on, get the fuck up.

The cut over my knee was deep, but I've had worse injuries before, and with the help of Alex, I tried to get to my feet. My ankle felt like it was about to explode as pain shot through like fireworks.

The rocks below were not helping the situation. I needed to shift all my weight to the other ankle, but it was near impossible without solid ground. I just wanted to collapse.

Sweet mother of fuck! It kills—let it end now. The other hikers were right, this was torturous. Maybe we should have turned back at the main viewpoint. Who was I kidding trying to attempt this, I'm not a hiker, and I'm certainly not dressed for it. Stupid idiot, scorned my inner voice without the slightest sympathy.

There wasn't much further to go, but every step was more agonising than the last. It felt like miles, but soft grass and mud started to come into view. There were only a few more excruciating steps to take. Pain after pain, the last rock gave way, instantly slipping from Alex's support like a sack of potatoes hitting the soft ground.

Never before had grass and mud felt so comforting and there was coolness in the breeze that I hadn't felt since we were on the ridge—it was bliss. My body jolted as if it had received an electric shock. It was pain. It wasn't over yet. The throbbing continued to get worse. It looked like it was to be my first visit to the hospital in New Zealand. Funnily enough, Alex was with me for my last visit to the hospital in Sydney. That was after a concert in front of the Sydney Harbour and Opera House, where falling off my friend's shoulders straight on to broken glass had resulted in my finger nearly being sliced off and needing multiple stitches.

With Alex's help, I dragged myself off the floor. Mordor had defeated me and the quest had been forgotten. I hobbled and dragged my pain-ridden body over the grass and through the tree line. Soft dirt and cover from the high canopy blocked out that giant ball of fire for some relief. The tiniest breeze floated through, but after a full day of stagnant air, it felt like a hurricane had swept through. Life was all around us once more— birds sang through the trees, leaves rustled, bugs buzzed around, branches snapped in the distance. After a day of complete silence in a desolate world, to see colour and hear the sound of forest life was music to the ears and helped with the pain. With solid ground below, I was able to walk on my own, but in pure agony. The soft dirt of the forest ground provided cushion as much as it could, but of course, it wasn't that simple. We had to climb up and down through the forest. Exposed vines acted as support and rope to climb on to higher ground as we followed the signs. Every step caused a throb, but having to put all my weight on the right ankle, both were now ready to explode.

"Can you hear this?" Alex stopped in her tracks.

Past the birds and buzzing, and there it was.

"Yeah, I can. Where though?"

It was as if we had found a pot of gold at the end of a rainbow—traffic in the distance, hope, or more so the end of this treacherous journey. The quest would be complete after all, just when all hope was lost. With each step, it got louder. A smile for the first time in hours cracked through the dirt caked on my face. It even masked the pain for a while; or my body had just gone numb. Light pushed through the tree line—we were so close to the end. But would the bus to take us back to our campervan still be there waiting?

Yes, it was. The driver was just finishing up his smoke. I had never been so happy to see a bus.

"Just made it… two more minutes and you would have had to walk."

Without saying a word, after one last push, we jumped onto the public bus happy this day was over. Right now, there were no feelings but I knew when the pain eased, I would look back at this day as an incredible adventure.

Peasant in Neverland

Malt wine and fumes of coffee fused with the burning cherry birchwood danced in the bitter icy fresh air alongside the constant chatter and clattering teeth all around. A magical and very unique atmosphere I had not felt anywhere else was generated from the melting pot of tourists, backpackers, thrill-seekers, and adrenaline junkies, with the added sprinkling of locals.

Once anybody experienced this melting pot, it was hard to leave this picturesque town. For most of the time it felt like being in a fairy-tale. Especially with the view of the frozen lake and snow-dripped mountains in the background from the outside seating area of this café. Travellers from all over the world hid under woolly hats, brightly coloured puffy jackets, and matching pants and floated through the walkway between the café and lake. Most of them buzzing around like colourful bees, either returning from or heading to another extreme activity.

The majority of them passing through for a few days and dialling up the adrenaline to the max before moving on.

This was winter in Queenstown. The South Island of New Zealand was known as the adventure capital of the southern hemisphere, and Queenstown—or Neverland as those of us who didn't leave liked to call it—was the epicentre. The bitter air bit at my cheeks only to be melted by crackling flames emanating from the fire pit to the side. The winter sun bounced off the sheer white mountains and just added to the surreal fantasy feel of this town. While travelling through with Alex, I had just a little taste of the unique energy, but it compelled me to return once she returned to Australia.

From the moment I returned nearly four months ago, it was like living in a thick bubble where the outside world didn't exist anymore. Alex, who I've kept in touch with, thinks I'm spiritually connected to Queenstown—that's why, even as broke as I am, I love it. Sure, I could feel the ambience and atmosphere, but it definitely wasn't a spiritual thing, I don't believe in that mumbo-jumbo.

A pink glove slid in front of me and placed another coffee on the wooden bench accompanied by a familiar Canadian accent.

"So, apparently, my loyalty card had two free coffees. So, you're welcome and we finally have some luck! And FYI, I hate that you like sitting out here."

"It's nice out here, feels tranquil and we've got the fire to keep us warm. Better than sitting inside our frozen cabin." A smirk grew as my mouth lifted from under my three hoodies to feel the bitter air as Amy sat beside me.

"True, but not better than sitting inside the café. Amit, my feet are frozen and I'm wearing three pairs of thick woolly socks and Uggs."

Only Amy's face—or rather just her purple hair—was visible as she hid under layers of clothing and a thick jacket with all hoods up. The coffee had barely sat on the table a moment and it had already started to go cold, but it was free, and free always tasted good—especially when you were broke.

"How was work?" I asked while taking a sip.

"Same as every day. Pretty darn shite. Tourists coming in and out of the shop, asking me ridiculous questions like I'm an expert skier or snowboarder. Don't they know I just work in the shop for very little money and am not an expert? It's annoying, I hate it. And I have to sell and rent out gear for people to have a great time when I can't afford to do it myself. Ahh, that's better. Rant over." Her huff was not a welcome breeze, turning icy as it hit my cheeks.

"You sure?"

"Yup. Anyhoo, how was your day? Ready for work? Over the hangover?"

We both shuffled along the bench, getting closer to the fire. Being a local in this town was not as adrenaline-fuelled as it was for the tourists passing through, but partying practically every night was. While the adventurous overpriced tourist activities created the electric atmosphere during the day, it was after dark when Queenstown really came alive. Locals finished work and hit the bars, and all the tourists fuelled up on adrenaline let it all out in the bars and clubs so the electric atmosphere exploded.

"Yeah, just about over it… didn't do anything though, nearly froze to death in the cabin, went outside to feel some warmth. Got some noodles for dinner, sat in this café watching these tourists pass by."

"Oh, well, don't get too wild, you should slow down all that excitement," she sniggered.

"Yeah, I know, right, some might think I was an adrenaline junkie backpacker."

"By the way, you went to the shops…"

Before she could continue, a pack of sour worms Haribo sweets appeared on the table.

"Amazing. That's my dinner sorted then. But seriously, will you get food vouchers from work today, Amit? We need to go shopping soon. We need real food."

"I dunno, I've tried swapping the drinks vouchers for food ones, but no dice. I'm done with living on noodles. I didn't live on noodles ever in Australia, no matter how broke I was. And I'm dying to eat a Fergburger."

"Stop it, Amit—I hate being so poor. Can't we just rob a bank?"

More tourists flooded the walkway, some stopping to take pictures of the lake and domineering mountain ranges. Some stood on the wall trying to get the perfect selfie to show off on their social media accounts, while we sat here like paupers drinking free coffee. Amy hated it here, not just because she was poorer than she'd ever been in her life, but because it reminded her of home.

Like me, home was a place she never wanted to return to. It was, in fact, my fault she was here. I had convinced her to skip over from Sydney when her visa ran out, selling the town to her. And while, for most of us, no matter how broke we got it was a fairy-tale town, for her, it was a nightmare. She also had the same luck with money as I did—none. It wasn't a great combination.

*

All types of monkey species, sloths, snakes, meerkats, wild hogs, wise elephants, and tigers made up this zoo—but this wasn't an actual zoo. This was the late shift in a Queenstown call centre for backpackers. The day shifts were made up of the normal, head-down-and-get-work-done sensible ones. Then there was the night shift. All the wreck heads—most spent their days either recovering from hangovers or snowboarding or partaking in another extreme activity, and their evenings working then partying.

Like the rest of the late shift, my pockets were stuffed with more drinks vouchers, but again, there were no food vouchers. The vouchers were handed out as incentives for making sales instead of doing nothing. They were accepted by local bars, which is how we were able to get drunk most nights while having barely two pennies to rub together. It was the end of another shift, and like every night, there was only one destination for everyone—the bar!

The bitter mountain air tried to penetrate through and the thirty-second walk to the other side of the building felt like thirty minutes. As we got closer to the safe haven of the eXtreme bar, I shot through the single door, bursting up the wide stairs of the open sports bar, straight to the bar and the welcoming heat. I'm from England, but this is the coldest I have ever felt, it may as well be Antarctica. The welcome warmth helped in the fight to push coldness out and bring feeling back to noses, ears, fingers, and toes. Winter in Queenstown was no joke, but that's what happens in a valley town surrounded by snow-capped mountains.

Free drinks vouchers wafted across the bar—the two barmen knew what most of us drank and lined them all up. They had been expecting us, just like every night. A perfume of stale oil, chips, and chicken wings filled the large open space. With my beer in hand, I walked past the pool tables that filled the open space to the usual spot near the smoking area.

Vibrations started to shoot up my leg from the old Nokia phone, I'd missed Amy's call but a message popped up:

"Don't go to the bar tonight, come straight home, we are FUCKED! Like code red FUCKED!"

Sounds important. She wouldn't call like this if it wasn't—she said code red.

My inner voice was right… she wouldn't say code red it if it wasn't super important and she's normally in here waiting. The beer disappeared down my throat as quick as it appeared.

"One more?" asked the ginger-bearded barman.

For the first time in my entire residence in Queenstown and coming to this bar, my head shook to say no. For me to say no to alcohol after work was something unheard of. I was the guy who was synonymous with the phrase 'just one more' and kept people out drinking until the early hours. One of the reasons we all drank so much was to numb ourselves from the Arctic weather outside. This was one of the rare occasions I needed to battle it sober. My limbs were not looking forward to it.

Pinewood Lodge had been home for the last month and was pressed right up against the mountainside. I burst through the door before a potential storm swept through. Unlike most places, it was colder inside than outside with the lack of heating. Another reason we got drunk most nights, to feel some heat inside. We had got royally screwed over when choosing the cabin, but in truth, we couldn't afford much more. The other option was to sleep outdoors.

Amy was nowhere to be seen in the tiny space that was meant to be the living room. This wasn't the usual cosy winter wooden cabin—it was just a mobile unit like the ones schools use when they're doing building work. Wrapped under two thick duvets, Amy sat in the middle of her bed facing the door with just purple hair flowing and eyes overflowing like a waterfall, she didn't even wait for me to step inside.

"We're fucked, they're kicking us out at the end of the week!"

"What do you mean? How? We're paid up, they can't just kick us out!"

"Yeah, until Friday, but then we have to leave. We have been here five weeks, it's the maximum they allow. They've already booked people in from Saturday. Amit, what are we going to do? We can't afford anything else... we're going to be homeless!" She made no attempt to wipe away the free-falling tears.

"Friday? Well, we can just go back into a hostel until we find another place. This place is an ice-box shithole anyway."

"That's the problem. They're all fully booked through the weekend. Amit, everywhere is fully booked… hostels, hotels, Airbnbs—everything. I've been ringing all afternoon. There's that festival this weekend and places have been booked for months. We're going to be homeless… like actually homeless!"

Since Australia—well, my entire life—being broke and running out of money wasn't a new concept, money came and went. There have been days spent without a penny and then days flushed with money. But there had always been a roof over my head. Those words were like bullets piercing through my heart, causing my body to fall back on to my bed. There are not many lower levels to sink to in my life, but this was a new one.

"Fuck my life!"

My head started to spin as I tried to think how to get out of this latest predicament, but one of my inner voices wasn't allowing me to think straight. It was that parallel life again—on the one hand, amazing, living in a fantasy fairy-tale, and on the other hand, reality kicking me in the teeth. I just couldn't win.

Homeless? Fuck off, are you kidding me? How the fuck are we gonna be homeless? Fucking homeless!

Relax, it will work out… it always does, something will turn up. It has to, ah, bollocks—let's just get pissed and figure shit out tomorrow.

The white foam ceiling tiles that also wrapped around the walls felt like they were caving in.

"I hate this place," Amy wailed as the dam burst.

"I've got $75 worth of vouchers, think that will help? Shall we just get drunk and figure it out tomorrow?"

"NO! We need to sort this tonight. This is serious, we need to figure something out. I'm not being homeless."

Her purple hair erupted like a volcano from the duvets… that might not have been the best thing to suggest to her.

"No hostels at all? Not even base? I can call, they know me from staying there before?" I tried to get back on track.

For the first time, Amy swept away the tears falling off her cheeks.

"You can try but they said they had nothing. There is one option… it's not sensible at all, we could end up being in an even worse situation next week. But we won't be homeless this weekend."

Both my ears and eyes perked up a little like a dog being brought a treat as I leant forward on the bed.

"Rob a bank or go to the casino, put everything we have on black and hope for the best?"

"I think my idea is riskier. We just say fuck it. Fuck life like this. We put whatever money we have together, go over to Wanaka for the weekend, come back on Monday, the festival will be over and hostels will have some space again. I don't see any other option."

"Fuck it, let's do it. Figure out what we have and how to survive next week I guess."

See, no need to panic. Money comes, money goes. Let's go fucking snowboarding. Fuck you, life!

This is a stupid idea—how am I even thinking about it?

Oh fuck, I'm doing it.

"I'm just so fed up with feeling like crap all the time. Amit, I haven't genuinely smiled since I arrived and that was over two months ago. I need an escape from this nightmare. I know you love this place, but I hate it. You work full-time and have no money. Whatever happens next week happens."

"So, how are we gonna do this then? Put our money together, but what about getting there, equipment, passes, and all that? It costs money that we don't have."

"What I was thinking was to use what we saved for next week's rent money. We don't need it anymore. We can use it to rent a cheap car, food, and a cheap hostel and save the rest for a hostel next week until you get paid. I can get all the equipment from work and my boss has a ski pass I can borrow for Treble Cone."

"I have a couple of friends who work on Treble Cone, I can ask if they can sort us out with snowboards. Looks like we've got a plan. Can't afford to eat a proper meal, but can go snowboarding," I added.

It was the plan.
And plans... they always work out how they should.

* * *

There's nothing quite as embarrassing as walking confidently into a restaurant, sitting down, looking at a menu, and high-tailing back out because what was meant to be cheap was out of your budget. So, instead, we opted to sit in the car park of a supermarket eating cheaper than chips snacks. As much as we didn't want to think about it and had made a deal to leave the worries for our future selves, it was there. The niggle that we couldn't overspend, we needed to keep enough money for rent when returning to Queenstown, and that meant no restaurant meals.

However, we had got over it. We were not homeless, and the crappy rental car hadn't fallen to pieces nor broken down again as it slowly climbed up the tight sludgy mountain edge. There were a few moments it seemed like it would give up and even fly off the edge. But with the combination of the tyre chains, Amy's continuous seduction of the car and her Canadian driving skills, it kept going. Even if my heart thought otherwise.

Treble Cone was one of the most popular snowboarding and ski resorts in the area, and the higher the car climbed, the more another New Zealand picturesque postcard view opened up. However, it was only once we somehow made it to the top that we could see the whole breath-taking view. We were higher than most mountains, getting a bird's eye view of other ice cream-covered peaks and icy rivers and lakes flowing through. At this point, I didn't even care If I didn't get on a board—this was more than worth it all. An old friend of mine, who was part of the original group I'd met in Australia, called out and ran over, pouncing to wrap her arms around me. She lived in Wanaka now and worked in the ski resort. We had met up and got drunk a few times in Queenstown before, it was always great to see her. Stories of our hostel in Sydney were never in short supply but they would be saved for tonight as she had invited us out with her housemates.

She gave us a quick lowdown of the slopes and the conditions, and had saved a couple of boards for us to 'rent', but not pay for. She knew a trick so we could have them for free, and even organised a couple of beginners' 'how to snowboard for dummies' lessons for me, which was much appreciated. Amy being Canadian was quite adept at being on the slopes. I, however, was all the gear, but none of the ideas. Fully kitted in black snowboard pants, knee and elbow pads, a snowboard jacket, face mask, goggles, and the board, which was a little taller than me, it was time to hopefully not break any bones.

Even after the more-than-basic lessons, it was going to be a painful day, and before even attempting the main slopes, a few runs on the baby slope needed to be mastered. The lifts up the baby slope were not the standard chairlifts, but a dangling pole with a plastic plate around it—the drag lift. Children made it look easy, wrapping their legs around and sitting on the plate while holding on to the pole as the lift dragged them up.

Looks easy enough, if they can do it, it can't be hard… I don't know why Amy was making such a fuss. Let's do it.

With one of my boots attached to the board and the other remaining free, I waited for the next pole to arrive.

Easy, just do as the kid in front did. Wrap around and sit on the plate and hold the pole, foot on the board, but don't put pressure on it, just let it loosely slide up.

Oh, what the fuck! Why's it so loose?

The pole wasn't sturdy at all, my body weight had not been accounted for. These lifts were designed for light-as-a-feather kids, not slightly overweight adults. The wire holding the pole up instantly loosened, causing the pole to swing like it was in a hurricane. The seat span but the lift didn't stop. It rose up, pulling on the pole and seat, rocking my balance. My board dug into the soft fluffy snow, in an instant, my grip on the pole loosened, my body twisted up into a pretzel, and before I could think, I was eating snow.

Amit: 0, Children's Ski lift: 1.

Laughter streamed over from my two friends and from other children.

It's fine, no need to feel embarrassed, it was my first ever attempt. The next one will be much better.

The next pole came around, but it swung free—that wasn't the right one. Another was in sight. I gripped the pole once more, tighter this time for more control, the seat rode up in position to feel my body weight. A smile grew on my face in achievement.

Wait, why I am spinning?

My brain concentrated too hard to stop spinning, forgetting about the board. It started to gather snow like a plough. In trying to lift it, all control and balance was lost, and snow greeted my mouth once more.

Amit: 0, Children's ski lift: 2.

OK, this is not easy at all. These kids are all laughing at me. The little shits!

One by one, they jumped on, making no big deal of it. It didn't matter if they were on skis or a snowboard. One even started to show off and jumped on like he was Spiderman. I was not going to get outdone by some little brats. With all the kids sliding up the side of the baby slopes, I looked back to my two laughing friends who offered no advice or encouragement. The coldness was seeping through to my bones, I needed to get up there. I gripped the pole once more, tight and in both hands, moving it up until the seat was in place.

Gotcha!

There wasn't any spinning, just moving in a straight incline up the side of the slope. Nobody had advised on how to position the board other than to let it slide freely between the mounds of snow gathered on each side of the lift. It caught something—a panoramic view passed my eyesight, my body weight pushed the seat down, and all control was lost once more. It was either keep getting dragged along and cling on for dear life or let go. I was not going to let it defeat me. In a feeble attempt to cling on, the board clipped the ground, all of a sudden, I was doing my best sloth impression, my back dragging against the icy ground below but clinging tight to the plastic seat above. My loose foot swung where my head should have been, my head where my foot should be, grazing on the snow, collecting it in my hood, with chills shooting through my spine. Not like I wasn't cold enough already. There was no choice but to let go. Back on the ground, rolling to the side, a wooden fence the only protection from sliding off the steep cliff edge, which I hugged like a koala.

Amit: 0, Children's ski lift: 3.

"See you at the top," a familiar voice laughed out.

A growl met Amy's voice. She was expertly riding it to the top.

Wait, how was she doing it? She was taller than me. It's not fair.

Saving myself from any more embarrassment, I fully unclasped the board. There was more than halfway to go but, using the fence as support, the board over my other shoulder, I started to climb on foot while mumbling like I had Tourette's syndrome.

To make things worse, my calves were burning, it was like climbing up the volcano in Tongariro again. Snow sucked my feet all the way in, and I expended so much energy trying to dig them out with each step. From the bottom, it seemed like a slight incline, up here, it was so steep.

Amy had already been down the slope and back up the lift by the time I reached the top and collapsed on the floor. She cast a shadow over my body, with her purple hair poking out the side of her bobbled woolly hat, smiling down.

"See, I told ya… not so easy, huh?

We both sat on the top edge of the slope watching the kids jump off and zoom down without a care in the world. It reminded me of being a child, having no regard for safety, jumping off ramps and slopes on my BMX, or rolling down muddy hills. Back then, pain didn't last, bones were broken, but there was no fear. Now, the pain lasts, and the fear of breaking bones was there but so was the competitiveness. The kids doing tricks felt like taunts.

They already laughed and embarrassed us on the lifts… we gonna let these kids do us like that? We need to get bigger air than then. Time to be Mr Extreme.

Remember how we used to skateboard—it's just the same but without wheels and on snow.

Skateboard? What the fuck you on about? We could barely jump off the curb without falling. Twenty-nine years old and you wanna beat some kids. Grow the fuck up. Plus, we cannot afford medical bills. NO TRICKS!

They were at it again, but for once, I needed to listen to the sensible voice. I was older, I needed to let go of that macho bullshit bravado when it came to sports—and I definitely couldn't afford a trip to the hospital.

Amy was on her feet, strapped in and ready to go. My feet were in the boots and I cranked up the fasteners too tight, nearly cutting off circulation. She smirked with her arms folded, swaying from side to side slightly, but her smirk felt mischievous.

"Why are you smirking like that for?" I asked worryingly.

"No reason… come on, get up."

She had her camera in hand, waiting as my hands pushed into the firm compact snow, lifting slightly, but the board slipped from beneath. I was back on the floor.

"That's why. Thanks for the perfect picture." Her laughter filled the air as I smacked against the ground.

It wasn't just hers… hysterical laughter and pointed fingers came from the kids too. Her comment was met with a growl. The board lodged into the ground, my palms pressed into the snow once more lifting up, this time getting to my feet. But instantly, they tried to grab onto thin air. It was no use, the board slipped from underneath and my back was reacquainted with the snowy ground.

"Oh, come on, give me a break!" I growled from deep within as my body thundered and clattered on to the ground. "Ouch, that hurt."

The creamy sky above, to my surprise, wasn't filled with spinning cartoon stars as I expected, instead, I just heard hysterical laugher from Amy and the other kids.

"Glad you're finding this so funny. Some advice would be nice," I growled once more.

All the visions over the last couple of nights of looking like a professional snowboarder, jumping metres in the air, doing fancy tricks, had all but gone. Even with one of my inner voices trying to convince me otherwise. I couldn't even get up the baby lift or stand upright on the board. A few of the kiddies took their places on the edge, sliding off with no concern. Snowboards and skis attached to these tiny humans were no obstacle. Once they were all gone, it was just the board, my body, and the snow. This time, though, I rolled on to my front, lifting off from my knees and pushing from my palms slowly getting upright.

"Haha, I did it!"

As if it was the biggest achievement of my life, I marvelled at standing upright for more than a second. It was a huge win. The next challenge, though, was to actually get to the edge and head down the slope.

Remember, I'm goofy… right foot forward.

Millimetre by millimetre, the board edged slowly forward, shuffling until it was in position.

Bend the knees, push forward, toe, heel, toe, heel. Nice and slow, no getting competitive and NO breaking bones.

It's times like this there was a definite need for adult supervision. The other inner voice was pleading to just let rip, but I was not listening to it.

More kids had jumped off the lift and whizzed past—a part of me wanted to push but I blocked them out, like a snail, knees bent, balancing, letting gravity do its job. Any time the pace quickened, my toes lifted, digging the back edge of the board into the snow to slow down. More than five seconds passed without falling.

I'm a natural. I got this… go faster. Oh, wow, look at that view…

The incline dipped, cold air pushed against my cheeks, there was more speed building.

No. Concentrate, damnit! Slow down!

The grey-and-orange board slid against the pure-white snow.

Heel, toe, heel, heel, heel, bit of toe, heel, right foot firm, left leg loose.

"Woo, look at you, be on those mountains in no time. You might want to go a little faster though," shrieked Amy as she literally ran rings around me like an eagle stalking its prey.

"Nope, this is as fast as I'm going for now. Fuck off. Leave me alone and let me concentrate."

She didn't need any convincing, leaving me in her powdery wake, zooming off like a roadrunner. My eyes quickly averted back to the snow and board. In my mind, I was cutting through the snow, catching pow, but that wasn't the reality. A bluster of wind kicked up some loose snow and rasped past in a blur. I lost my balance, my arms instinctively tried to act as wings, flapping like a bird. What was I doing thinking I could fly all of a sudden? Gravity was pushing me in the opposite direction as my body crashed to the solid ground. It was not as soft as the top and my bum felt it, letting out a painful yelp.

"Get used to that, you have a whole day of it," laughter came screeching from the lift, Amy was on her way back up already.

Her laugh got louder at the sight of my middle finger, before I rolled on to my front, using the same technique as before, lifting from my knees and knuckles. The board was already sliding away, but in the opposite direction to where it should be. The front lip pushed in, causing more speed than needed, but then dug in too much. Before I knew it, snow was on the menu once more, much to the delight of two little girls on skis.

Fucking little shits.

Bellowing out a heavy sigh, teeth clenched, pushing up from the knees and knuckles once again, this baby slope was not going to win—I was!

Fuck you, I'm getting down there.

My eyes flicked from the bottom of the slope to the board, which had started to move again.

Heel, heel, OK, too much heel, toe, toe, push forward on the front leg, there we go, nice and steady, that's it, gently does it.

I was starting to get the hang of it, there was no sign of Amy or her mocking voice. However, roadrunner kids constantly zipped past in an endless train, but I hadn't lost balance or fallen for a few minutes. The bottom of the slope was in sight, close enough to let go of the mental handbrake.

Go on, feel the speed, just let it rip—feel the rhythm, feel the speed, feel the ride, Amit, it's snowboarding time!

My speed started to gather, I could feel the cold mountain icy air breezing past, the board was a magic carpet, flying across the snow. Everything passed in a blur. Instinct took over from being less cautious, my board pushed back and forth, gravity pushed further, but a thought popped up.

Oh, shit, wait, how do I stop naturally?

There was only one viable option—to fall backwards, finishing the last part of the slope sliding down on my back.

"Fuck, yeah! I just snowboarded without breaking any bones!" I laughed.

OK, it wasn't anything to brag about, especially going that slow for most of the way down.

"Took you long enough!" Like a ninja, Amy slid up from behind but remained on her feet. How did she do that magic?

"Ready to go up again? I've been following you for ages. I don't want to spend all day on the baby slope. It's getting boring." She motioned towards the poles.

Following me, when?
I did not notice at all, but peering towards the mocking poles dangling away, I nodded, they would not get the better of me. I released one foot free of the clasp, rotating

to make sure there was still movement. The ankles survived, the boots were doing their job. I flipped on to my front once more, but the technique was met by laughter.

"What the heck are you doing?"

"Getting up. It's the only way I can stand upright."

"You do not cease to provide entertainment. Fabulous!"

Back on my feet, my free foot rested on the board, sliding over to the poles as I closely studied her movement and how she took to the lift with ease. I copied exactly what she did.

Now why couldn't she have gone first the first time round? So easy.

We had passed halfway, snow started to build on the board.

Come on, come on, we can make it.

I tried to resist the urge to flick the snow off the end of my board. But there are times when an urge kicks in, resistance is needed, but in the end, it's futile.

"No, what are you doing, you stupid thing!" Without any consent, my foot flicked.

"What? I didn't do anything," said Amy from in front.

"No, not you, my foot."

It had betrayed its command, the pole started to go like a bucking bronco. There was no taming it, control was lost, it was swaying from side to side, the board was out of the smooth slope and into the rough. A mouthful of snow followed and I was face-down, splattered on the ground once more.

Amit: 0, Children's ski lift: 4.

The fence provided support once more, my calves burned with each step, but this time, they were joined by stretching hamstrings as I dragged myself up the remainder of the hill towards Amy's laugher.

"So, so close. Next time you will make it all the way up."

A growl was the only response warranted once again.

Ready to go once more, pushing forward, I had more control this time. I instantly picked up speed, the board pushed back to slow down, but not quite to the snail's pace of the first attempt. From right to left, knees bent, less tense, letting instincts take over, letting if feel natural. I gathered speed as gravity started to push once more—in an attempt to slow down, I dropped back on my ass, but this time, bouncing straight up using momentum. That was a new trick. A kid flew past like a rocket.

You gonna take that from him? Come on, we went slow the first time. What's the point in going slow? GO— after him! groaned the inner voice.

No, don't listen, no…

It was too late—the kid was the target. Speed picked up, and in my mind, I must have been going 60, even 70 miles an hour, but as other kids were zipping past, it can't have been that fast.

However, everything passed in a blur, much quicker than last time. The board hit a bump, separating from the ground, with nothing but air in between.

Holy fuck, my first jump, catching some air, baby!

My heart decided to take cover in my throat while beating as fast as I was going. I must have been at least an incredible two inches off the ground, but it felt like two metres. With my arms outstretched, time slowed down and the board felt like it was trying to escape.

"Ohhh, fuckk!"

While my face was the first to feel the snow, my legs continued to fly past my hips, curving my back the way it shouldn't go. The board smashed the back of my head before rolling back out and I was unable to move.

"Owwww, fuck, that hurt. Pain, so much pain."

I was so used to falling by this point, the snowy ground didn't even feel cold any more. A pink snowboard came into eye line.

"I think I broke my back. I'm paralysed, get me the air ambulance," I moaned.

"I have to give it to you, that was some impressive Superman shizzle."

She completely ignored my statement, instead, encouraging me to get back up. Moving was not an option, but the little fuckers zipped by and each one tried to spray snow over my broken body, which prompted me to push up. There was no longer any pain, none at all—despair turned into delight.

"Fuck, that was pretty cool. I picked up some good speed there."

"Yup, much quicker than your first attempt." She nodded favourably.

It could have been the adrenaline pumping through or just the numbness, but that fall was like a jolt of electricity surged through my body and I wanted more. I wanted more speed. The little kid inside me was ready to unzip the adult suit and burst out to play.

A few more of these rides, then hit the actual slopes, get some real speed, and the adrenaline cranked up to full speed.

After a couple of more rounds on the baby slope, and a quick stop at the overpriced bar, it was time to hit the actual slopes. This time, I carefully studied the way people sat on the metal chairlifts, three to a seat, getting in position and feeling the metal seat against the back of their legs before they sat back. My heart thumped the higher we rose over the mountain, the baby slope looked minuscule and the view from before looked so far in the distance. Amy had taken the lift in front—I was sandwiched between two brightly coloured boarders talking to each other about the amount of fresh pow there was. I worked with people who snowboarded and knew a few snowboarding terms, but there was no need to engage with them. White land started to get closer—we were reaching the top. It suddenly hit me.

How the fuck do we get off?

I peered at Amy in front, keenly watching. Her board hit the ground as the lift turned. Seamlessly, she slid off to the side with just one foot clasped.

Oh fuck, this is gonna be hard.

Solid ground hit the bottom of my board, the two either side slipped away naturally. I, on the other hand, tried to slide off, but like a clumsy apple, rolled off to the side, my free foot not fully on the board, catching snow, and tumbled towards Amy.

However, unlike the mocking little brats, nobody paid attention up here. It was only while looking around that a new world opened up. A winter wonderland for adrenaline junkies. All over the vast white peak, bright colours were doing all types of crazy flips, insanely high jumps, and landing like ballerinas on boards.

Maybe we should go back to the baby slope and try these ones tomorrow.

Nah, fuck that, this is awesome. Look at the height these guys are getting.

If ever I felt out of place, it was here, but part of me felt like I belonged up here. This was just at the peak where people were practising before taking their routes down, which, on the noticeboard close by, were colour co-ordinated from easy to difficult.

It was definitely the easy one for me.

* * *

We returned the rental car at Queenstown airport—the weekend of not giving a fuck was over and as soon as the airport doors slid open, not only did a bitter gust of wind hit but so did reality. Neither of us brought our smiles back with us from Wanaka. We both looked at each other, shaking our heads.

"We fucked up hard, what the fuck are we going to do?" I asked.

There was no reply, she hadn't said a word for a while now. A few days ago, it was future Amit and Amy's problem. Well, now, it was very much ours and we hadn't just gone over budget, but by having a carefree, happy, joyful weekend of not giving a fuck, we blew the budget. All of it, down to our last seven dollars.

What the fuck are we going to do? Where the fuck are we going to sleep tonight?

We had reached Frankton Road, which was the main road leading into Queenstown—even catching the bus back was too expensive and had to walk back. We reached as far as the enclave, walking around the edge of the huge lake that Queenstown hugged around Frankton Road. Cars zoomed past; instinctively, Amy popped her thumb out.

"I can't walk back all that way. We need to hitchhike back."

Luckily, at the third attempt, a car stopped for Amy and took us back to Queenstown.

The sun disappeared behind Queenstown Hill and darkness owned the sky. All the bars and restaurants had their outdoor fires and heaters lit. Tourists, young and old, from all over the world buzzed around the streets, all returning from their activities, ready to hit the bars or relax with a warm hearty meal. We needed warmth, food, and a place to stay. I needed smokes and, no doubt, Amy needed sour worms—we could barely afford either. We decided on a beer instead. I still had vouchers to use and slipped into one of the cosy little wooden cabin-type bars that accepted the vouchers. An open log fire roared out from the middle of the open bar. Instantly, my body started to thaw and feeling came back to my bright-red nose, toes, and fingers. Amy gulped the beer down, asking for another voucher. My eyes drifted back to the roaring fire as I wondered what to do.

We were broke and homeless in Neverland! The lowest point in my travelling life to date.

Tuk-Tuks and Scams

Utter chaos. There were no other words for it. Relentless, never-ending chaos and it was coming from all directions. And it wasn't even the heart of the city— just the outskirts! The constant ear-bursting horns papping from mopeds, all other vehicles, other unrecognisable noises, and the traffic was never-ending. It hadn't since we arrived in the early hours. We had stepped out of the hotel straight into a dysfunctional orchestra of noise. In an instant, the humidity wrapped tight, squeezing the life out of me while caking me in the same dust that covered the broken path and roads. *'Welcome to Bangkok, enjoy your stay,'* said the sign at the airport last night—how could anybody enjoy this madness?

A knife was needed to cut through the thick orange glinted air. That giant ball of fire pulsated down but was barely visible. The side street covered in wooden broken-down shacks and crumbled concrete buildings didn't provide any reprieve either.

How the fuck are we going to survive this? I'm dying, melting away. And the noise—when will it stop?

My skin felt like it was melting, and my insides were on fire; Australian heat felt like a walk in the park compared to this. It wasn't even a case of getting in the shade, it was all shade, but the humidity was so suffocating.

"There it is, this is the one she said about," Alex pointed to an orange pastel-coloured building, her bare arms glistened from sweat.

It was hard to tell if that was the actual colour or just the glint from the visible smog. This was a new experience, and I had no idea how I would get used to it. A new culture awaited to experience—one I didn't have much knowledge about. All I knew was this was going to be a completely different experience to Australia and New Zealand.

We were both leaving a trail of sweat behind, this oven was unbearable, so much so, I couldn't even smoke. A wrinkled face popped up out of nowhere trying to sell us a paper, saying something in Thai, but we just apologised not understanding her words, shook our heads, and sidestepped her. Our pace quickened towards the café as we kicked up more dust—all the buildings, even the overgrown tropical plants, were caked in it. It was like walking into heaven after spending time in hell as a blast of Arctic air wrapped around us as if somebody had put the fire out. My lungs welcomed it and sucked in the crisp cool air I had become accustomed to in Queenstown. My sweat was even jumping for joy at being frozen as I moaned in relief.

"Ahhh, that feels so good, I can breathe, I think I'll stay in here all day." I basked in the cool café with my arms spread.

Finally feeling the shivers from sucking in as much icy air as possible, my eyes popped open from behind the dusty sunglasses to see a Thai girl shorter than me with her hair tied up as tight as humanly possible.

"*Sawasdee ka*," she sang out in the softest of voices.

Alex bounced the same response back, as did I.

"Hi, err oh, *sawasdee ka*."

Both of us had learnt a few basic words last night, knowing this was our first experience of a foreign country, although Thailand was popular with backpackers and tourists, we'd been told learning a few basic words goes a long way with locals.

"No, no, sir, you say *sawasdee krap*. This is man's way. Women say *ka*, man say *krap*," she giggled back like a schoolchild, hiding her mouth behind her childlike fingers.

The smile on her face didn't waver as she educated us nor when she led us to a small square table close to the air-con unit the Arctic air was blasting out from.

"Sir, would like to turn off the air-con?" she asked.

"No, no keep it on, make it stronger if you can. It's so hot outside."

"Yes, the smog makes worse."

Leaving us with a couple of laminated menus, she waddled away a few metres with her notepad and pencil, keeping an eagle eye on us. Alex had already created a mountain of wet tissues trying to wipe the sweat and dirt from her face. She wasn't as concerned with the menu as I was.

"OK, I know what I want. Easy." Alex only glanced at the menu for a few seconds.

"Did you even look at the menu? Let me guess, just fruit?" My eyes peered up over the top of my menu to see her outstretched body on the wooden chair soaking in the air-con.

"No. Yogurt and juice too."

It was probably the best option, but the thought of a proper English fry-up—eggs, bacon, sausages, black pudding, beans, tomatoes, and toast—the whole works—had floated through my mind, but this was Thailand and there was no chance of that.

"Sir, for you?" The Thai girl waddled back with her beaming smile.

"Yeah, can I have a fried egg on toast... I don't suppose you have any bacon?"

"This, sir?" her eyes took to the menu, scanning before pointing to something that resembled ham.

"No, bacon, not ham."

"Sorry, sir, I do not understand this."

"No, it's OK… just the fried egg on toast with an ice coffee." My shoulders lifted and dropped effortlessly.

Alex quickly ordered her fruit with no issues. Her face looked like it was dripping off just as much as mine, but the air-con was solidifying us back together.

As the girl waddled away, the sound of her flip-flops clapped over the tiles. I peeled my wet back from the back of the seat, leaning forward and noticing the ashtray beside us on the table.

"Can I smoke inside? Sweet." My eyes lifted towards Alex while lighting the smoke, "Alex, how the fuck are we going to survive out there? Look at the state of us just walking a few metres. It was less than five minutes."

"We will be OK, we just have to get used to it. But I do not want to stay in Bangkok long."

A plume of smoke lifted from my cigarette, A sigh of relief followed from my mouth, nodding to her comment and finally able to enjoy a smoke. We were excited to travel together again, it had been nearly a year since our camper-vanning trip and we felt far more experienced. Thailand was super popular with backpackers and tourists, somebody even said it was the backpacker superhighway—everybody goes through it. However, we were fully aware this was going to be completely different to anything we had experienced before.

A gecko took my attention, scampering across the pastel-green wall into one of the cracks. The café was small, lined with a few tables and chairs. My eyes veered over Alex's shoulder to the wall-to-wall window. Everything outside looked like it was melting.

The little Thai girl waddled back over, carrying the oversized tray with precision and handing over Alex's breakfast. She beamed at her chopped selection of tropical fruit, yoghurt, and freshly squeezed juice.

Maybe I should have got the fruit selection.

"So, so good." Her eyes opened up, savouring the taste.

The waitress returned with the same oversized tray—unlike Alex's, mine didn't look tasty in the slightest. What was meant to be a fried egg looked like a runny boiled egg poured over bread.

"Sorry, can I have the eggs cooked, this looks very raw, and the bread toasted?"

"Sir, there is something wrong? This is what you ask—egg and toast."

"Yeah, but cooked. You've just given me a raw egg and bread. It's simple, fry the egg and toast the bread."

"Sir, you would like an omelette?"

"No, just a fu—" I stopped myself from swearing and calmed my voice down. "Can I please have a cooked egg and toast?"

That friendly smile was plastered on her face, but it was clear to see she was not understanding my request for cooked food. However, she did take it back.

"See, you should have got fruit. Well done for not swearing, but now you make trouble over nothing," Alex beamed while tucking into her breakfast.

"She didn't have a clue what I was saying, Thai food has fried eggs on it, they know what a fried egg is. Why was it so hard? No, not causing trouble, I don't know much about Thailand but I do know I'm not getting thrown into a Thai jail."

The girl could be heard saying something in Thai followed by a lot of crashing and banging from pots and pans behind the curtain.

Well, my food is definitely getting spat on. Should have just got the fruit.

I let Alex enjoy her breakfast. The chalky walls took my attention as the gecko crawled out of one of the many cracks, scurrying across and hiding in another. It was playing hide and seek with itself. The Thai girl came back with my food. This time, the egg had been nuked and the bread was still bread. Without lifting my head, I could see Alex shaking her head. She probably thought I would erupt, but I smiled at the girl and thanked her.

"It's your own fault," Alex laughed as soon as the girl was out of sight.

"Yeah, thanks. So, we going back to the hotel afterwards to wait for it to cool down a bit, get our bearings, and figure out what to do?"

"No, we go explore. We have to get used to the heat, Amit. No hiding."

"Woman, do you want me to die? I'll melt." My voice inadvertently raised a notch.

"You will not. Enjoy your rubber egg."

She pulled out the tourist map of Bangkok that the hotel receptionist who recommended this place had given to us.

"So, we do a tourist day today, get it out of the way to say we've seen it, then we start exploring more further away before leave to the villages. All this big Buddha thing, the golden temples, markets, then Khao San Road."

"So, you want a proper tourist day while it's the hottest day ever?"

"Today, yup, today we do this," she replied before taking a sip of her juice.

"We gonna take a tuk-tuk or take a taxi? There's a tuk-tuk driver out there, he's been staring at us for ages. Think he can tell this is our first day here?"

"Yes, I think so. It's cheaper than taxi." Her head swivelled around to the window to the guy leaning on his black-and-yellow tuk-tuk.

"OK, so remember what we were told… agree the price before we get in. On the street, we're in control, in the tuk-tuk, he is. We're gonna have to haggle."

I lit another cigarette, knowing it was near impossible to smoke out there. Alex tried to get an idea of how much it would cost to get to certain destinations. The girl gave her a rough price for each. She was talking in hundreds, which was another thing to wrap our heads around—the money. Thai baht was the local currency, and it came with added zeros, but everything was dirt cheap—the added zeros made no sense. We tried to make sense of the exchange rate, but as I learnt in Australia, it was best to work off local prices and not try to compare everything to the prices we were used to. However, the money was going to take some getting used to.

The bill arrived, but it was more than we calculated. A service charge and a tax were added on. I tried to argue it, but Thai girl stuck to her guns.

Wait a minute, so I'm paying more than I thought over the worst breakfast in history? Feels like I'm getting scammed.

Alex must have seen the look on my face and just shook her head at me as if to say, *Stay calm.*

I did and just popped a note with lots of zeros on top of the bill, hoping to get the correct change back.

Not leaving a tip for her.

She came back with the change, crumpled little paper notes—for all we knew, it could have been fake money she gave back. She didn't like that my food had remained untouched and just ignored me as we said goodbye. She went from friendly to rude very quickly.

No sooner had we cracked the door open, it all came flooding through like opening a furnace door—the noise, the papping, the dust, and the unforgiving heat. It swept through, and in less than a second, my cooled body was on fire once more while being choked from the humidity. The noise made everything overwhelming, especially when the tuk-tuk driver pounced like a cheetah on a gazelle.

"Where you go? You need tuk-tuk? I take you anywhere. Cheap, cheap."

It was too much; my brain couldn't compute properly. It was stimulation overload. Instinct took over and my legs started to walk away, but the humidity sapped my energy, my body was like a pierced water hose. He didn't give up easily, jumping in his tuk-tuk and stalking us like we were prey.

"Where you going—it's your first time? Nothing this way. I take you."

Even though I had travelled for three years and saw myself as experienced, he saw a novice. And that's what we were again. Did we stick out that much or was it because we were the only 'foreigners' on this dusty old side street? Both of us were summoning the courage to stop and negotiate a price but kept aimlessly walking in the wrong direction of the hotel, adding to his conviction of us being lost tourists. I knew we had to haggle but I'd never done it before—never had the need—but finally, my feet came to a halt.

"How much to Khao San Road?" I asked with some bass in my voice like it would make a difference.

I don't know why I said Khao San Road, that was meant to be the last stop, but I said it and wasn't going to change the destination at the risk of sounding like a dithering tourist.

"Very cheap for you but you want to see the city? Too early for Khao San. You go there in the night party, I give you city tour." The brown-orange tint of his teeth appeared and matched the air around as he nodded.

"No. No city tour, just Khao San Road please."

It took us by surprise when he gave a price much lower than the girl in the café had suggested. We didn't know what to do. I had prepared to knock his price down. I looked over to Alex and back to him.

"That's the price? Can't change it, that's what we pay, and you take us to Khao San Road. No city tour."

"Yes, I take you to Khao San," he replied while ushering us into the back of the tuk-tuk.

That felt way too easy and left an uneasy feeling in my stomach. The last three years have taught me that if it sounds too good to be true, then it probably is. But there were no other tuk-tuks around and we had walked too far away from the hotel. We took the chance and slid into the back of his three-seater open tuk-tuk.

Ah, fuck it, let's see what happens, he can't change the price now. First day in Bangkok, time to get involved in the chaos but keep alert.

I knew the signs to look out for—as did Alex. Both of us were street smart enough to know if we were about to get fucked over.

He spun the tuk-tuk around and drove back up the side street, past the café, and turning past our hotel on the main road and dove straight into the chaotic traffic without any regard for safety. Instantly, the paps shot through like rapid-fire machine guns. A swarm of mopeds surrounded us and every other bigger vehicle on the road. Both of us were poking each other and pointing out the most random things on mopeds.

In just a couple of minutes, we had seen a family of seven crammed on to a little bike, pets in the footwell and seat, even a guy carrying a wide screen TV, barely able to see the road. They were like ants covering every little gap in the road. My eyes felt like they were popping out, witnessing this craziness on the roads. The mix of fumes from exhausts, dusty roads, all types of spices from vendors and street stalls fused with the heat to create the thick, stale oily air, mixed with the humidity and made it so hard to breathe. The only reprieve came while there was a little space. The driver was able to speed up a little for the slightest warm breeze to pass through. The streets were manic, mopeds pulling out all over the place—I was almost certain we would crash at some point.

It wasn't as if the driver was being safe either, yanking the tuk-tuk in and out of different lanes. This was just as bad as the crazy pilot on the castaway trip, with no regard for our safety. Fear of death was becoming quite a reality the more he pulled in and out, even people on their feet were just walking out in front of traffic, playing chicken with death. Not once did it occur to us that he knew what he was doing, and this was just a normal day for him.

It was carnage on the road. Thankfully, hiding behind sunglasses, my fear couldn't be seen, but it was running through my body as it must have been through Alex's as neither of us said a word. Both of us kept trying to grip onto the tuk-tuk's rails.

"You are not used to seeing this? Very normal for us. No need to be scared." The driver must have noticed the pure shock on my face.

He cut through three busy lanes like a knife through butter and somehow didn't hit anybody but faced an endless torrent of angry paps. He took a sharp turn off the main road and into a back street. Instantly, my spider senses tingled.

Where the fuck's he taking us? Why has he pulled off? This is where he tries to jack us and fuck us up—this is why he was so cheap, implored an inner voice.

My top lip started to curl up and my eyes turned serious. Alex noticed—she knew this look, placing her hand on my thigh to calm me down. But she leant forward.

"Hey, where are you going? Why did you leave the main road?" Alex demanded before I could say anything.

"You don't like the traffic; this is shortcut. It's OK, you relax," he nodded back through the rear-view mirror.

Fuck that, relax in the back streets of Bangkok? Shit, I've seen too many movies, you're going to try and fuck us over. Nah, mate, not us. I will fuck you up if you try anything.

My eyes were peeled as he turned from one alleyway to another backstreet, with nothing but a few homeless guys and wild dogs roaming, looking for scraps. He turned on to another road, which was more much more open with locals going about their day. Most of the shacks were mechanics, food, and spice stalls. The next turn, the shacks turned into built-up shops, mostly garments, and busier with an increase in tuk-tuks, which put our minds at ease a little.

OK, maybe we were quick to judge. But don't drop your guard, this could be a trick.

He drove through, but slowly, talking to passers-by— he was obviously well known along the road—but then he came to a stop.

"Very, very hot. I go quickly for a drink. You can look in this shop, very good, cheap, cheap," he strongly suggested.

It doesn't seem right, why would he just stop like that and why tell us to go into a shop? Keep an eye out.

There didn't seem to be other tourists or backpackers along the street, just a few locals—most of them hanging out on the side the driver went off to.

"It's too hot to just stand here, shall we see inside. Get out of the heat?" Alex wore a face of confusion, but shrugged, sliding out.

"No, I don't trust him, something isn't right here." It was sweltering, but I shook my head.

"You don't trust anybody, but look, there are people around and it looks like a normal shop. We look then leave."

I shrugged and followed tentatively behind. Instantly, the cold Arctic blast hit and we both hurried into the shop, caring about nothing more than letting our bodies cool down.

"Sawasdee ka, sir… shoes… not allowed, sir." All I could hear was a screech.

My eyebrows pushed together as I shook my head. *No way, I'm not taking my shoes off, my feet have been boiling and frying in them since the morning, they will stink the place out.*

"Please take off, or outside." The lady pointed back outside.

I didn't understand why she was making such a big deal, but it obviously offended her a lot. Alex had already slipped out of her flip-flops and was looking around the fabric store we'd walked into. We had no reason to be in a fabric shop, but the air-con was bliss. The Thai lady followed Alex like a shadow, trying to persuade her to buy something. It wasn't just a friendly suggestion, but quite forceful as she shoved things in her face. Alex didn't take kindly to that but tried to remain calm.

"OK, let's go, she is getting annoying now," Alex fumed—she was losing her cool, which never happened.

For a moment, I didn't want to open the door, knowing what was waiting outside, but Alex didn't want to hang about. The driver was still relaxing and chatting across the road as I called him back. He wandered back, looking bemused.

"You do not buy anything? So much good thing in there for you. Cheaper than London."

"Yeah, that's great, but I'm not interested in buying fabrics. I'm a backpacker, I'm not going home in a week. Just take us to where we want to go please."

"Yes, yes, OK, we go now," he responded while starting up the tuk-tuk.

I flung my melting body back into the seat next to Alex, shaking my head. He pulled into another street and came to a stop again.

"Now what?"

"I drink too much, I need to use bathroom. Short break. This shop very good. You go look." He turned back, smiling.

Why the fuck is this guy getting us to go into shops?

The humidity was too stifling to sit still, and again, we reluctantly slid out of the tuk-tuk and into the store. Once more, we were welcomed by a girl, but this time offered a cold drink. We both accepted and there was no mention of taking our shoes off. It was a store full of tacky souvenirs, which neither of us were interested in—the only thing that appealed was the air-con.

The girl tried to get us to buy gifts, and once it was clear we were not interested, she became quite rude and that was our cue to leave. We both stepped back out into the scorching heat and thick air. The driver was already waiting.

"You not buy anything again?" He looked quite dismayed.

"No, we don't want to buy anything, just take us to Khao San like you said. Nowhere else. Don't know what game you're playing, but we ain't interested. Go back to the main roads," I huffed but tried to remain calm.

He nodded back, not saying anything for a while. Alex pulled out her map, checking it as he finally joined back on to the manic crazy main road. The chaos was all around again, constant papping, never-ending traffic, swarms of mopeds. Alex kept an eye on the map, checking against big statues and buildings we passed like the Royal Palace Gardens. It seemed finally we were heading in the right direction. But then he cut off again, swooping and swerving past a pack of dogs. There were so many dogs just roaming the streets. Again, he stopped on a road full of local people, where meaty spices, the clanging of woks, and frying engulfed the air. The smells from the food court and the carts lined on the side of the road filled my nostrils and were very appealing.

"You want to get food? Very good here," he asked casually.

I was starving, but out of principle, I declined. As much as I tried to remain calm, he was winding me up and the heat was making me very irritable. My blood was boiling. Alex didn't even try and stop me this time.

"NO! Just take us to where we want to go. For fuck's sake, stop fucking with us."

"Hey, you not be rude. I am being nice to you," he took exception this time.

"No, you're not. You keep taking us to random places we have no interest in. Not once have we told you to stop. You are not our guide. We don't want a guide. You're a tuk-tuk driver. We agreed a price for you to take us to one place, so take us there. Or we get out and find another one!" The pressure cooker exploded.

"The price I give is to take you to Khao San, but to stop on the way. This is why so cheap. If you want to go straight, then price is more." He started to smirk, shaking his head.

"What? No, fuck off. We agreed a price and that's it. Take us there now."

"Or what?"

"We get out, give us our money back!"

We both jumped out of the tuk-tuk, imploring him to give us our money back, but he refused. Even Alex was starting to get annoyed but was calmer than me. The driver refused, just laughing, which wound me up even more. Alex must have noticed the way my fists started to ball up—new foreign country or not, the red mist was returning. Her palm pressed to my chest as she made eye contact and pushed me back.

"Amit, calm, not here. No. We sort it, but not like this. Be calm."

She had a way of making the red mist pass. My fists un-balled and I stepped back but shot daggers at him with my eyes. One of the locals must have heard the commotion and walked over asking what was going on. The driver fumed in Thai, but I jumped in trying to explain what was going on. The local seemed to have a go at the tuk-tuk driver and turned back towards me.

"This is scam. You pay already?"

"Yeah, but we want it back."

"You pay me, no give back," shouted the driver and pushed me away.

I stepped back up to him, the switch was nearly flicked, but Alex flung her arm across my chest.

"Amit! NO!"

Once more, I backed down.

"You lied to us, we asked you to take us straight there, so give us our money and leave," implored Alex.

The local stuck up for us and others joined in, all imploring the driver to leave. He did, but without paying us back. I tried to shout out but it was no use, he was gone.

"You need be careful of driver like this. If tuk-tuk too cheap, then scam." The skinny local turned to us, shaking his head.

Scammed on the very first tuk-tuk driver ride—just my luck. It had not been a good start to the day so far, in fact, it was a horrible start to life in Thailand. I felt stupid and naïve. I was meant to be an experienced traveller, but it just showed that being in a non-Western country for the first time, this may as well have been my very first day as a traveller. All those instincts, being street smart, and being aware of signs to look out for clearly needed to be sharpened up. In that moment, we were very much the stupid tourists. But on the other hand, it could have been a lot worse… he could have actually tried to jack us up.

Bangkok was a big city and we had no idea where we were. It didn't take more than a few steps in the suffocating heat to realise we were the only foreigners around. Not a single other traveller or backpacker was in sight. Locals eyed us as if to say, 'What are you stupid tourists doing here? You don't belong here.' The strong smell of overused fried oil got stronger the further we walked down the narrow street. Each side of the road was comprised of local food carts and stores.

One frying bugs in a huge wok, another with a basket of honey-roasted crickets as if they were a selection of nuts. The further we walked, the more bizarre the foods and smells became. Shark fins were advertised through glass windows, dried skins—pigskin, snakeskin, and all sorts—and chicken feet hung in front of carts. Mopeds readily rolled up to them, all ordering and driving off. Chickens and hens ran free across the road, while others were crammed into cages and some were even on leashes.

They eat this stuff as snacks like they're nuts or crisps... talk about culture shock. This ain't for me.

We quickly turned off the road just to get away from the putrid smell of meat, salty fish, shrimp paste, and stale oil. But the smell was replaced with rotting trash and my eyes were on the lookout for any rats that might be harvesting the rubbish.

Where the fuck are we? We seriously need to get back on to the main road, I'm not getting lost in Bangkok on my first day.

It wasn't the rats that we needed to keep an eye on, both of us twisted round upon hearing the rumblings of a growl.

Its eyes looked a little demonic, ribs showing through, and the growl grew as it took a step closer. The street dog was joined by another—they were like hungry hyenas looking for scraps and had found a buffalo and a gazelle lost in their territory.

Show no fear and just keep walking.

They both started to follow, but the growls turned into barks—turning back once more, we saw they had started to fight over scraps they'd found in the trash.

"The poor things," Alex pouted, watching them fight.

It was unfortunate, I loved dogs, but they were street dogs, hardened, and wouldn't hesitate to bite. They too were something else to have to get used to.

"Can you hear that?" I stopped us in our tracks.

Noise, a lot of it, like loud chatter, papping but not relentless. We surveyed the street until we saw a large group of people walking in and out, getting on and off a cluster of mopeds.

"There, it's busy, that must be a main area."

The closer we got to the cluster, the louder the noise grew—all types of high to low pitches, people going back and forth, but we couldn't understand a word of it. There it was in front of our eyes—pandemonium.

"Have we just found the black market?" I asked, watching the chaos in front of our eyes.

"I think so," Alex replied timidly.

The Wall Street trading floor was probably more civilised than this large open-air market. Hands were waving all over the place, people shouting, bartering, haggling, it was crazy but a welcome sight.

"We have a look inside. We are here. Maybe you find your flip-flops in here," Alex was no longer timid but excited.

"Or maybe not in here, been scammed already. We're gonna need to learn to haggle at some point, but I was thinking of starting off somewhere quieter."

"Quieter? Amit, this is Bangkok, there has been nothing quiet since we left the café."

She had a point. Making sure all our valuables were in a safe place, we took our first step into a Thai market. Shouting was volleyed from one person to another, it was carnage, worse than any Black Friday sale, flea market, farmers' market, or free-for-all. Vendors jumped out in front of us, trying to get us into their market stalls, people shoved and pushed their way through, there was no orderly fashion, no respect for personal space, even little old women pushed through. The open markets sold everything from fake designer handbags, clothes, belts, watches, jewellery, snacks, sports jerseys, shoes, sneakers, and wallets. My head was in a spin trying to make sense of it all. We were barely choosing our own path, just being pushed in the general flow like being caught up in a strong undercurrent. Every few seconds, my hands made sure my valuables were safe, while Alex wore the green backpack on her front with her hands over the zips.

We were pushed into another section that was a little quieter, providing a little personal space while walking. But that gave vendors more opportunity to call out, and some even popped up in front of us, trying to get us to buy fake goods.

"There's one you can buy from." Alex spotted one, a market stall full of flip-flops.

"Nope, not here, it's all a bit too much."

"OK, I'm going to try. I want these pants. So comfy." She had seen something she wanted—loose cotton elephant-print pants.

We stopped for a second, paying attention to how people haggled back and forth, but it was just noise and in Thai. We didn't understand a thing.

"There, Amit, look—another one for you. It's quiet here. You have to try."

"Yeah, I know. Fuck it. Let's do it. I'm brown, haggling should be in my blood."

The vendor had already locked eyes with me, knowing I was looking into his stall. Before I even stepped in, he was in my face—personal space was out of the window again as he beamed. That was the next lesson in cultural difference—there was no personal space allowed.

"Hello, sir, you need flip-flop? I have good quality, cheap, cheap."

Does every fucker in Bangkok say those words? asked one of my inner voices.

Right, don't let him control this. I'm in sales, I control the narrative, get that ego out. I'm in charge here. We've already been fucked over today, not happening again.

The vendor had already started to pull his choices out, but I ignored him, trying to walk off.

"I'm just looking."

I needed to be rude and arrogant back to him. Every time he stepped closer, I walked away, even when he had a nice pair, on principle, I moved away to show him who was in charge. He didn't like it, nor did he leave me alone. Just like with Alex, as soon as I reached for a pair, he would spring in saying they were an excellent choice and he could give me a good price.

Bro, let me look at them first. Get the fuck out of my face.

It got to a point I had to sneak a look without him noticing any that took my eye. However, there was one pair I found... this was it, time to haggle.

"How much for these?"

"Good choice, for you—special price," he beamed and gave a price.

"No, too much." I shook my head.

"No, no, brother, good price, very good quality. This is very special price for you." He was holding the flip-flops.

"Nah, come on, it's too much."

Again, I shook my head, but my face didn't match the smile on his—mine showed no emotion, it was poker-face time. My counter-offer was less than half of what he proposed, which he laughed off, saying that was too low. I shrugged back.

"That's my offer."

I was sticking to it, he tried to lower just a little from the original price, but I didn't budge. He tried again, but once more, I stood my ground. He looked around huffing and fuming.

"No, sir, too low."

My face was a stone wall, I was getting fed up with this back and forth. Alex was done and dusted in this time frame, but this guy wasn't playing ball.

"That's the offer or we go somewhere else."

"OK."

What, he just said OK, did I win? Did I just get a price down to what I wanted on my first attempt?

I wanted to smile, but kept up the stone wall poker face. His smile was gone… was it because of the defeat? It wasn't. The flip-flops were returned to the rack as he shrugged and started to usher me out—well, more like push me out like an unwanted rodent.

"OK, you leave now, you don't buy here."

Alex tried to reason with him, but he didn't want to know.

"What did I do wrong? Is that not how to haggle? I stuck to my guns, didn't back down, why did I get the dickhead?"

"Aww, he didn't like you like the girl at breakfast and the tuk-tuk driver. Amit is not making friends today," she laughed, wrapping her arms around me.

"Fuck him, I'll get some another time. He just didn't like that I didn't back down."

That was us done with the market. We needed to find our way out of the maze somehow, but following other people, we were just going in circles. Finally, somehow, we stumbled out, back into the thick hot sweating open air of smog—and apparently, in another country. Somehow, we walked out into China. Chinese music sang out, food stalls covered the street, Chinese symbols and colourful red-and-gold buildings with golden dragons rose up. It was obviously Chinatown and a recognisable reference point on the map. There was so much going on all over the place—so many people, so many voices shouting out in broken Thai, English, and Chinese. We found a quiet spot and some open air, but the thick musky air still felt suffocating in our throats. Alex pulled out the map, but before it was fully open, we were jumped on and harassed.

"Where you want to go?"
"Are you lost? I'll help you."
"Brother, do you need a lift?"
"Tell me what you want, I will show you."

They all came from different voices, random hands tried to snap the map away, but we kept hold of it while also making sure none of our belongings were taken.

"Fuck off! Leave us alone! Back the fuck up!" I growled back at the vultures.

Fuck's sake, is this what Thailand is like? I'm not liking this at all.

We had escaped the clutches of the tuk-tuk drivers. Alex was able to check where we needed to go but turned to me.

"Just relax, calm down. I know you're getting angry, and the heat is not helping, but try to calm down. We have to cross the road."

How do you cross a road where the traffic is relentless and never stops?

The two of us stepped up to cross the road lining up with others, my mind was racing as quick as the traffic passing by.

This is fucking suicide.

It seemed like it, but others were dancing with death, making it to the other side. Nobody was paying any attention to the traffic lights or the zebra crossings. We kept watching as others crossed, our legs unable to move.

"Hey, first time crossing? You just gotta go. One pace, straight line, don't dither or change pace and they will just swerve out of the way," said a blond-braided backpacker as she smiled back.

Her smile left with her body as she casually floated across like it was an empty road.

Fuck it, we need to do it, somebody take the wheel.

I looked across to Alex, she just nodded back ready to dance with death. That was it—in unison, we took a step but immediately stepped back as a papping moped soared past. My heart exploded. I've jumped out of two planes, off cliffs, been in a plane with a lunatic pilot, submerged in an ocean, but nothing had been as scary as this. We both looked at each other, laughing, waited until a larger group of people formed, and once they went, so did we. I couldn't look up, the dusty concrete road was my focus. Mopeds swerved past, some so close a breeze whispered through, every step prompted a harder and quicker thud of the heart, followed by, "Oh, momma, I'm gonna die. Oh, momma, I'm gonna die."

How have I not been hit yet?

I felt like a lizard crossing a stampede of buffalo. They came shooting past from behind and in front—this was the worst obstacle course in history. Somehow, I'd made it to the concrete island in the middle of the road intact. But now the traffic was coming from the other side. Again, I waited for a few people to cross first, sucked in some thick air, and went again. One step after the other, rubber tyres whizzed past, but there was no looking up, just one step after another. I knew by looking up I'd be a deer in the headlights and that would mean a visit to the hospital or the morgue.

However, a screech got louder, as did the papping. It made my eyes lift and nearly pop out of their sockets.

"Oh fuck! I'm gonna die!"

A truck had slowed down, but a moped jumped out in front, it was on a collision course with my body, my heart was trying to escape as much as my eyes. With the moped only inches away, I braced for impact, but it swerved just enough, missing my toes by millimetres.

Fuck, fuck, fuck!

As soon as it passed, my feet kicked into gear, moving through the traffic. I wasn't thinking any more—adrenaline had kicked in and instinct took over once more. The other side was getting closer but the constant papping wasn't helping, was it aimed at me? I didn't know. My foot hit the pavement and my first instinct was to check all body parts were intact, then it was to look for Alex. I was alive, my heart felt like it was about to explode once more. But I had done it, so had she, we had survived crossing the death-trap road. As soon as I felt the pavement, my body wanted to collapse.

Coming back to my senses, an explosion of vibrant colours, noise, music, and the smell of noodles took over to create an electric ball of energy. Alex was spinning on her heels, taking it all in but I wasn't feeling it. For a moment, the thick air was forgotten about, but it soon wrapped around us once more.

"That was some scary shit. Fuck, I nearly got hit a couple of times."

"I know, I saw it. This is why I stand on the other side of you, so you get hit first," she beamed back.

"Oh, cheers!

*

Night had fallen on the first day in Bangkok and we had found ourselves on the famous Koa San road strip. Bars lined each side of the street, billboards and signs were lit up above, and the street was packed full of tourists, holiday makers, and backpackers. We had made friends with two male backpackers who were negotiating a price from a vendor. They had convinced us to try a local delicacy, and with a few beers down, I was game keen to be the centre of attention. He handed over my stick, a deep breath was needed as I laid eyes on the jet black deep fried scorpion in my hand.

Alex closed her eyes and winced a little before giving it a bite. I drank the last of my beer before sliding the scorpion into my mouth. The crunch shot through my ears as my teeth bit down. My brain was expecting something disgusting but, surprisingly, my teeth continued to crunch—the taste was familiar. It was like eating a burnt chicken wing. More beer was needed, it didn't look like it was going to be an early night.

We survived our first day in Bangkok, but we had to survive the night!

Paradise Hurts

"What do you mean it's gone missing? HOW?"

"Gone, sir, we do not know where."

The small, clean-shaven Thai man in his pristine white shirt who sat in the safety of the little office on the other side of the iron bars simply shrugged back like it was a normal thing. I flung my arms into the air, wanting to rip off the iron bars, but instead, pointed to one direction of the train track.

"It can only go either that way," my finger pointed the opposite way, "or that way. How can a train go fucking missing when it was on its way here?"

As with every day in Thailand so far, my wet t-shirt clung tightly to my sticky burning body. Every inch was soaked, but the clerk in his ironed white shirt looked fresh. He remained calm with his arms folded.

"Yes, sir, I sorry, we do not know."

Another torrent of abuse was fired, but he was impenetrable. Before another assault was just about to fly out, fingers pressed against my chest.

"Just calm down, stop being an asshole, it's not his fault. There is nothing he can do, and no point you getting angry for nothing. It will not make the train come like magic. You know all the time in Thailand the transport is late. We have this all the time."

"Yeah, but that's those stupid overnight busses, not trains in the middle of the day!" I fumed back.

Alex slid in between me and the clerk, breaking my glare and pointing towards the open-air waiting room like I was a naughty child before apologising about my behaviour. I dragged my heels towards the wall-less waiting room like a deflated balloon. While she dropped on to the concrete bench and went back to her book, my feet carried on dragging towards the shade just outside the white concrete walled entrance. Before I could even lift my cigarette, like sharks smelling blood, a clamour of tuk-tuks kicked up dry dust and started clamouring around. But one got the jump.

"You need a lift, where you go, I…"

Are you for real? You've seen me come out here for a smoke before, you know there hasn't been a train pass through, are you going to take me hundreds of miles to Phuket? Idiot!

His words were instantly met by my raised palm as I looked away and lit the smoke while leaning against the wall. It was one of the tricks we had learnt in Thailand— simply waving them off while not making any eye contact or giving them any opportunity to start a conversation. They all retreated back, assuming their napping positions, and near silence fell. It was just the sounds of grasshoppers and crickets in the nearby shrubs and rustles in the overhanging palm trees.

It was our third day in this little village south of Bangkok—three days too long. Having got out of Bangkok after just a few painful days, we'd been hopping through towns and villages along the way to the tropical islands in the south. We thought the local villages would be calmer, but it's fair to say this missing train epitomised just how Thailand had been so far. Barely anything had gone as it should have. My cigarette burnt down to the butt and I returned to the waiting room. Two little kids were playing around on the floor while Alex's head was in her book. A local was at the clerk's window, presumably asking about the train.

"Leave it, Amit. Just sit down. It will come when it comes," Alex intervened just as my foot lifted.

My body slumped back on the concrete bench, head draped over the back, eyes closed behind my sunglasses. Thailand had been a comedy of errors from the very first day—a shit show. Thoughts started to drift as I tried to figure out where the train could have gone missing.

I felt a sharp dig into my ribs, making my eyes pop open as my head snapped forward in a little daze. It hadn't all been a dream, I was still in the waiting area.

"You were snoring, you were sleeping for hours, and I think the train is coming."

In an instant, I was in front of the iron bars—the clerk had been replaced.

"Train to Phuket? Found it yet?"

"On way, sir… coming soon." His brown eyes looked back at me and he nodded.

"You serious? Two tickets, second class." It was the best news I'd heard all week.

It didn't even matter where or how the train went missing, it was on its way and that's what mattered. We were done with the little hops and skips from town to village and wanted a tropical island to escape from all the chaos. He handed over the tickets and pointed to the closest platform. Alex must have seen my jump of joy, the ticket, or both and joined, heading to the platform. The comedy of errors was hopefully over.

We had fallen for the most stupid of scams on our arrival to this village. In not our proudest moment, we found a nice hotel, which was within our budget, but on arrival, we found out why—it was out in the middle of nowhere, but the real scam was that it was half built! That was just one of the misdemeanours here. Another was trying to communicate with an old Thai lady who spoke no English and having to mimic a chicken. There was Alex's weird breakfast that freaked us both out—she asked for a boiled egg and got a half-developed egg-embryo—they call it *balut* and the locals think it's normal. That's not to mention the constant hounding we received, transport being late, unreliable, or going missing like today.

All of a sudden, an older, very frail and wrinkly Thai man approached. We both stopped laughing, thinking he was going to ask for a handout, although nobody had since Bangkok. He just studied us both, flicking from Alex's face to mine. We smiled back, but there was no reciprocation, just more flicking of his eyes between us before he walked away.

What the fuck was that?

"This place so weird?" Alex burst out laughing.

Before I could answer, the old man popped up again like a ghost.

"You are Indian?" he asked.

"No, English," I replied.

He looked at Alex while scrunching his wrinkles together.

"You are English?" he asked her, slightly more confused.

"No, German." She shook her head as I did.

He nodded again and walked off. She looked at me mouthing, "What the...?"

The frail old man was back again, looking at both of us and pointing in confusion.

"But you are brown and you are white? Why you speak English good and you not?"

The poor old man, who had probably not met many foreigners like us before, looked bamboozled—he just couldn't comprehend, like it had just blown his mind. Whatever shit feeling and grumpiness we both had was laughed out of our system right there as he toddled off again.

I jumped up, re-enacting what had just happened, but as I did, I saw it—hope.

It was only seven hours late. Another cultural lesson from Thailand... never rely on anything to run on time. As the train got closer, it looked decorated. It was... in humans. Some sat on top, others hung off the sides. This was to be our first train experience, and by the way previous transport—from tuk-tuks to buses—had been, I wasn't looking forward to it. There was sure to be more culture shock in wait.

* * *

The hollow wooden slats of the jetty bounced under excited backpackers' flip-flops and bare feet, desperate to get on to the island after a two-hour boat ride from Phuket.

"This is more like it… this feels like the tropical Thailand I imagined," I beamed, feeling the ocean breeze on my face.

The ride over from Phuket was eventless, it was amazing, nothing went wrong. The boat just soared through the type of ocean I hadn't seen since the Great Barrier Reef—a baby blue and emerald fusion with streaks of lime green running through. We took our time coming off the jetty. I was still in awe of the smaller limestone islands along the way, which gave it much more of a Jurassic feel. Ko Phi Phi Don was the first of many of Thailand's southern tropical islands we wanted to visit and do nothing but relax. In the short time we'd been in Thailand, the chaos and constant noise, not to mention the humidity in places had been so draining. We were ready to unplug from it all and just enjoy island life for a while.

From aerial pictures, it looked like two limestone islands connected by a flat stretch of land, almost like a natural bridge. The two main stretches of beach lay on both sides of the flat land, while the forests and jungle grew out of the limestone islands. Alex said it looked like somebody had taken a bite from both sides of an apple. The core being the flat land and the uneaten apple ends being the hilly forests. This side of the beach was mainly used for boats ferrying travellers over and traditional fishing boats, but the other side was apparently the public beach, which was lined with beach shacks, bars, and beach huts—including ours. Commotion started to take over my ears as we approached the sandy beach.

"Accommodation? Cheap, cheap. You need hostel, hotel, guesthouse, beach hut?"

I thought we got away from the noise. I just want some peace, why is it so hard?

From children to old men, a handful of them had lined up to greet newcomers with laminated sheets and folders, trying to entice backpackers. They got hold of many in need of accommodation, but those of us who had organised it beforehand waved them off. As we made it through, another Thai man jumped in front of us, shirtless and with white shelled beads around his neck, his dark dreadlocks swinging away.

"Hello, friends, welcome to Heaven. You have accommodation already? Where do you stay?"

Alex waved him off while smiling.

"None of your business," I snapped back.

"But it is, I have your keys if you already have accommodation," he laughed.

"What?"

That made my feet dig into the pale sand, nearly losing my flip-flop. The smile grew on his face as he floated over, bouncing a wooden tray of keys.

"This is small island—I hand out the keys to your accommodation here. It's OK, you can relax. Looks like Thailand has stressed you out, brother."

Alex gave him the name of our beach hut, he nodded and searched through the box and picked out the keys.

"Ahh, excellent choice. You have an amazing view."

He whistled somebody over who, without asking and in one fell swoop, slipped off our backpacks, flung them on to a wooden wheelbarrow, and was off with them.

"Oi… where the fuck you going?"

"You have definitely been on the mainland too long. Relax, he is taking your bags to your hut for you." Before I could give chase, the guy wearing beads stopped me.

"Yeah, this country is stressful as fuck," I responded.

"I know, that's why I live out here—*hakuna matata*. You have a little climb; he will drop your bags for you." His finger reached halfway up the forest on the south side.

"Nah, we're not up there, we booked a beach hut." Following his finger to a row of huts pressed against the forest on the hill, my sweaty head started to shake.

"See, beach hut." Alex showed him the printout.

"No, this is correct, it is a beach hut overlooking the island on this side, just not directly on the beach." He, in turn, took a look and confirmed the name of the hut.

It was the correct booking—we had been done over again. Shaking my head, I stormed off kicking the sand in a huff.

That's what we get for trying to be smart and booking from the mainland.

Alex apologised, telling him how we'd had no luck in Thailand so far. I heard him call back, saying, "This island will give you all the luck back. Enjoy your stay, friends."

Yeah, right, I'll be the judge of that.

The palm trees on either side of the sandy walkway stood tall and the palms waved in the breeze as if to shake off all stress while welcoming people to a magical tropical paradise. Music—mainly reggae—grew loader with each step. The sand below faded to reveal large stone slabs as the pathway to the little square. Wall-less open-air bamboo shacks on natural wooden stilts surrounded the square, each one of them either a café, bar, or restaurant. I prepared myself for menus to come flying from all directions like everywhere in Thailand and to be harassed by the menu holders, but they didn't care. Instead, all we got were hellos and smiles from them all and quick reminders about when happy hour was.

This was a new experience in Thailand. Instead of overzealous Thai waiters, braided and dreadlocked backpackers in bikinis or Chang beer vest tops held on to the menus just talking to each other. There was a very hippy vibe—one I didn't mind at all. It was a nice change of pace. Our hut was perched up on the hill against the tropical forest behind the bottom corner of the square. It was bliss walking without being harassed, I was even bouncing to the assortment of music. Large overgrown vegetation and palm trees provided a very wild look against the little wooden huts dotted along the long shallow steps towards our hut.

"Do you think there are snakes in here?" asked Alex as she walked in front with her eyes floating around the fauna.

"Dunno, maybe, it is a tropical island, and this forest looks quite untamed. I've not seen snakes since Australia."

Up until now, the thought hadn't crossed my mind, but now my eyes joined the hunt.

I hated snakes but shrugged them off like I didn't care about them. However, there was one animal I loved but had not yet seen in the wild.

"I heard there are wild monkeys here though, I wanna find them… can't wait to see them."

"You might get lost with them, or they take you home to your family," she teased back.

The hut came into view with our backpacks waiting by the door. It wasn't quite the bamboo hut directly on the beach, but it did have an incredible view. The ocean in front, a brief glimpse of the beach, reggae music, and the sound of the sea, the forest directly behind and a nice open patio area to relax on. It definitely beat a half-built hotel in the middle of nowhere.

I lit a cigarette and, falling back on the wooden garden chair on the patio, a smile naturally formed on my face for the first time in Thailand since the old man at the station nearly a week ago now. My eyes were closed as I took it all in—the whistles from the foliage, the sea singing, Bob Marley soothing from the square. All of it combined swept through my mind, emptying all the stress, frustration, and anger that had built up. Nature had become therapeutic.

"Ahh, looks like Amit is happy and relaxed?"

"Yeah, you know what, I think I am. Feels so tranquil. I'm liking the hippy vibe. Maybe I'll become one. Peace and love, man!" I said, waving a peace sign in the air.

"You would be the angriest and grumpiest hippy ever. But you are right, it feels very tranquil."

Although the music filtered up to the hut, the sounds of nature were in control, like it was singing a soothing song.

"Alex, listen… no fucking horns papping, I can't hear any mopeds, no screams of

"massage", no traffic. I can relax without getting hassled. I forgot what that felt like. Now it feels like we're in the tropics."

"I know, so good. But we need beer, shall we bring some back?"

"Yeah, ice-cold beer… we should bring some back now, then check out some bars later."

My eyes were closed, drifting in and out with the waves, but then, suddenly, my eyelids sprang up. There was one thing here that wasn't going to allow full tranquillity. Mosquitoes! They had already restarted the war from the first day in Bangkok. While Alex looked for the mosquito spray and got freshened up a little, I hit the square, grabbing a few bottles of Chang beer, which was cheaper than Chang water.

With the beers cracked open, icy cold fizz sliding down my throat, the sound of nature, and the sea lapping in the distance fused with Bob Marley's 'Three Little Birds' floating in the air, it was pure bliss. My mind started to drift away, almost void of all thoughts. All the bad luck and all the mishaps of mainland Thailand were gone. Life had been playing its game of fucking with me, but there was a reprieve—hopefully.

Queenstown popped into my mind—those last couple of months after returning from the snowboarding trip. This was a world away from the rabbit hutch of a house I'd moved into. Amy left to go back to Canada soon after the weekend away. She just couldn't deal with being so broke any longer. By the time I left, I was at ease with the decision not to pursue sponsorship or a second-year visa. New Zealand was magical, and Queenstown will always be Neverland, but it was time to leave the bubble. I didn't know what was next, just that I didn't want to go back to England. Thailand was an impulsive decision after Alex said she wanted to travel through it before heading back to Germany. My thoughts evaporated and so did all sound as dreams started to appear.

After a well-deserved nap, we it made into one of the bamboo huts in the square for happy hour. It didn't take much to twist our arms and the hippie backpacker staff convinced us to get on the cocktails. Both of us were stretched out on the padded mats that filled the bar. Nobody was bothering us, no hawkers, no beggars—it was like this wasn't Thailand any more, just a tranquil paradise. The buy-one-get-one-free cocktails had gone down a treat as we tried different combinations. One of the hippy backpackers had told us about the fire shows and beach parties on the other side of the island, but neither of us were in the mood to party that night. This was just too relaxing.

Another two cocktails arrived—these ones as blue as the sea; we didn't even ask what was in them.

"This is the life, right?" I smirked, moving the umbrella from my drink.

"Yup, so freaking good. We stay here for a while I think, but this can be your life for good."

"Yeah, maybe not in Thailand, but yeah. I have no ties or commitments to anything, anyone, or anywhere now, I'm completely and utterly free as a bird."

"Just like how Amit likes it. But has to learn to be calm, to understand locals more and be like them."

My fancy cocktail glass raised up to cheers hers. I sat up a little more, adjusting the floor mat and nodded back.

"Exactly. Weird, isn't it? Like if I got sponsored in Australia, I wouldn't have experienced New Zealand, wouldn't have felt whatever it was in Queenstown, and we wouldn't be sitting here right now."

"I told you before, it wasn't the right time for you. You don't like to be settled; you need to be free. How do you say in English about the spirit flying?"

"Free spirit?"

"Yes, this. You are a free spirit. Before you go to Melbourne, you feel trapped so you become angry like an animal in a cage. Afterwards when we in the flat, even then when you try for sponsorship you were miserable, but you do this for your grandad. And then in Queenstown after your friend leave, you feel bored because you are stuck, and other people leave. One day, you will settle, just not yet. Maybe one day you want to go back to England, who knows."

The cocktail went down too easily—another was called for. There were a few other backpackers dotted around but none were being lairy. There was such a calm atmosphere, but darkness fell over the island and we realised we'd missed the sunset from the viewpoint. Dim candles were lit all over the bar and the square, adding to the tranquillity.

"There is not a chance in hell I will ever want to go back to settle in England. Never. You know it's my black hole. Maybe visits in the future, but never to stay." Lighting a cigarette, I shook my head.

"You should never say never—you don't know what you will feel in the future. But I know you do not like it there. Your past is always going to be there."

Slurping the last of her cocktail, she called over to the waitress to order a pizza for us. We were going through a stage of having eaten too many noodles and rice, we needed Western food. Talk of England brought back the memory of my grandad. I smirked to myself, thinking about what he would have said about me being on a tropical island in Thailand with no plans whatsoever, other than to keep travelling somewhere and to see where it leads.

"You're thinking about him. I can always tell when you are. You miss him a lot." Alex must have seen the look on my face and she smiled.

"Yeah, every day. Just thinking about what he would say finding out I have no address, no home, just floating wherever life wants to take me."

"He would be proud of you. He knows you—he knows you can't settle in one place."

Our new orange-and-red cocktails were placed on the tiny wooden table in front of us, but there was a gust of wind that blew through as if a warning before the pitter-pats came from above. Droplets started to fall on the sandy concrete outside and it didn't take long for the rain to come down in sheets. The island was about to be under siege.

What the fuck? It's a tropical Island, just our fucking luck.

Long wet sniper bullets took down the candles dotted around the square, more rained down against the tropical vegetation sounding like it was going straight through the leaves. Wind rasped around, cooler than usual. The attack became stronger once rainy machine guns got involved, spraying quicker and covering more ground. A huge crack from the heavens above followed before it opened up, raining down an aerial bombardment.

Everybody inside the hut moved back, trying to keep cover, but it was getting stronger by the second, louder and heavier. The hatched roof was shot at by a thousand rapid-fire machine guns, the ground outside covered by relentless non-stop bullets of water. The full force was unleashed. I'm from a country where it rains for the majority of the year, but I'd never heard it so ear-piercing or heavy as this. We were stuck in a bamboo hut in a monsoon, and it was awesome. I kept willing it to get heavier, curious to see how strong it could get. There was hardly any space between raindrops, one after the other falling with the full might. This must be what an ant feels like when a bucket of water is thrown over them.

We're on an island in the middle of the ocean, not close to land. We could be hit with a tsunami. Remember, we already passed through the devastation still left in Phuket from the one that hit there.

Relax, it's just a monsoon. Tsunamis are caused by earthquakes. Just enjoy this monstrous rain.

Alex sat there with a wide smile, almost hypnotised by the rain's power. It was like an energy rose the harder the rain got, and the way it hit thick palms and vegetation. The thatched rooftops had started to leak through. For a moment, I thought about running out into the rain, but quickly thought better of it. The violence in the monsoon was so peaceful and mesmeric. All of us under the thatched roof were hypnotised by it.

* * *

There was no evidence left from last night's monsoon, which, turned out to be just a passing tropical storm and not an actual monsoon. They were regular occurrences and, as the waitress explained, a monsoon devastates the island much more than the odd few broken branches. But this was a new day with no cloud in sight, and that giant ball of fire was tanning and burning bodies laid out all over the white sandy stretch of beach—including Alex. She was out there exposed to its full rays. I, however, lay sprawled out about a foot behind under the safety of the shade provided by the overhanging palm trees. The only time she had moved all day was to jump in and out of the sea, while I played the old game of hide and seek from the sun, which was looking to burn me to a crisp burnt chicken wing. My eyes were on another target—it was the mission for the day, just a few feet away, tied to a couple of thick coconut trees—the hammocks. They were occupied, but I needed them in my life.

For now, though, the near pure-white grains of sand rolling between my fingers and toes were enough to provide the relaxing entertainment. The soft lapping waves were telling a story while rolling on to the beach—this was definitely the life. Everything was calm, the waves, the slight ocean breeze, the birds sang melodies rather than abrupt chirps, there was a mellow ambience and people smiled all the time. None of the other backpackers were loud or obnoxious. It was as if everybody had fallen under the same spell of total relaxation.

My body sprang up to check the hammocks, but it was a false alarm. It was also nearly time to move again, the sun had shifted position. Instead of moving into the shade, I placed my wallet, smokes, and lighter next to Alex, which prompted her head to lift.

"What do you do? Moving again?" she asked.

"Not yet. Back in a bit."

Smirking, my feet left the towel, sinking into the sun-soaked white sand, letting smooth grains roll against my toes, which lasted all of a second before they shot off the ground.

"Fuck… HOT, HOT, HOT!"

My toes danced across the top of the sand like a lizard skipping by to the sound of Alex's laugher and those I pelted past, until they landed in the cool water practically sizzling like sausages. It didn't take long though for the coolness to run through my body, pushing all the heat out and letting out an almighty sigh. Since the Great Barrier Reef, I had started to push myself and had got braver in the sea. Not to the extent of going as far out as most people, but I was comfortable with getting at least neck-deep—especially if the sea was as clear and calm as this one. With only my head exposed to the sun, whenever it got too hot, I sunk underwater to cool down, and like a bobbing float, popped back up. It was in moments like this I had learnt to just stop and take a minute to soak it all in, letting it penetrate deep that this was my life now. It wasn't just a week's holiday or a few months out of my normal life, this was permanent.

This island was paradise. Looking out to the two hills on either side of the stretch of beach, the tropical trees behind added to the masterpiece. From the life I came from, to say I spent two years in Australia—albeit fucking around for the first eight months and things didn't go to plan—then a year in New Zealand being broke as a joke, but falling in love with it to being neck-deep in the ocean, looking back at a tropical island. If I had said this would be my life even six months before arriving in Australia, nobody would have believed it. Shit, I wouldn't have believed it. Who knows where this crazy life of mine will lead in the future?

Like a plum, my freshly shaven head sank under the water once more, cooling from the sun before bobbing back up. It was times like this I wished I still had long hair.

No, that was just a phase. It looked horrendous. No grunge phase ever again.

The early 2000s were my grunge phase, but that was another life ago. This life, though, required me to get out the sea before I turned into a shrivelled raisin. The light breeze kept my wet body cool for long enough to dance across the firepit sand and back to safety under the palms. The hammock was still occupied. Alex lifted herself on to her elbows and smiled wide but said nothing.

"What?" I asked while reaching for a smoke.

"Nothing. Just happy to see you like this. Not stressed, being calm, enjoying. You are happy and no bad Amit demons. I like this."

"Told you, I think this hippy beach life is more me, I've just never known it before."
She shuffled a little more, adjusting her bikini and sat up placing her book to the side.

"I think you have connected with the island. You can feel it is soothing you, like you were with Queenstown."

"No, I'm not connected to it. Yeah, I can feel the atmosphere, calmness, and ambience, but I'm not spiritually connected to it. It's just nice and relaxing. Don't start with that mumbo-jumbo again."

"I never say this. I just say you feel at home, comfortable, and happy."

"You were about to, I know you were."

She poked her tongue out like a lizard before she strolled away towards the sea.

Why aren't her feet burning like mine did?
I dropped back on to the towel, shades back on, giving my eyelids permission to close for the afternoon. The leaves above rustled softly as the breeze felt like a feather brushing over me. The gentle rolls of the waves were only interrupted by light chatter in the distance. I was practically breathing in the serenity. This island was such a contrast to the never-ending bombardment of noise on the mainland—noise I didn't want to go back to.

Droplets of icy cold water landed on my body, causing my eyes to spring open and my body to squirm to the laughter of Alex's voice.

"Wakey, wakey. Time to go." She found it so amusing watching me shudder.

"Oi! No need. Stop it!"

"Wake up then, we go to the viewpoint to watch the sunset soon. We have to climb the steps."

Fuck, why steps? Can't they just put a lift up? This is meant to be a relaxing break, not physical work.

I ignored the inner voices' moans—the viewpoint was meant to be incredible. That morning, we had got talking to the backpackers in the next hut down from ours and they said it was one of the most incredible sights they'd seen so far.

*

Overgrown vegetation on either side of the concrete and sandy steps trapped the heat, making it harder to breathe with each step, and without any breeze, it was energy-sapping. Giant palms and thin lacy vines overlapped, weaving through the thick trees and trunks. It was the perfect spot for snakes to hide—if there were any—and monkeys to play through. There had been a few howls, but no sign of them yet. Sweat dripped from every pore on my body, leaving a trail on the ground. Once more, I felt like I was on fire while Alex floated up. Along with other flip-flop-clad backpackers, nobody was in a rush, everyone was just taking in the tropical scenery. As the ground opened to a bare patch of the forest floor, something that shouldn't have been there appeared.

Why is there a couch in the middle of the forest?

The brown couch under the open bamboo hut looked ominous. If it was a resting point, it wasn't exactly enticing. It was more likely home to all kinds of bugs, insects, and fleas.

Other than bugs, there had been no sign of any larger wildlife, not even any lizards—maybe they were just staying away from the edges and remained in the dense untouched interior. The thick still air started to break. A refreshing cool breeze floated by as the canopy opened up like the sunroof of a car. Gasp after gasp filtered down as other backpackers made it to the top.

The small opening around the top of the hill allowed for an incredible 360-degree view of the island and the surrounding Indian Ocean. It also provided the perfect view of both sides of the island.

It does look like an apple being bitten from either side.

Boats trawled in, carrying new backpackers and supplies on one side of the core, while on the other side, the side we were on earlier, the turquoise calm sea lapped the beach. The hill on the opposite side of the island was on level ground to this one. And behind it in the distance, the sun was in place to make its descent to go and torment another continent. Alex had found a spot on a large limestone slab to lie back on. I noticed most others up here had a beer in their hands.

Where did they get them from? Surely, they didn't carry them up, the beer would be boiling.

It warranted an investigation—she asked another backpacker, who pointed to the Thai man selling them. It didn't take long before we had an ice-cold Chang in our hands too.

Full attention was on the giant ball of fire. A golden glaze spread through the sky until it was on fire. The island below turned into a shimmering silhouette. It didn't matter how many sunsets I had experienced in my travelling life, they never became any less phenomenal. Gasps filled the air as the sun sank behind the island. The golden glaze lighting up the sky became brighter, but darkness had started to roll in from above. A few people were more interested in posing for pictures, not even looking at the sunset.

While a few years ago it was only 'flashpackers' who carried smartphones, they had become an everyday accessory for most backpackers and, in turn, a new craze had exploded—selfies. All of a sudden, backpackers were taking pictures of themselves, posing like they were on a modelling shoot and uploading to social media for others to like and comment. I wasn't quite privy to that world just yet, forking out so much money for a phone didn't make any sense. Alex, however, did possess a smartphone with a good camera. She snapped away, taking pictures of the sun dropping into the sea while I sank back another Chang beer, soaking it in with my eyes.

The lower the sun dropped, the bigger it became, bursting out a fiery vertical beam across the horizon and lighting up the ocean surface. More gasps, more snaps, more poses took place as I laid on the slab, feeling the moment. Another one to add to the collection.

A golden sheen spread through the sky for a few minutes before the sun completely disappeared, the island remained a silhouette in the navy-blue night sky. Our backpacker neighbours we had met earlier were right—it was an incredible sunset and fitting for this island how calmly it went down.

However, it wasn't perfect, the enemy was already out, nipping at my legs, which my hands were already slapping away at. As much as I wanted to lie here all night, the mosquitos were a sign to leave. Other backpackers streamed down the steps in a rush to get back on to the beach or into the square in time for happy-hour cocktails. We were no different.

That was until a crowd gathered towards the bottom. Photos were being taken by excited backpackers, and it was only when I saw what they were looking at that my eyes and mouth sprang wide like I had found a long-lost family member.

"Monkeys!" I joyfully yelled.

For the first time in Thailand, the adult suit was unzipped, and the inner child burst out, jumping around like the monkeys. An ear-to-ear grin was cemented on my face, my brain instantly turned primitive. While others took pictures and walked away, I tried to get closer, wanting to embrace my lost cousins. My feet had already started to shift closer as if I had turned into one myself—all rationale, all sensibility had disappeared. Neither voice inside warned me not to get closer, both were actually encouraging it. One monkey locked eyes with me and all I could hear was a faint cry from Alex telling me to be careful. What did I need to be careful about? I was approaching a family and the monkey looking at me wanted to embrace. Like a giddy child being licked by a puppy, I embraced the monkey as it crawled and climbed on to me.

Holy shit, there's a wild monkey on me.

It used my body as a climbing frame, up my leg, over my back, and perched on my shoulder. Its scent was strong and musky, but its grey fur felt so soft. I felt such an affinity with monkeys—it was even my grandad's nickname for me as a child. My mind was in a spin as Alex tried to get a picture. Others laughed, also taking a few snaps. Alex couldn't get the shot, it wouldn't stay still, looking in the wrong direction, its butt practically in my face. In trying to get it to look the right way, I lifted my hand…

"Fuck mother fucker! Ouch, fuck!"

Pain shot through my hand as I felt a sharp clamp and release. Luckily, it didn't stay clamped as I shoved it off, pulling my throbbing hand away. The onlookers gasped.

"Fuck, shit, it kills. The fucker bit me!"

My reaction was to growl and roar back at the monkey, but it jumped around, screeching back and getting the attention of the other monkeys. I had already backtracked towards the crowd, which was dispersing in fear. Alex grabbed my hand to investigate while I was shaking it around in agony as we got on the move down the rest of the steps. Some who saw the incidents asked if I was OK, one advising me to go to the medical centre.

Can't believe the fucker bit me. What the fuck was the need for violence? I was just trying to be friends with my long-lost cousins. The little fucker!

"It's OK, there is no blood. But we should get it checked out," Alex relieved my fears.

Bite marks were visible on the outside of my palm, but no skin had broken—there was no blood. It was a relief, but we didn't stop moving.

"No, it's fine, just need some ice on it, it didn't break skin. It's OK, I don't have rabies."

"It doesn't matter—we go and get it checked by the doctor."

That was something I didn't want to do, mainly because I didn't have travel insurance and didn't want to, nor could I afford a big bill.

"It's fine, honestly, it doesn't feel too bad."

But if it's swollen or hurt tomorrow, we get it looked at.
Agreed!

It was as if she was more scared than I was from the way she kept examining the hand. Other backpackers who saw it asked again how I was as we headed back down—that was not the encounter I had imaged to have with my primate cousin.

Candles had lit up the little square just like the night before. My hand pulsated like it was about to explode, I needed ice quickly. We jumped into the same bamboo hut as the night before, asking for a beer and a bag of ice. Alex explained what had happened to the Australian backpacker who had served us for most of the previous night, and who also thought it was a good idea to get it checked out. However, I wasn't listening to anybody. I just needed alcohol and ice. As the beer came, I chugged it back, but a giddy feeling ran through me.

"I just got bit by a monkey. That was awesome."

"No, that was stupid, it could have been really bad, Amit."

"But it wasn't. It's all good. I think I want to stay on this island forever."

She shook her head, laughing, but also concerned. That just summed up my life—being provided with something I'd dreamt about, but at the same time, life fucked with me

In the Jungle…

The Indiana Jones theme tune started to get louder, but it wasn't bursting out of any speakers, it was booming internally as the thick, rough rope pressed tightly against my moist palms. The wooden slats underneath my feet didn't feel safe at all, they bounced more than a bouncy castle would, but it didn't deter me. The others used the safety of the sturdy concrete bridge, but where was the adventure in that? There was an unsafe, could-fall-apart-at-any-time rope bridge to cross, and even with my gammy foot and limp, I was going to make it across the death trap.

OK, granted, this rope bridge wasn't thousands of feet in the air attached from one cliff edge to the other with nothing but an abyss below. In truth, it was only about fifty metres away from the murky river flowing below—not a raging river either—and it was attached from one river bank to the other. But that didn't make a difference in my mind. Today, I was Indiana Jones, deep in the Thai jungle. That part was true. One foot tentatively stepped out on to the creaking loose wooden slats, the other hesitated for a second before following.

My friends were already waiting on the other side, Alex bellowed out to hurry up, but her plea was ignored as I tried to concentrate, bouncing in rhythm with the wavy rope bridge, slowly stepping from one wooden slat to the next. Sharp pain pushed through the sole of my injured foot as if somebody had stabbed a spear through it. The pain shot up through my nerves, causing jerk reactions, which didn't help with keeping my balance on this bridge, but my moist palms held tight enough to start feeling rope burn. By now, it should have healed up, enough time had passed, but having the foot trapped inside my trainers in the heat was probably not the best idea.

Fucking thing, had to happen to me, didn't it, yelled an inner voice.

Well, whose fault was that? Royally fucked up this time. Even pissed Alex off, and that's virtually impossible, responded the other

I sucked in thick, humid, sticky air—the jungle on the other side of the bridge was waiting, the giant ball of fire was behind the vegetation somewhere, out of sight but the heat was telling. Pain was not my friend today. Once more, my slashed foot pressed against the wooden slat, not even the comforting sole of my shoe helped the injury—also known as a 'full moon tattoo', which I had acquired in Ko Pha Ngan. It wasn't something I requested, I just acquired it out of pure drunken stupidity. At some point during the famous beach rave, I had lost my flip-flops, and after drinking so many alcoholic bucket cocktails, without a care danced around on the beach where my foot met a sharp shard of broken beer bottle. The wound was so deep, it required stiches. Instead, Doctor Amit decided it was better to let it heal naturally with the aid of sticky stiches. It wasn't working out too well so far.

In the weeks since the injury, I had made sacrifices and missed out on a lot of activities and excursions. While I spent more time in guesthouses doing nothing but dwelling on my stupidity, Alex had enjoyed more adventures, especially in the jungle areas of Thailand. Along the way, we had been joined by two friends of ours from Sydney and started to travel together. The group dynamic had shifted a little, not as bad as travelling in a group in Australia, but compromises had been made. However, they didn't affect me so much as most of the time I was laid up trying to heal my foot. Today was an occasion I was not going to miss out on, but first, I needed to conquer this rope bridge.

Loose slats that needed to be stepped on carefully—so they didn't lift like a trapdoor straight into the river—signalled the halfway point. My hands gripped the rough rope tighter to stop the swaying from side to side up and down—it was a good job I didn't get motion sickness, but I needed painkillers, which were in Alex's daypack. She didn't trust me with them. Each step saw me swearing and wincing. The pain had got so strong, it took away any enjoyment or sense of adventure of crossing the bridge and the Indiana Jones music had faded. It was like a sauna, a sulphur sauna in my shoes, which stung the open wound, causing bolts of pain to shoot up my leg. To make matters worse, the rope burns had started to get worse, making me regret this decision, but it was too late to turn back.

"Hurry up! Come on, Amit," Alex bellowed out once more.

She was not sympathetic to the pain I was in because she had implored for me to get the stiches, which I refused. The slats started to rise and become sturdier, the end of the bridge was in sight, green vegetation growing into the mountains, and the brown rusty dirt ground running along the riverbank came into view. I had made it across without the bridge falling apart, snapping, or throwing me into the river, but the win came with a price. Instantly, my body collapsed on top of a fallen thousand-year-old thick tree trunk, wanting to kick off my shoe but knowing that if I did, it was never going back on. Throbbing was not the word to explain the pain shooting from my foot—it was so painful, my body went limp and

I nearly bit into the thick bark still wrapped around the fallen trunk.

My three friends, the other two coincidently also German but from different regions to Alex, asked if I was OK.

Yeah, I'm fucking tip-top, no pain at all, growled an inner voice.

"No, it hurts. Alex, can I have my painkillers? They're in the bag."

"Can you walk? We need to head along the river from up here then go downhill. Will you be OK? It is your fault you do not listen. You should have just used the normal bridge and not be stupid as always," explained Alex from under her shades as she bounced in her elephant pants and tank top.

I do not need a lecture right now.
"Yeah, I know, I'll be fine, just need a few minutes."

An all-too-familiar eye-roll met the comment, but the agony pulsated through my body. However, it provided a welcome respite and a few minutes to reflect on how a childhood dream had become reality, one I told my mum years ago I would do—which she laughed off at the time but left us all conflicted. Today hadn't just been about trekking deep into a Thai jungle, but also the chance to visit an elephant sanctuary and become Mowgli from *The Jungle Book* while riding an elephant through the jungle.

There was no denying that while riding the elephant, my inner child had burst through the adult suit and I enjoyed every second while peering through the foliage on the lookout for Bagheera, Shere Khan Baloo, and Kaa. It was only once the ride was over that regret had set in. I started to think about whether the sanctuary was ethical or not, it had been advertised to be, but then again, so had the tiger sanctuary. That place left me feeling sick seeing all the drugged-up tigers. The tiger tattoo covering my right calf showed my affinity to the majestic of all animals in my view, but I only had regret about that visit too.

The tiger was my favourite animal, sharing personality traits like being misunderstood, it was a protective animal with a reputation of lashing out. Although many tiger attacks are made out to be unprovoked, that was not true. They only attack if they feel threatened or are provoked too much and then they will rip heads off—a bit like me.

But there was no point dwelling on it, what was done was done and it's all about learning from mistakes. The painkillers had started to kick in, a cigarette rested between my lips and I lit it before detaching from the dead fallen tree trunk. All eyes were instantly on the hunt for things moving around in the dense green foliage and trees above, especially monkeys. Since the biting incident, I hadn't had the same enthusiasm towards them.

Dry rusty dirt kicked up from the ground. My limp had got worse and my injured foot dragged like a broken part hanging off the bottom of a car. Mobility had become an issue, the girls had floated away in front without much concern, however, Alex kept swivelling her head back just to make sure I was still in view. Every movement from either side of the foliage prompted my eyes to turn into sniper scopes, looking through the dense covering of palms and vines, but there was nothing was in sight, jungle animals were the masters of disguise.

The rusty dirt ground disappeared and turned into flattened overgrowth—I was certain the jungle's inhabitants probably had eyes on me. However, away from the buzzes, zips, crickets, and croaks, another sound had started to demand my attention. It was hidden from view, but everybody knew what it was. The girls let their ears lead the way as I trudged behind almost managing a smile. My inner child wanted to burst through the adult suit but was physically incapable at this point.

"Can you hear that, Amit? We go check it out, yes?" beamed Alex

"I'll be right behind you… well, from a distance, go. Go find it."

"OK, we see you there, we might be in it by the time you get there."

That was not a surprise, the three of them disregarded any concerns or fears for anything living in the jungle and were on the hunt. The canopy had closed overhead, but beams of sunlight shot through like lasers; all the foliage reflected different shades of green, but as the girls disappeared, I stopped for a second to take it all in, to feel it all.

I'm alone in a Thai jungle, this is as close to The Jungle Book as I'm ever going to get. Fuck my life, this is incredible, but it hurts so much!

Why does life like to hug and punch me at the same time so much? asked the other inner voice.

Laughter, screams, and giggles broke my thoughts and my ears perked up. For a moment, I had forgotten about the injury and rushed in their direction, pushing loose vines and giant leaves out of the way but came to a stop before hitting my stride. The gushing became louder as I hobbled closer, adrenaline started to pump in anticipation. My inner child was desperate to burst out, but just couldn't.

My friend's beaming smile greeted me as I reached the opening, another fallen trunk—much smaller than the one I had rested on—acted as a bridge, but there was no way I could get across it with my foot. Alex and another friend had come prepared and stripped off into bikinis, sitting on a ledge under the naturally formed waterfall, laughing and screaming out in joy. Their inner children were definitely out to play. A smile grew, just hearing and seeing the water crash to the stream below dispersed the tension, pain, and stress that had started to weigh on my shoulders. I had not felt this light since before the monkey incident. While the three of them played around in the water, it gave me a chance to rest my foot while being calmed by the gushing and crashing of water.

My mind drifted away, their laughter remained in the background, the beams of sunlight pushing through provided some entertainment and, for once, things felt peaceful in Thailand. Apart from the islands, there hadn't been much of it. My thoughts ran back to leaving Ko Phi Phi Don and heading over to Maya Beach—the island beach made famous by the movie, *The Beach*. We spent a couple of nights out there... well, sleeping on a boat anchored on the cove through the night and all day on the beach. Although we had seen just how touristy Thailand was since arriving in Bangkok, being out there was another first-hand experience of over-tourism.

It was a far cry from the movie, where a bunch of backpackers had set up camp on a secret island. In real life, Maya Beach was covered in tourists like ants over a sugar cube. Through the day, there wasn't a grain of sand in sight, tour boats took over the shoreline like a naval invasion. Luckily for us, we were sleeping out under the stars on the boat—well, actually, it rained the two nights we slept out there, which meant we did have the beach to ourselves for a few hours in the morning and ate dinner on the beach in the campsite after the hordes of tourists had left. But, as awesome as it was, while we ate around a campfire on the beach from *The Beach*, my war with mosquitoes raged on.

My thoughts returned to the jungle, luckily, there were no other tourists as most took day tours to the sanctuaries and organised routes through the jungle—we, on the other hand, decided against it and just ventured out.

Imagine if a panther or wild tiger appeared? I'd be fucked with this foot.

Why on Earth would you plant that seed? fumed the other inner voice.

I dunno, just thinking of The Jungle Book.

Luckily, the girls had their fill of fun in the waterfall and broke the idiocy running through my mind.

"You OK?" asked Alex.

"Yeah, well, as much as I can be. Was just thinking of Maya Beach and panthers. That place was covered in tourists, but it's so peaceful up here."

"Ahh, yeah, swimming with the plankton at night was so much fun. I miss the islands. But come on, we go more. Wait, panthers? Why? No, actually, do not say, I do not want to know."

Gingerly rising to my feet, I could feel the swelling, having the foot open in flip-flops felt so much better than being trapped in a hot shoe in this humidity—it felt hotter in there than some hot springs I'd experienced in New Zealand. The four of us headed down the steps, following the stream, knowing it would lead back to the main river. With our eyes peeled once more, we pushed back foliage and thick vegetation. Sounds of the jungle—crickets, hisses, and buzzes—emanated from all around like a surround-sound speaker system. Flying bugs were on the attack, attracted by the sweet drips of never-ending sweat from my body.

We're fucked if this stream doesn't lead to the river.

Why, what could possibly go wrong being stuck in a Thai jungle with the possibility of wild tigers and panthers lurking?

It didn't take too long for the river to start opening up, I didn't realise before, but one of our other friends had a map in her hand, she knew exactly where we were going. We were not venturing blind around the jungle at all.

"If this is us with the map, we are for sure lost in here," sniggered Alex.

"What you on about? We've never got lost, just always discovered," I sniggered back.

"Yes, you believe this if you like." She rolled her eyes.

Her comment was met by a wink and smile as the stream attached back to the wide murky brown river as the rusty dirt road greeted our feet. But there was a little cry from my foot as we stepped back on to dry, hard ground.

"Look over there, shall we take one of these instead of walking?" One of my friends pointed to the river.

Civilisation had appeared, it seemed we hadn't gone as far into the jungle as we first thought. A few locals had built flat bamboo rafts to ferry people downstream. It didn't take long to notice a tour group waiting to head down the river. But we all agreed it would be a good way to travel and it would provide my foot with more relief. The tour group rushed through, making sure they got on to the rafts first—there are some people who feel so entitled. One of the girls wore a long flowing dress and heels as she struggled to get on to the raft. Her poor partner had turned cameraman as she barked orders at him while posing.

If only she gets her heel stuck in the bamboo grooves and falls in, sniggered one of the inner voices.

This had started to become a common theme, especially with social media on the rise. For some reason, travellers had decided that they were models and tried to portray travelling as some glamorous lifestyle.

"You serious? You're in a jungle, everybody looks like crap, feels like crap, and you're going to tell and show people you were actually dressed like that?" I growled.

"But the worst thing is, people will believe it. They think that's what all travelling is like, then when they start, their bubbles are burst. How many people did we see in Sydney thinking one thing but seeing it was another?" replied one of my friends.

She was right, this trend of glamourizing travel life, especially backpacking life, gave a false image. So many people see it, get swept up in the fancy Facebook and Instagram pictures, and think that's what it will be like. Here we were, all sweaty, in grotty clothes, and there she was in an outfit not suitable for getting around the jungle. How was she trekking through in heels and how did that plush white overflowing dress not have a speck of dirt on it?

My attention was finally diverted from the fake Instagram model as a raft pulled up to the side of the muddy bank. The local directing the raft helped us all on to the long bamboo tied together with vines, imploring us to sit. I didn't need to be told twice. He stood to the front, pushing a long bamboo oar like he was a gondola guy in Venice. Although we were level with the river, the raft took our weight, and calmness floated across us all. Bamboo was such an amazing material, it was so durable and strong—they used it for everything in Thailand, from bridges to huts to drinking straws. The jungle felt so peaceful and quiet as we drifted down the river, the giant ball of fire peeked out from behind the trees along the bank, even the throbbing emanating from my outstretched foot couldn't take away the relaxed feeling.

However, one thing did interrupt the ambience and that was the squeals coming from the raft in the distance as the annoying overflowing dress girl continued to bark orders at her poor would-be photographer. Although she was on another raft, I'm pretty certain everybody on those that followed were willing her to stand too close to the edge and fall in the river—I know I was. My ears felt ready to bleed from her voice, even birds flying cross from one side of the bank to the other were squawking for her to shut up. If there were any crocodiles in the water, they were probably being deafened by her too. Alex and the girls happily took snaps of the serene scenery and of each other the further down we drifted, but then we started to pick up speed. The local advised we would be getting off soon as the water was about to become dangerous. It seemed the calm river was about to turn into rapids. That was confirmed as he pushed us towards an open grass clearing, my head shook.

"Even in the jungle there's a tourist trap," I huffed.

Rubber dinghies lined up along the bank, the local had bought us to a white-water rafting start-off point. I wasn't sure if the girls were already aware of it or not. If they were and this was part of their plan, I was a little jealous. There was no way I could do an activity I loved with my injury. The last time I was on rapids was in Queenstown.

"Did you know this was here?" I asked Alex.

"No, but it would be so much fun to do," she beamed back like she did know but did not want to admit it.

"Yeah, fun for you guys, but I'm going to have to be a spectator," I moaned back.

"Aww, poor Amit, has to sit out so much. See, if you had listened to me and had the stitches then you could do by now."

"Yeah, well, you know why I didn't. You guys should do it, though."

"We will see if we can."

The raft pulled right up to the bank—this was the hard part. Somehow, the overflowing dress girl had managed to get off the raft with no problems, however, as I tried, this raft became unstable. The girls were off and on to solid ground, but as I got up, it drifted away. They couldn't help but laugh as I stood on my knees trying to keep balance. The local, who, for some reason, thought it was the middle of winter in his long-sleeved shirt and jeans, tried to push us back. The river was not as calm as it was all the way here, and the raft nearly got swept up in the lightest of swells. I remained on my knees, which had started to dig into the bamboo, but I couldn't get back to my feet either. He got us back, the girls hadn't stopped laughing, all three held oars and sported life jackets and helmets, ready to get into the dinghies already.

"That was bloody quick, you did pre-arrange this."

"No, we don't. Do you want to join?"

"You know I can't, so why ask!" My face dropped, feeling like that kid who gets left out.

"OK, that tuk-tuk driver, he agreed to be our driver when we finish. He will take you to the finish point. We meet you there."

Eventually, I managed to get on to the bank. Looking over Alex's shoulder, a lonely short Thai man stood leaning against an orange tuk-tuk. In the time it had taken me to clamber off the raft, they had managed to sort everything out. It didn't feel right.

"You agree a price with him? You haggled, right?"

"Of course, we sorted but you pay. It's cheap."

There seemed to be something quite dubious about all of this. They knew my thoughts on overpriced tourist trap tours. The three of them were called over to their rafts, while the tuk-tuk driver called me over. Begrudgingly, I dragged my feet and hobbled over towards him.

"Hello. Your friends say you need to have a ride to the finish spot. You pay first then I take you. It's ok, we have fun, on the jungle express."

"The jungle express?"

"Yes, my baby… best vehicle in the jungle." He patted the metal roof rack of his tuk-tuk.

He danced around the tuk-tuk, asking if I wanted to stay here longer, explore the jungle more, or be taken to where my friends will finish their rafting. I opted for the latter, mostly because I didn't trust him, and who gets into a tuk-tuk in the jungle?

Well, if I get kidnapped today, it's Alex's fault and they will know who did it.

Fuck that, I want to go white-water rafting. Fuck the foot, chop it off. This is Thailand, sure it's easy to get a new one somewhere on the black market.

The driver introduced himself, names just never stuck, but I paid him and as the girls set off screaming, I headed down to the finish point with the driver. I didn't even take in the view, I was just thinking how much fun it would have been on the rapids. They were having the adventure while I was here. But a thought did pop up.

"How strong are the rapids?"

"Oh, not too strong. Not very scary at all," he replied.

Well, that was somewhat comforting, but I still would have rather been out there on the river.

"So, does the river turn into a giant waterfall or is it just rocks causing the swells?"

"Waterfall is long away, many kilometres."

The fear of missing out was easing a little. Finally, my eyes decided to take in the view, but there wasn't much of one. We were just driving through a small track with vegetation climbing up either side and hanging above.

"Are there any wild animals out here?"

"Yes, yes, many, but not see many. Deeper in. Monkeys, lizards, snakes. Maybe others too."

"Any wild tigers, panthers, or big cats?"

"Maybe, yes, maybe. You want to go and see? We can go."

Seeing animals in so-called sanctuaries and wildlife parks is one thing, but seeing them in the wild in their own territory is another. However, my eyes were peeled for any monkeys… this was not the day to be bitten by another one.

"Yeah, maybe when my friends get back yeah."

"I can take you all later when your friends finish. The route now goes up into the mountain. I previously was the tour guide. Take people up by foot, sleep in the jungle, but you know too much walking I do not like. Not without opium. This is nice opium in the jungle. But I make the road now with tuk-tuk."

This guy has mentioned opium a lot—and what's he mean he made the road?
"What? How can you drive the tuk-tuk through the jungle? What, like on a main road?"

"No, no. I do many times and my friends, we make a trek for the tuk-tuk because we become lazy to walk all the time. Can be very tough walking. Tuk-tuk easier and more fun for you to sit."

"Yeah, maybe, I'll see what my friends are saying."

It sounded a little weird, but at the same time, riding through the jungle rather than walking did sound more appealing. I just didn't know if I trusted him enough.

"My friend, do you like opium? We can smoke before your friends get back."

"What? No." My eyes instantly shot towards him; this conversation had taken a turn, alarm bells started to sound internally, my guard was coming up and my fist started to ball up in anticipation of any funny business.

He stopped the tuk-tuk, pointing up to some smoke high in the dense mountain, laughing.

"My friends, they are there. You know guide for jungle trek, they smoke now, we go and join them—you like to try opium with me? It's very nice feel."

"No, I don't want to try fucking opium—fuck me, take me to the finish point. That's it."

He started to laugh and explain how when he was a tour guide, he and other guides would meet up to smoke opium in the jungle. He had just gone from asking if we wanted him to drive us through a jungle to admitting he was an opium addict. I don't think we would be going anywhere with him.

Thanks, Alex, for hooking me up with an opium addict who wants to take me deep into the jungle in his tuk-tuk.

"How far to the finish?" I quizzed.

"We are there soon."

Paranoia had started to creep through, my eyes were on the road now—more concerned about his opium confession than what lurked in the jungle as I kept an eye out for any sudden movements from him. However, he was true to his word. It didn't take much longer for us to arrive at another opening in the trees. The river had come back into sight, and abandoned rubber dinghies and oars could be seen on the wet grass of the riverbank. As soon as he stopped, I jumped out, but he pointed up to the mountain again.

"You are sure you don't want to try? We can go now, I know quick way."

"No, fuck off!"

I just really told a local tuk-tuk driver to fuck off in the middle of a Thai jungle, and one he knows very well— not the smartest idea. I started to back away, heading closer to the river bank, but he didn't follow. It was only after he drove off that I looked around and noticed a hammock by the river. My foot cried out for some elevation as I dragged it over to the hammock.

Relief swept through, any time having a hammock to myself was pure pleasure. It didn't take long for it to sink in that I was on a hammock in the middle of the jungle in Thailand with the rushing river right next to me. This, in any other circumstances, was utter bliss. However, the wound and having an opium-addicted tuk-tuk driver lurking around didn't fill me with ease.

The hammock was too relaxing, my guard was dropping, and the river was sweeping away the paranoia. But just as I was fading, screams from the river started to howl through, pushing the sleep away—the girls started to get closer. German accents and familiar laughter filled the air. They had returned, all alive and in one piece, and I hadn't been attacked by an opium-addicted tuk-tuk driver nor any panthers or monkeys.

"Amit, oh my, you missed such a fun time, so good. Not as strong as the one I do in Lake Taupo. You remember I did this in New Zealand."

"Yeah, I remember. Good that you had fun."

"And you, how was the ride?"

"Yeah, so you chose a weird opium-addicted tuk-tuk driver to bring me here. He wanted me to go and smoke opium with him in the jungle."

"Oh, this is why you hide here? He is so weird?"

Before I could reply, one of my friends joined us. It seemed like the opium addict had got her on board with driving through the jungle. The girls thought I was being too paranoid, pointing out he seemed like a lovely guy, and as much as I didn't want to get back in a tuk-tuk with him, I was outvoted. And what other choice did I have... to stay in the jungle alone? No, thanks.

His yellow tuk-tuk wasn't the typical type you get in Thailand, he had two benches running along the back, more like a tuk-tuk pick-up truck. And the roof covering was a much sturdier silver metal roof rack. As we started to pile in, he suggested getting on top of the roof.

"No problem, very strong, you all can sit on top. An experience, ride on a tuk-tuk roof through the jungle. Like Safari."

Before he had even finished the sentence, the girls had climbed up, and even with my foot, I joined. All four of us slipped on to the roof rack, holding on to it before giving him the all clear.

Now this is a different type of experience. Who else can say they rode on the rooftop of a tuk-tuk through the Thai jungle, driven by an opium addict?

Wait is he high now? Is that why he suggested it?

It was too late to dwell on it… he was on the move along the same track he drove through, but then cut into a trampled tyre track through the jungle. It was obviously the one he said he and his friends created.

Let's just hope he isn't taking us to an opium farm or kidnapping us.

The voice was ignored as my arms flew up into the air, dancing as we sat. Music played from one of my friends' portable speakers as screams and laughter filled the jungle—more than likely waking up any sleeping animals we passed along the way. The deeper we headed in, the thicker the vegetation became, and the introduction of a new game of dodging branches and vines started. One person was always on the lookout, calling out when a flailing branch was in sight, thankfully, it was still light and the sun shone through while we had the protection of the canopy above. Who knows where the opium-addicted driver would take us, but at least I was surrounded by good friends who were enjoying life without a single care in the world.

Jurassic Bliss

Anthony Bourdain once described Laos as a country that was "as sleepy as the Mekong River itself". If memory serves right, he called it "a land that time forgot, full of mystique hidden from the evolving world we live in". Bourdain was my travelling hero, hours upon hours were spent watching his documentaries pre-travelling life, and that description was all I needed to know I had to experience it myself one day. Back then, it seemed like another unrealistic pipe dream. But here I was, not just experiencing it but feeling it, breathing it in.

I felt it course through my veins while the soft current of this part of the Mekong River carried my weightless body downstream. My arms and legs reached as far as they could, the waves barely put in any effort, lapping up against millennia-old boulders. Birds sang just as softly high up in the vegetation that enveloped the ancient domineering limestone mountains—it felt like a Jurassic world. My eyes snapped open. I was on the bank, my body wasn't floating down the river, it just felt like it was.

What is this feeling? I love it, can I bottle it up and sip from it every time something pisses me off like Thailand did?

Fuck Thailand, it's over, stop thinking and dwelling on it, live in the now, this is all that matters.

Laos had the complete opposite effect on me to Thailand, both physically and mentally. Laos didn't cater to tourists, it wasn't the backpacker superhighway, it was raw, basic, and nothing but soothing. It was as if it opened its arms up with a hug and provided comfort rather than punching me, having seen the shit-show that Thailand was.

Dry gavel rolled between my fingers and even that felt soothing as my eyes kept on climbing up the limestone mountains on the other side of the wide riverbank. The thick green vegetation covered the perfectly carved limescale, which added to the prehistoric feel of the place. I half expected a dinosaur to roam through or a

Teradactyl to fly over. In fact, if one had, it wouldn't have been a surprise.

It was exactly the environment that was needed—the perfect setting to let my thoughts roam free. It was nice to have space for my brain to breathe. In Thailand, apart from the islands, it was all consumption, on the go all the time, having to be on guard 24/7. Alex kept going on about how we'd had a spiritual connection with Laos. That notion was shot down by me, but there was something, the strongest feeling I'd felt, more than Australia and New Zealand that was for sure.

It was becoming a common theme, although I didn't believe in having a spiritual connection with places, there were stronger feelings, vibes, or some sort of a connection with certain places than others. I didn't understand or grasp why it happened, but it did. Maybe one day I'll have the understanding or the answer to why. Right now, I was just enjoying this feeling of calmness and hearing nature in its rawest form.

Hours had passed by sitting on the bank, letting my thoughts drift down the calm river, and not even the humidity was a bother for once. The only thing that did concern me was the slight tingle on the sole of my right foot—months removed from the night of the injury and it still hadn't fully recovered. As each day passed, there was more regret at not having it stitched up properly. Once it healed, the scar would be a permanent reminder of another mishap and bad decision.

Nothing I can do about it now, let's go explore somewhere.

Pebbles dug into my palms as I finally got to my feet, breathing in the salty river air and letting it reach to the depth of my lungs before exhaling slowly.

A few locals were scattered along the bank, getting on with their lives, not too concerned with this imposter almost floating along the riverbank. One took my attention—an older frail lady, with wrinkled skin drooping off her bones. In recent months, the more we've been around locals, the more I've realised how us 'travellers' go off the beaten track to get a glimpse of local life but never really consider we're strangers intruding on their everyday lives. We are fascinated to understand and see 'local life' because it's the other end of the scale from most people's everyday rigorous boxed-up, all-consuming life.

Like this old lady, here I was just watching her do her laundry. There's nothing special about that, we all do laundry. It's because, by sight, a feather would have been too strong for her, but the way she beat the clothes with a long wooden paddle against the rocks, it seemed she had the strength of a bear. This was normal life for her, but for a Westerner like me who would throw clothes in a machine or hand them in to a laundrette, to see this traditional way was fascinating. It wasn't just the laundry, it was other things, farming, construction, maintenance, everything was done using the elements they had at their disposal and making the most of it.

Her big brown eyes lifted as she squatted on the bank, smiling. Her eyes looked like they were full of experiences and stories. She may be poor compared to

Western wealth, but it seemed like she was rich in life and experience. That's the type of wealth I wanted. I didn't care about money, I wanted to feel the happiness, richness of life and experience. She nodded back, there was such a softness in her deep eyes but then she lifted the paddle in my direction and said something in her local tongue, which I of course couldn't understand. But as was the case through parts of Thailand, language didn't always need to be spoken—body language and actions said it all.

The initial reaction was to decline her offer, but this was something Alex and I were changing about how we travelled. Instead of just saying we experienced rural local life by just watching people, we had started to get involved, to further understand things from their perspectives. Although in Thailand I may have refused and been paranoid she was going to rip me off somehow, this was blissful Laos and I accepted her offer.

My feet dug into the muddy bank, making my way towards her on the rock, she pointed to some clothes, then to the river as if to dunk them in and then to the soap. I followed her instructions as her smile showed off her toothless gums. For some reason, it reminded me of my own grandma. Although I was British Asian, I'd grown up not caring about my own culture, and although my gran had spent most her life in England, I could picture her doing this. Which is maybe why I accepted the offer.

She handed over the paddle, instructing me to beat the clothes. Oh, if only this was Thailand… I would have so much aggression to let out. But as I beat down against the rock, she stopped me, shaking her head. Her actions showed she wanted me to hit down harder, so I did. But instantly, the paddle nearly flew out my hand as the vibration from hitting the rock shot through my arm. She laughed, turning to another local, saying something in their language, no doubt along the lines of '*Look at this tourist, he has no idea*'. I gave it another go but the vibration shot through stronger once more. This time, she took the paddle away.

I stayed a little longer just dunking the clothes for her, neither saying a word to each other but laughing as she expertly hammered down on the rock, she didn't lose grip of the paddle, she was the expert, and I was the clueless novice.

Eventually I got to my feet, my body was soaked but it had been an enriching experience, one I was glad to have, she pushed her fingers together, moving them to her mouth. I knew what this gesture meant—she was asking if I wanted food. This time, I politely declined, not that I didn't want to try her home-cooked food, just I didn't want to intrude more than I already had done. I thanked her before moving along the bank again.

Life in Vang Vieng moved at a snail's pace. To be honest, I loved how life was lived here although it was as basic as it could get—it was underdeveloped and locals like this old lady used the elements around them to aid them through life. It made me think of life, how it's interpreted in different societies, from the Western world's hunger for consumption and greed to developing countries getting by with what nature provides them. In the Western world, we're born into a life where we're told to do this and that, make sure we have achieved this by that age, or you're deemed a failure. Society dictates life, people are sucked into the world of consumption, wanting material possessions to show off their success. Fancy clothes, the newest high-tech gadgets, bigger houses, faster cars, more money—none of that means shit.

There are many people in the world who have nothing, people like this old lady who had probably lived the most simplistic and basic life but had the richness of this natural beauty around her. She more than likely understands life, natural resources, and nature more than most, but will be deemed uneducated because of where she is from. It's truly a humbling experience being around locals like this and puts into perspective so many first world problems I think I have. Although it was brief and no words were exchanged, the experience I just had with her, sharing a part of her life, that will stay with me forever.

My eyes were still fixed on the locals getting on with their lives. This is exactly what I wanted long-term travelling to be for me. Not to just do the touristy things, visit 'must see and do or top 10 this and that'. It was to be around locals and to not just see their perspective but feel it. I wanted to feel a place, take in as much as I could, get a taste and understanding of their reality. I wanted to be on ground level with them, not looking down from an ivory tower and have hired people to be 'authentic'.

My thoughts had drifted as far as I had walked, a small bridge connecting to the other side of the bank, the river at this point had broken into smaller streams and these handmade wooden and bamboo bridges acted as interconnectors. Things were so basic here, even the bridges were not constructed with any engineering precision. They were, however, a testament to locals using whatever resources they had and put together a structure that was strong and sturdy enough to carry people over from A to B. In this case, it was just wooden beams with added support of bamboo nailed together. It looked like a mess, but it wasn't about style, it was pure practicality—it did the job and that's all that mattered.

My feet happily stepped over the loose unvarnished raw wooden slats without any worry at all. I could imagine if this was in Thailand during the first few weeks, I would have moaned and groaned like an entitled brat, but by being in the region for so long, I had complete faith in the bridge holding up. As much as I hated Thailand, it had been a good education of letting go of certain Western pre-conceptions like health and safety for one and the ability to adapt was growing.

Coming off the bridge, my body was submerged in the long uncut wild grass. I moved past the wooden houses on high stilts before reaching the dirt track. Open fields on either side led away from the main area of Vang Vieng. This was a day to just let my feet wander in whatever direction they wanted, explore the local area and get lost. I used a cluster of limestone mountains in the distance to get my bearings—as long as they were in sight, I knew which direction to head in and wouldn't get too lost.

Remember, though, Alex isn't here to stop me. If I see monkeys, I CANNOT go chasing them.

Yup, but I can chase waterfalls if I come across them.

The open fields either side of the gravelled dirt road seemed to sprawl for miles. My reference mountains were stationary from behind while others grew in the distance through the dusty air. A smile was permanently plastered on my face, just as permanently as my clothes stuck to my skin. That weightless feeling carried on from the riverbank, thinking of the old lady as I floated through, taking in the scenery, stopping to watch a hot-air balloon pass by.

We definitely need to do that before we leave here.

A cigarette pressed to my lips while I floated down the gravelled road as a local carrying a bundle of cut bamboo walked past with a smile. She wasn't just carrying the bundle, she rested it perfectly on her head. Who knows how far she was carrying them and where to. Things like this would never happen in the Western world, but here, it was normal life and nothing out of the ordinary. The gravelled road started to come to an end, the mountains were still behind me. There was an urge to go off track into the mountains thick with vegetation, but knowing my luck, I'd get lost deep within the Laos jungle, so I thought better of it.

Remember that's where I came from… when I go back, this is the way.

The mystery of where the bamboo was cut was revealed—a local man in one of the open wooden shacks was slashing them into pieces with his manual machine in a workshop. He too returned a smile before I passed more small open shacks. It was the way in Southeast Asia, all types of local businesses set up—from blacksmiths, stone cutters, and fabric stores to snack sellers—crammed into each other on a dusty road. But this felt more surreal with backdrops of luscious vegetation and limestone mountains surrounding the area.

The heat was becoming unbearable the further along I walked—plastic chairs and tables enticed me to step inside, greeted by a huge wall-mounted fan. It was an open shack café. Instantly, I plonked myself down in front of the fan.

Ahh, that feels better, it's baking out there, I swear I must have lost so much weight just sweating since constantly being in this heat.

Eyes looked in my direction, a few locals scattered around realising I was not one of them, wondering why a traveller was in a local café and not in the main town. It was a look that had become familiar through the region and wasn't concerning any more. There wasn't any hostility, smiles and nods were shared. It was another contrast to Thailand, how people here were so genuine. Even though we didn't speak the same language, dressed differently, unlike Thailand, nobody tried to rip me off at every turn.

With an iced coffee—which had become an addiction—ordered, I lit another cigarette. This had also become another favourite pastime, to sit in local places and just people watch.

Remember in Melbourne, that first day, thinking I ordered a coffee but it was a dessert. That would go down a treat right now.

Shit, yeah… wow, that was so long ago now, I remember not even being able to go for a beer alone back then.

A plastic bag with a straw poking out was placed on the table—coffee in a bag had become an everyday occurrence—and I passed over the paper-like money, which was received with a little nod and smile from the hunched up old man.

Laughter and chatter filled the open space from the four old men sitting at one of the tables. As my cigarette burnt down, my eyes lingered on them. I had no idea what they were talking about, but they seemed very comfortable with each other. I thought they had probably been friends all their lives, grown up locally, and potentially never left this area.

"May I join?" asked a strange voice.

"Yeah, of course," I replied without hesitation, looking back at a local man covered in car grease, wearing a fake Chelsea football jersey.

"You are English? You are a tourist, you like football I see?" he asked inquisitively, having noticed the England football jersey I wore.

"Yeah, but not Chelsea, and not a tourist, I travel long-term."

"Yes, backpacker. We used to have many here. For tubing. Not so many now."

Tubing in Vang Vieng was quite infamous among backpackers in years gone by. I had been told many wild stories—the notorious event, however, was banned a few years back after a number of deaths. Well, one version of it was banned. It used to be a river bar crawl. Backpackers would sit in their rubber-inflated doughnuts, start by caving, then on to the river to drink from the river bars, play drinking games, consuming as much as they could as backpackers do, and make their way down the choppy river waters. From the stories I heard, it could end up being quite dangerous and that was proved by the deaths.

While tubing was still allowed, selling alcohol along the river like that was prohibited. It was now a sober activity. In fact, it was what Alex was doing today. As much as we travelled everywhere together, we had got to a point where we needed our own space once in a while.

"I've been told it was quite crazy when there was drinking involved with the tubing," I replied.

"Yes, very much. You know Laos is still a new country to tourists. After dictatorship finished, the doors opened to the world. But not many tourists. Some in Vientiane, but here so quiet. Until this tubing—and boom—so many foreigners drunk everywhere. Why do you do this?"

His question stumped me a little, unexpected, like I'd instantly become the spokesperson for all backpackers throughout history. I wasn't quite sure how to answer, but taking a sip of the iced coffee, lighting up another smoke and offering him one, I took a minute to think about why certain backpackers act the way they do at times.

"Honestly, it's the freedom, especially for younger and first-time backpackers. We Westerners come from such an intense closed environment, to feel this type of freedom we just go wild."

"But you should travel to see and discover."

"Yeah, that's true, but it doesn't work out like that at times. We lose where we are, have no regard or even respect at times. It's like it's not our country, so we go nuts. And it's worse when there is a place where drinking is encouraged."

"That's not fair on us, we live here, this is our home. You backpackers do not have respect?"

"It's not everybody… you shouldn't generalize it for all backpackers. But it does happen, I was the same when I started to travel four years ago now. I even forgot that I was travelling. I just partied like there was no tomorrow. But most of us, we change the more we travel, we learn, we get more understanding of local life."

With my ice coffee finished, I asked for another and continued to explain.

"There isn't a manual on how to travel, so we learn as we go. It's only once we start to get experienced that we learn different. But not everybody is like that."

"Well, I am glad it got banned here, we lost money from tourist, but do not have to see drunk foreigners and vomit, fighting, sex everywhere now."

He stubbed out his cigarette as his brown bulging eyes looked over towards the counter and he asked for a cold drink in his local language.

"That's the thing as well—money. You can't always blame it on travellers. So many tours, even countries, encourage drinking and partying. They entice us with it. In Australia, all up the east coast, in New Zealand, in Thailand, so many tours entice backpackers with it, boat cruises, island hops, cave dives, jungle treks, you name it. I'm sure it was the same here with tubing. It was advertised and encouraged by the companies and how it impacts local life is not considered."

The longer I had travelled, the more I noticed it and started to recognise the business side of travelling, like the curtain had lifted, or going behind the veil to see another side of it. So much of it was about enticing younger backpackers to get as drunk as they could. It was evident everywhere in Thailand, especially on the islands. The full moon party was once a secret rave, now it was so commercialised. There was a party for every occasion, full moon, half moon, no moon, jungle rave, waterfall rave. Backpackers ended up getting the blame for ruining places, but it's local governments and tour companies that encourage it because of the money it generates. I was seeing it and experiencing it with my own eyes.

He lifted himself from the table, leaving grease marks on the plastic sheet before shifting his hair, which matched the jet-black grease, smiling back and nodding.

"I am happy now, traveller we get now are more respectful and take time to see our wonderful country. We do not have the same money as other country, but we have beauty. I hope you enjoy your time in Vang Vieng. If you need ride anywhere, my garage is just next door. I can take you on tuk-tuk."

With that, we said our goodbyes and he was gone with his glass bottle of Coca-Cola. His views on backpackers and tubing were very clear. It was an unexpected conversation to dive into, I wasn't expecting to explain a backpacker's mentality to a local today, but that was one of the joys of sitting in a local place—never knowing what conversation would strike up. It was random but enjoyable and it's always good to get local perspectives, especially on how they viewed us backpackers. It was fair to say we didn't have the best reputation. It's something we don't really think about, how we treat a place or how locals view us. I'm sure if the lady doing her laundry could speak English, she would have had her own stories about backpackers back when drunken tubing was a thing—after all, she used the river as part of her life.

My plastic bag was empty of coffee, and it was tempting to get another sweet refreshing bag, but it was a slippery slope. It was like having a beer… one or two is ok, but the third, that's the tipping point to drinking all day or night—the same could be said for my addiction to ice coffee, although there are worse thigs to be addicted to.

It hadn't been a wild adventure day like I'm sure Alex was having, but it had been full of local discovery and insight. And, life hadn't fucked with me, in fact, it hadn't since arriving in Laos. Either it was taking a break or the atmosphere here wasn't letting it get through. Before long, the dirt track greeted my feet once more, farmers and workers out on the fields either side were finishing up for the day as I headed back towards my mountains. One of these days, I was going to head out towards them to see what was there. There was so much untouched landscape out here, so much to discover and explore.

Local kids were out playing on the streets, it reminded me of my time growing up, a time before the internet when all the kids on the street would get home from school, desperate to go out to play. Back then, some were out straight away, others were trapped, made to do their homework, pining as they watched the others from their windows. Before starting to travel, being a child was the last time I could remember actually feeling any happiness—it was such an innocent time. It was good to see there was still a place for people playing out on the streets.

*

Alex's lips were attached to a straw, sucking in her favourite watermelon juice, her eyes glued to the book in the wall-less restaurant area of the guesthouse.

"Hey, how was tubing?" I asked while sitting down to join her.

"Ahh, so good, relaxing, amazing views and I met new friends too. We go meet them later on. And you. How was Amit alone day, shaved your head and…?" she beamed back.

"Did some laundry."

"No, you not, the clothes are still in the room."

"Yeah, not ours… I helped a local woman on the river do hers, then just wandered around, explored a little, had a random chat about what tubing was like before, and how backpackers behave in places. You know, normal day."

"Oh, very cool. So, you help this woman, but you cannot bring our clothes downstairs to the laundry? But good to see you have another calm day. But remember last time you were this calm, a monkey bite you." She laughed back, rolling her fingers through her short blond hair.

"No monkeys in sight this time."

"Amit, I have fallen in love with this place. So, so nice. On the tubing, we go out of the town on the river and come back. The scenery is so wow. The mountains so good. We HAVE to explore them."

"I know, right? I went down to the river and just chilled, felt like I was floating down it and I was so tempted to just go off towards the mountains and explore them. We're in no rush, let's just stay here."

"We both have a great day then it looks like. You are very floaty now, yes?"

"Yup. Was such a great day, you know one of them where I've not done much but take in a lot and it feels so fulfilling. So, you hungry? Wanna get some food?"

"Starving, the people we meet later, a Belgian girl and a guy from I can't remember, but he tell me there is a good food in that bar that always plays *Friends*. There in the corner of the bendy street," she nodded back, bouncing to her feet.

I nodded. I could tell she was getting hungry by the way she tried to explain that.

It didn't take long for us to get ready to head back out. The bar she was talking about was just off the main road, along with what must have once been the main backpacker area. Three or four multi-story wall-less bars lined the road full of TVs showing constant reruns of *Friends* and *Family Guy*. I guess they left the bars open in hope backpackers would return one day. We headed up to the top floor, which overlooked the rough grass below, a number of makeshift bridges hammered together for the smaller crossings, the main river, and limestone mountains in the distance. It was the perfect spot for the sunset too. But it was so cloudy, the sun just looked like a red beam pushing through the sky.

As was customary in most places and becoming normal, I took off my shoes at the bottom of the seated mats. Relaxation had no limits here, sprawled out on the padded mat with a cigarette between my lips and a cold beer on the way. Alex mowed through the menu ordering her beer too, but was more interested in the food.

"This place is perfect. Look at this view, it can't get any better."

"Don't say anything more. Just enjoy quietly. Because you know what happens." Her finger instantly pressed against my lips to shush me.

Both of us turned and became lost in the view, the sun slowly started to drop, heading behind the limestone mountains, creating a deep purple sky. It was so surreal, the quiet ambience just added to its mystical feel. Anthony Bourdain was right. Everything he said about Laos had been true from the moment we crossed over the majestic Mekong River. A breeze wafted through just as the sun went out of sight for another day. We both returned to lying on the mats as did a few other backpackers scattered around the huge bar. Our beers sat on the small table glistening, ready to be consumed.

"Alex, I don't wanna leave this place. It's so perfect," I exhaled before taking a sip of my beer.

"No, you say this in the islands too. You want to stay for now, but you will get too bored
because it's too peaceful for you like the same there."

"What you mean too peaceful? It's what I want," I said, sitting up a little.

"Oh, come on, Amit, you know by now. Your brain doesn't allow it. When it feels you're too comfortable, it messes with you. It tells you that you have to mess things up. This is you."

I didn't realise this was a counselling session… who needs a therapist when Alex is around? professed an inner voice, presumably because she was right.

"Go on, explain, Dr Alex," I sniggered.

"Look, it's like this. You want and love to have peace because you never had it in your life. This is what you look for everywhere. But when you get it, when things like this happen, you make it bad because you need conflict, you need drama, or things to mess up. It stimulates you. You want this, but you need crazy." She smiled, taking a well-deserved sip of her beer.

"Well, OK, so in other words, you're saying I'm fucked no matter what I do?"

"Yep. You are a restless soul. Maybe one day you find complete peace and you find a home. A real one, a place you feel at one and belong in. That will be where you want to really settle. Not here, you just like this feeling right now like on the islands in Thailand. We stay here longer but soon you get bored."

She knew me better than anybody else, so who was I to argue her diagnosis. Dammed if I do, dammed if I don't. With that out there, my eyes took to the menu before it got too deep and I changed the subject.

"Did you order any food yet?"

"You are just going to ignore what I say and think about food straight away?"

"No, I heard what you said, no point just going around in circles about it and I'm hungry."

"OK, so we order now, I'm starving too. I get the fish."

"Think I'll get the pizza," I replied while scanning the menu.

"Oh. You do this. You know what happens. You order Western food when you know it will not be like normal. Then you moan that it's not cooked properly. We travel for so long now you know this happens. Look at where we are—you think it will be good?"

"I know, but I'm dying for a pizza. Getting fed up with eating rice and noodles all the time."

"Yes, me too, but it will not be good. This is why I get fish. You know there is more than rice and noodle."

I sighed. She was right again. Every time I'd ordered any Western food outside of major cities, it was under or overcooked or just tasted like crap.

"Alright, fine, no pizza. Just something local. Again."

"Aww, Amit turned into baby Amit now. See your brain is already trying to make conflict. I am right and you know it."

Her comment was met by a smirk and my middle finger before I pulled out another smoke and ordered another beer. There was nothing appealing on the menu to jump at, so it was another night of chicken and fried rice. With my back pressed against the mat, I noticed just how many TVs were spread around—for such a poor country, how were there so many of them and why were they still all switched on? It made me think of what the local had said. If this bar gave any clues, the place must have been heaving with backpackers at some point. I could imagine the carnage they created and left behind. It was bad enough on the islands in Thailand and how we were in Queenstown. It was something I had never considered before.

All thoughts were lost when our food arrived, and we both sat up. Alex's whole sizzling fish with fresh chillies was laid out, while my chicken and fried rice was plonked on the table. Opening it up, she lifted every single bone in one go to show it was perfectly cooked.

"Smells so good. See now Amit wants the fish, not his rice and chicken."

I shook my head, pretending I was happy with my own choice.

Bollocks, that fish looks so much better.

The smell of her fish overpowered the fried rice and chicken, and judging by the look of satisfaction on her face, it tasted as good as it looked. My food… well, it tasted of oily fried chicken and fried rice with too much soy sauce. My eyes shot around to see somebody else had ordered a pizza, it looked good enough.

I made the wrong choice. But if that was the size of the mishap I was facing, then I will take it all day long. I couldn't wait to explore and discover more of this incredible peaceful area.

Land that time forgot, right?

Yup, exactly like Anthony Bourdain said.

A Mekong Kinda Day

It was still pitch black; my eyes were barely open whilst hiding under my hoodie as the wooden boat that resembled an oversized canoe rocked to the motion of the calm water. Alex, on the other hand, was full of beans as usual. It didn't matter how long we travelled for, I still hated that disgusting floaty morning spring in her step. There was just no need for it.

"Oh, come on, Amit, look at all this. We are on the Mekong River with a local and going shopping with her."

Her words prompted a little snarl for getting me out of bed to go shopping. I didn't care where we were, at the end of the day, it was buying fruit and veg on a boat—it was nothing to get excited about.

"If this was Laos then you don't care waking up early, you will be so excited, but because this is Vietnam and you don't like it, you be a big baby," she sniggered.

She had a point… if this was the wonderful, mystical Laos that I missed so much, I would probably be in better spirits, but Vietnam hadn't done it for me. I felt nothing towards it. I don't know what it was, but Alex loved it here and everybody we had met loved Vietnam, I just had no feelings towards it. In fact, I was the only person I knew who didn't like Vietnam—I missed Laos too much.

Finally, my head lifted and my eyes opened, but I could barely make anything out along the river. The banks were hidden from sight, but there were noises, rustling like people were moving around. However, without visuals, I couldn't confirm what the noises were, which put me on edge a little.

What are those noises and how is this old woman even steering without any light?

Forget that, how did Alex manage to get us on a boat with this local?

There were two reasons we'd come to Can Tho from Ho Chi Minh City—firstly, to get to Cambodia, and secondly, for Alex to experience a river market on the

Mekong Delta. I was only interested in leaving Vietnam. What we didn't realise was just how many tour companies advertised an 'authentic river market experience', which instantly put us off. We had learnt—especially with our experience of the world wonder, Ha Long Bay—how anything that had grown popular became a huge disappointing and overpriced tourist trap. Incidentally, that was the last organised tour we had done. It seemed the 'river market experience' had gone the same way. Alex didn't give up though and somehow found a local to take us on a trip—she didn't say, but I'm sure some money must have been exchanged. Alex had met this lady a couple of nights before and befriended her, even though she didn't speak a word of English, so I'm not sure how that worked.

As we floated down the river in the darkness, a cold breeze snapped, biting at my cheeks every time I tried to look up to make out what the noises were. I could just see the local lady standing at the end of our boat as she lifted the giant wooden paddles she used to steer it. She hadn't said a word yet, just smiled in my direction as the boat gently floated down the river. She lifted one paddle out, rotated the other underwater, and alternated between the two. We had just set off, but it looked like tiring work. She lifted both paddles out of the water, letting the boat drift as another boat came into view—his lantern the brightest light on the river. Our boat pressed up against his, which had used tyres on the sides for a soft collision. My hood lifted in curiosity as she spoke for the first time, instantly nattering away with the old man holding the lantern.

Well, at least we know she's not a mute... wonder if that's her husband?

My eyes wandered over his boat as the old man sat surrounded by metal canisters, snacks, and a rice steamer, like a mobile boat vendor. The aromas of strong coffee lifted and wafted under my nose. Alex had already started to order her coffee and steamed banana wrapped in a banana leaf. He looked over to me and I nodded, asking for two strong Vietnamese coffees. He poured the thick piping hot coffees and passed them over while chatting with the old lady on our boat. Once the exchange was over, he pushed us away; the long wooden paddles were back in the water and she continued.

I was in desperate need of the coffee, and once a few burning sips slipped down my throat, my eyes opened a little more as I tried to adjust to the darkness around us. Shadows started to appear on the river, slowly turning into grainy objects like an old fuzzy TV coming into slight focus. The noises, the chatter around us, belonged to other locals. Some were on boats like ours, but most were on bigger boats. Dogs started to bark from them, children moaned about being woken up, older men brushed their teeth from the edge of their boats as if they lived out on the river. Alex confirmed that they did. She had read up on Can Tho before we arrived and confirmed to me families live their lives out on the boats. The more my eyes were able to adjust to the darkness, people and objects became clearer.

These people actually live out here—it's not for show for tourists—that's pretty cool.

Alex looked in my direction, noticing the way I had started to take it all in, while she was enjoying her mushy warm banana. It had become her favourite breakfast in Vietnam.

"See, now you have your coffee, you are glad you came now and not just stay in bed."

"I'd rather still be in bed, I know you've been excited to see this, but we're just going to a market, there's nothing special about it."

Light finally started to lift just slightly. Colour wasn't in full focus, all the shadowy boats on the river looked a dull grey, and people came into focus. There were so many boats, the larger ones anchored down, the smaller ones like ours looking like they were racing each other, all heading in the same direction. But there were no tourists and no signs of tour boats, which was a good sign. Can Tho was where the same mighty Mekong we had crossed from Thailand to Laos—and the one I adored in Laos—split up into a maze of waterways and channels before connecting to the sea. This was the Mekong Delta, and luckily for Alex, there was more than just one river market. The one we were heading to was apparently just for locals and not the tourist one, but that remained to be seen.

An orange glint streaked through the sky, bouncing off the ripples of the river—and for once, it wasn't thick smog, just the golden rays as the sun started to rise. With that, more colour appeared, as did the wide banks of the river, and daylight started fill my cold bones with warmth. The locals on the boats just got on with their morning routines. A few people on larger boats were doing their morning stretches and some sat with their legs dangling off, watching the sunrise while drinking their hot beverage.

"Look at this, Amit, we are seeing the sunrise on the Mekong River. You see the sunset on this river in Laos and now you see the sunrise here too. So cool!"

She was right about that. It was an amazing sight to see, especially as the sun rose and the river and everything on it was covered in the warm orange glow.

My hood had slipped off and my sunglasses took their position over my eyes—the tingle of the warm air against my cold skin felt toasty. With more light came more sight, bright-green rice paddies revealed themselves along the banks and it was like the river came alive. The locals' near-silent morning routines turned into loud chatter from boat to boat and the hustle and bustle on the river had begun. The larger boats appeared not just to house families, but were storage for fruit and veg. Smaller boats transported the goods to where they needed to go, while boats like ours ferried locals in the same direction down river.

"Alex, is this a tour?"

"Yes and no—same, same but different," she replied with a childish grin.

"What do you mean?"

"So, the other day, I am walking around, I see local people with their shopping and I ask people how I can do this without a tour. One person who speak English a little, brings me to this lady. They talk and then she says yes, she takes us and only asks for little money. She is like a water tuk-tuk lady, but also she need to do her shopping."

"Right, that makes sense, I was wondering how you made a deal with someone who doesn't speak English."

She just responded with the biggest, cheesiest smile.

More boats started to pass us. It was rush hour on the Mekong, but still, there were no tour boats. My eyes lifted towards the lady steering our boat, still making the same motions with the long paddles, she let go of one to make a peace sign and smile in my direction, which I reciprocated. The giant ball of fire kept rising to show this part of the Mekong River in all its glory, the rice paddies on the banks went on forever on one side, while little channels broke away on the other.

Noise started to rise from the distance. It was all too familiar—a noise we had become accustomed to throughout Southeast Asia, but didn't expect to hear on the river. It was the sound of traders and shoppers. Alex perked up like a meerkat, her eyes dotting around to see where the noise was coming from, but there was no sight of it yet. I too started to get a little curious. The local steering us must have seen our faces and pointed down river, saying something we couldn't understand while beaming. Being around locals over the previous few months, both Alex and I had learnt to communicate and get by with body language and hand signals. It was a game of over-acted charades, but it worked. Alex turned to her, pointing out one of the boats housing watermelons and pointed down the river. The local understood her and nodded back.

"I think the market is around the corner, we're close to this one. The other lady I meet says this is just for local people, so no tourists here."

She was right, we hadn't seen any other foreigners, tour groups, tourists clicking away at their cameras or posing for selfies. We didn't even know the local lady's name, but she lifted one of the long paddles out of the water, using the other as a gondola oar, and manoeuvred the boat with precision around the corner. Mangroves and long grass started to take over the banks as the noise got louder. Large and small boats covered the whole river, fruit and vegetables were being passed back and forth, some were exchanging fish and rice, while others paid with money. It seemed like chaos, but something we had learnt during our time in the region was that it was organised chaos. To the untrained eye, like ours back during those first few days in Thailand, it was utter mayhem. But, in fact, this was just the way of life—they knew exactly what they were doing and it wasn't overwhelming any more, I was able to process everything that was going on.

Our boat pushed into the melee, scraping past boats being pushed on by others. Alex made sure her bag was safe from the uninvited hands pushing us along. The old lady who had barely made a peep to us replaced her beaming smile with a stern look and came into her own. She started to bellow out what seemed like instructions, pointing towards where she wanted others to push us. Getting close to a boat housing a mountain of pineapples, she went to work. Although I couldn't understand them, in my mind, all I could hear was, *Get your pineapples, lovely fresh pineapples, three for two, get your pineapples!*

For a moment, it took me back to being a child, walking through the Saturday markets in my hometown with my grandparents.

But here, the old lady was getting her haggle on like the pro she was, shaking her hands and head furiously at prices offered, then counter-offered. It was great to see locals haggle and their hand gestures were what I zoned in on to learn and see how they reacted to each other. Once she was happy, she pointed towards me. My neck snapped back in surprise—she was insinuating I help. I obliged. Being ultra-careful to stand, not wanting to rock the boat too much and risk falling into the river, I steadied myself as the trader passed over the pineapples. Once the old lady checked them over and was satisfied, we were pushed away and back into the melee before being pushed towards a potato boat, the old lady once again pointed in my direction, lifting up four fingers as if to say four sacks of potatoes.

Once the potatoes were loaded in the right position so the boat didn't lose its balance, we were pushed off again. I couldn't even see the banks anymore; we were lost in a crowd of boats being pushed one way or another by strange hands while the old lady was chatting away to other locals. Sweat started to leak from my body by just doing a little work, as the giant ball of fire was firmly in its place high up in the late morning sky, beaming down on me. I flung off my hoodie, but I needed some kind of breeze and there wasn't one in the middle of all these boats.

As boats that started to run out of stock shouted out for the transporter boats to replenish their items, it dawned on me—this was a river market, but only fruit and veg were being sold. On land, especially along the streets of Can Tho, there were so many markets selling fish and amphibians, and all the stuff in those stinking wet markets. Surely it would make more sense if fish and other seafood were sold on the boats, and fruit and veg sold on land. But, hey, this was a tradition that went back centuries, who was I to question it? She was ready for her next load, this time, pineapples. Again, she gestured for me, apparently, I had become her helper. But I didn't mind.

"Oh, poor Amit has to do work, you didn't even want to come and now you're helping this old Vietnamese lady. So good of you," teased Alex.

While we were pushed towards another boat, my eyes wandered as I watched all these locals, the back and forth, haggling away. Along with countless others we had the pleasure of meeting over the past few months, it felt good to be with the locals, to experience their traditions and see how they lived day to day. It brought a genuine smile to my face. For the first time in Vietnam, I wasn't surrounded by people trying to rip me off. This was genuinely a pleasant experience.

*

The old lady was done with her shopping, and we were out of the melee. In fact, she had turned into one of the channels rather than going back the way we came. Mangroves were lined up on either side of the bank, the bare roots exposed giving it a haunted feel, like something was lurking in them. But we were the only ones on this stretch of the river, it felt so peaceful. The boat fell silent as it sliced through the calm river, only the birds overhead disturbed the peace. The mayhem of the main river was long gone.

"This is so beautiful and peaceful, so nice feeling. See you are happy you came now, yes?" asked Alex.

"Yeah, you know what, I am. It's been a good experience to be fair. I mean, we did just go shopping for fruit and veg, but it was nice with all the locals."

"Always the same—moody and grumpy when I wake you up early, but when we start doing, you're happy to experience it. Next time we have to wake before the sunrise, no moaning."

"Can't promise that," I shrugged back with a snigger.

My attention went back to the mangroves and the giant bright-green lily pads that started to appear in front of them. I was half expecting something to pounce out of the water towards us or for a snake to reach out from one of the wiry mangroves. But thankfully, my overactive brain's thoughts weren't realised.

Beads of sweat hadn't stopped dripping from my shaved head, sliding into the strands of my overgrown beard as we turned into another channel. The giant ball of fire was beaming down directly and there was no shade to hide from it. The old lady must have noticed and started to say something, pointing to her traditional Vietnamese hat. I hadn't brought my hat, leaving so early in the morning. She reached down, picking up a spare. The last time a local offered us hats was in Hoi An, getting us to pose in them and then demanding money. I wasn't getting stung like that again. Vietnam was similar to Thailand, people looking to either get money out of you or scam travellers everywhere—well, in my experience anyway. However, it seemed this old lady was genuinely concerned about my exposure to the brute force of the sun.

I accepted her offer but was wary of her demanding money at some point—after all, she was practically a tuk-tuk driver. However, once the hat was on, I was relieved to feel some shade and the inner child broke out. It was probably culturally inappropriate, but as soon as the hat was on, I started doing ninja poses. Alex and the old lady burst out laughing, Alex taking pictures as I somehow felt like I had become Raiden from the *Mortal Kombat* video game. Our laughter was all that filled the open space on the river, Alex had also adorned the hat. Although the lady was, in fact, a water taxi driver, we all felt we were on the same level, laughing and joking, we weren't travellers and she wasn't the boat taxi driver, we were just three humans having a laugh together. If only we could properly converse with her, to get her views and understanding on life, what she thought of us travellers, how she viewed the world. Instead, we stuck to laughter, peace signs, and hand gestures. Alex pulled out a few snacks she brought with her, offering some to the lady. Smiling back, she obliged but pointed towards me. It took a minute to understand what she meant.

"You want me to steer?"

She nodded back, beaming once more.

"Yeah, OK, I've never done it before. Can't be that hard, right? You've been doing it all day."

I gingerly stood from my wooden seat, trying not to rock the boat, still conscious of falling into the river. She gave me a quick demonstration of how to row and angle the paddles, pointing to the banks, as I keenly watched.

She stepped away and joined Alex on the seat. The paddles were much heavier than I had anticipated, she had made them look so light. Instantly, I struggled—one would have been manageable, but two was near impossible, so I looked up, hoping for some guidance. She was too busy laughing with Alex at how clueless I was. They were bottom-heavy and so hard to grip, it didn't make sense—how did this old woman make it look so easy? As they dragged under the water, I just couldn't get the hang of it. But today was not the day to give up, and their laughter made me more determined to get it right. Gripping on to them, I pulled one, then the other.

OK, so I can hold them, now I need to find the right angles to steer.

It felt like pushing two heavy logs through the water. The paddles were not very wide and the angle had to be right for there to be drag.

Her arms must be huge, how the fuck does she do this? Come on, can't be shown up by an old lady.

"Amit, what's going on? You are not so good at this," teased Alex.

She was getting way too much enjoyment out of my struggles. Her laughter was almost hysterical. The old lady didn't seem bothered—it was like she was done for the day and it wasn't her problem anymore. One paddle dragged along as I tried to find the right angle for the other, but in doing so, the direction of the boat changed. We were on a collision course with the mangroves. I quickly tried to reverse the way I was rowing, but that made things worse and we were head-on with the bank. The lady did pay attention this time and started screaming instructions, but I couldn't understand a word she was saying. As much as I tried, it was no use. All we could do was brace for impact. My face squirmed, ready to crash and to face a barrage of unrecognisable abuse from the old lady.

The scraping and a heavy thud followed as we went into the mangroves. My eyes instantly started to look for snakes and even crocodiles hiding in them, but it was the Vietnamese anger I should have been more concerned about. The old lady took control of the boat, pulling us out, but we were stuck between the exposed vines. While trying to stop, I had gone in too hard, but she managed to pull us back out. She once more shouted something and pushed the end of the paddle in my direction. She wanted me to take over again like it was my punishment for messing up.

Wow, she's really done for the day.

She handed them over like I was her new apprentice, once more showing me how to do it.

Her scowl turned back to a joyful smile as she sat back down with Alex.

Don't think she likes me anymore. OK, concentrate, don't break her boat, get a get a grip of both, find the angles, one stroke with the left, lift out of the water, one stroke with the right, put left paddle back in but like slicing a knife through butter, then repeat.

Fucking hell, this is hard work. Look, we've got it straight. Keep doing it.

The old lady nodded and clapped in acknowledgement. I was doing it correctly, the boat was slowly moving down the channel, staying in the middle away from the banks.

I was getting the hang of it, getting a rhythm going, that was the secret. It was hard work, but enjoyable. The old lady had made no attempt to take back control, she was enjoying herself with Alex too much. Both were acting like best friends, laughing—mostly about me.

What's all this about? This is cool, but, lady, there is no way I'm taking us all the way back.

My arms were already aching, I wasn't used to doing hard work like this—especially in this heat—and I wasn't getting paid for this. However, my eyes bulged at the sight of the old lady pulling out a small machete from the side.

What the fuck is she doing? She's going to slice us up and throw us in the water! I'm sorry for crashing your boat!

Of course she wasn't, she reached back for a pineapple, sliced off the spiky skin, and went to work carving out a spiral from the fruit. It was something we had seen fruit vendors do before.

She was like a master sculptor, the way she carved away at the juicy sweet fruit. I was in awe of her craftsmanship, but I needed to concentrate on the rowing. She handed the pineapple over to Alex, who didn't hesitate to tuck right in.

Where's mine? I want some.

She went to work on slicing another—her machete skills were precise, but instead of handing it over to me, she tucked into it herself.

"Oh, poor Amit, mmm, it's sooo tasty and sweet. You would like it so much," teased Alex.

I couldn't even flip my middle finger back at her at the risk of losing control of the paddle. Momentarily, I did lose control, though, and the boat veered towards the bank again, but this time, I was able to steer it back towards the middle.

"You are becoming an expert. Maybe you can do this as a job, earn some money—because you are running out again."

I didn't need to be reminded that my funds were running low once again—but I did need to find a way of replenishing them. My idea was to hopefully last until Cambodia and find some under-the-table, cash-in-hand work on a Cambodian beach. In all seriousness, though, I needed a source of income sooner rather than later and a serious look into my options was needed. One option I wouldn't consider was going back to England. That was a no-go and it wasn't even home any more. The funny thing was, when I thought of home, my mind went straight to Sydney. Although it had been years since I left Australia, Sydney was the place I had felt most at home.

Not letting my mind drift too far, my concentration went back to steering the boat. My legs had started to feel heavy from standing for so long, it felt like hours since I had taken control to 'try it out', but if there were any onlookers, they would have assumed I was the local and she was the traveller.

My biggest challenge approached—trying to get the boat around the corner. The old lady offered some advice, acting out how to stick one paddle in but not lift it out of the water and to keep moving the other like I had been, slicing it into the water, rotating it and pulling back out to repeat once more.

How about you take control of your boat and do it yourself before we go straight into the bank?

I did as she had shown me—well, to the best of my ability. I didn't have enough control, my grip loosened, and fighting with the big paddle was useless because the boat started to turn but just not enough.

Ah fuck, here we go.

The mangrove grew closer, but it was the giant lily pad that took the first blow as the boat went crashing in. All I could do was say sorry. The boat once more scraped through the exposed roots, this time, crashing through another giant green lily pad. I just hoped I hadn't angered any wildlife.

This time, the old lady didn't shout, she just laughed and stood up to finally take over. I gestured that I was done. It was her turn to take over. I joined Alex on the seat. The old lady made it seem so easy to reverse the boat out and turn into another channel. She motioned for Alex to have a go. She seriously didn't want to steer her own boat—she must have been tired from rowing all day. Alex didn't hesitate in the slightest and joined her. Just as I had, Alex listened to her instructions, but this time, the old lady stayed and coached her through the first few strokes.

"Why couldn't she do that with me? That's not fair."

"Because she likes me more than you because you don't like Vietnam and I do," she teased, sticking her tongue out at me.

The old lady helped Alex a little while longer, even taking her towards the bank where she started picking long dry strands of bamboo from the bamboo trees, which had replaced the mangroves on this side. I was curious to see why she was collecting them. Once she had enough, she coached Alex a little longer before finally joining me on the bench. She reached back for a pineapple and finally carved one out for me. My eyes intently watched the small machete slice and slash away at the fruit as my mouth was literally salivating at the prospect of it. The fruit all over Southeast Asia was so much tastier and sweeter than any I had tasted before.

The pineapple disappeared into my mouth, devouring it as if I hadn't eaten in months. Alex was taking her time with the paddles, getting her rhythm—that extra coaching seemed to have been working. We were drifting down the channel very slowly, which allowed me to take in more of the scenery, bamboo trees shooting up into the sky. The old lady took the opportunity to pick up the dry pieces of bamboo leaves and started to do some arts and crafts. It didn't take her too long before she had made a little ring and a bracelet out of it. She just whipped it up in minutes and handed it over to me, which was such a sweet gesture. I wasn't one to wear accessories, but I instantly put on the ring and bracelet, which she appreciated with a thumbs up and laughter.

Maybe she does like me?

I showed it off to Alex, who laughed back as she concentrated on keeping the boat straight. Her beaming smile showed she was enjoying steering the boat.

"How's it going? Finding it hard?"

"No, I do not know why you struggle so much, this is fun. I feel like a local person. She likes you, huh?"

"Yeah, looks like I've made a friend."

"See, you would have missed all this experience if you stayed in bed."

"Yeah, glad I came along." I smiled back.

"Alex was right again, like always," she beamed.

The old lady wasn't finished. In the time we were talking, she had created another piece, this was more like an origami masterpiece. She placed a grasshopper made out of the bamboo leaves in front of us. It didn't just resemble one, it looked just like one. I marvelled at her work, so impressed by it, taking pictures of it, which she appreciated once more. She stood up from her seat and finally relieved Alex of her duty, pointing out that the channel was coming to an end. We had been on the water almost all day. As Alex sat back down, we both took in the scenery once more and the rice paddies came back into view when we were on the main river again. Everything we had passed in the darkness we now saw in broad daylight, showing just how many of the stationary larger boats there were, full of families living on them.

What I thought was going to be a boring day going to a market on a boat had turned into quite the fulfilling day, spending time with a local, steering the boat. In fact, although other days had been more 'action packed', this was one of the best I'd had in Vietnam. However, thankfully, our time here was coming to an end and I couldn't wait to hop over the border into Cambodia.

Vagabond

Even in the dead of the night, the air was warm. Moths, mosquitoes, and other bugs danced in the headlights to the music of constant horns papping from the never-ending train of tuk-tuks, taxis, and buses zipping past. For most of the Western tourists, travellers, and backpackers congregating by the side of the dry dusty road, it seemed like it was their first experience of it all as they were frozen, not sure how to cross.

You think this is bad, wait until you see what it's like during the day, sniggered my inner voice.

They waited for an opening, for something that didn't matter, frozen in their ways—for traffic lights to turn red and for the safety of the little green man to start flashing. Alex and I squeezed through the waiting huddle.

"You just have to walk, straight line, don't dither. The traffic will just go around you," I said to a group waiting for the traffic to ease off.

While they were apprehensive to take my advice, we kept walking to show how it was done. One pace, without hesitation, no dithering, through the papping and exhaust fumes choking out black smoke. Tuk-tuks, taxis, mopeds, and even larger vehicles weaved and swerved around us and other locals. Some only a toenail away but there was no panic in reaching the other side of the road. Crossing the road had become more frequent than putting socks on since being in the region. I remembered what we were like in Thailand that first time, when the blond braided backpacker gave us the same advice. It was the travelling circle of life, unexperienced travellers being handed advice, then becoming experienced, in turn, handing out the same advice. We had been doing just that with newbie wide-eyed backpackers through Vietnam and Cambodia, giving them tips and advice to help ease their transition into this wild region.

A pack of ravished tuk-tuk drivers waited on the other side of the wide road like hungry wolves, ready to pounce on fresh-faced travellers. But we were not fresh meat and they recognised that. Having travelled through the region for so long now, we wore the wear and tear of Southeast Asia, we knew how to blend in with the locals. Just like back in Sydney when a newbie arrived on the Kings Cross, all wide-eyed, surprised, in awe, or overexcited by things they hadn't experienced before, or the clothes people wear, their appearance, makeup, clean shaved, it was the same here. Travelling for long wears on you. Even our clothes, no matter how much they were washed, had the smell of Southeast Asia ingrained in them. It was like a deterrent. They much preferred tastier fresh faces, clean, pristine clothes, wide-eyed and, most importantly, naïve travellers to rip off.

Calls of, "I can be your driver for whole day, I take you very cheap," and, "You join the tour, it much cheaper for you," rang around like bait towards the fresh-faced travellers and tourists thinking they were getting an authentic experience. They were an authentic scam.

Poor suckers, if only they knew they were about to get ripped off.

Even roaming stray dogs ignored us now—it didn't matter how many times we washed our clothes, dirt, sweat, and musky aromas were fused into them permanently. This is what happens being a long-term traveller in Southeast Asia.

There he was, just like every day at the bottom of the dark narrow side street. His cart stationary, pressed up against a crumbling dry wall, pouring out tea and coffee. It didn't matter what time of day, this cart was never quiet of locals. It was too far off the normal tourist area in Siem Reap for any tourists to venture down. Most of them stayed in and around Pub Street—the touristy area. But locals and other long-term travellers knew this was the spot for the best coffee in town. The small Cambodian man spotted us and beamed.

"Hello, friends, coffee for you, sir, coffee and banana for you, miss?"

"Yes please, you know us so well already," Alex beamed as we sat at a small plastic table and stool some children would struggle with—very similar to the tables in Melbourne outside the cafés and everywhere in Vietnam.

"You are here very, very early today, not even light yet. Makes me very happy you come every day."

The sun hadn't even woken up yet—it was stupid o'clock, but it was another thing I had become accustomed to.

"That's because you have the best coffee in Siem Reap. We weren't sure if you would be here this early."

"Yes, yes, already here, very busy this time because people going to work."

Locals were up early, ready to start their day, passing through grabbing a drink or food. Some sat for a few minutes talking to other locals, while others rolled up on their mopeds, picked up their banana leaf parcels, and sped off like it was a drive-through. Through Southeast Asia, we had learnt that going off the beaten track didn't necessarily mean disappearing into the wilderness. Sometimes it was just a case of wandering a few blocks away from the touristy centres into local areas. It was like a different place altogether. It was another local we'd got to know who told us about this cart. Not something referred to on TripAdvisor or in a Lonely Planet book. This little side street was a world away from the famous Pub Street, but was only a few blocks away. The small clean-shaven man brought over two cups of piping hot local coffee, which he brewed himself, and placed the banana leaf parcel in front of Alex.

"You do not leave today, no?" he asked.

"No, we're finally heading over to Angkor Wat. See what all the fuss is about. To be honest, I'm templed out, I've seen so many of them now, and they all look the same after a while."

"Yes, I understand but Angkor is very special place for us. Too many tourists now but you will enjoy still.

You go to see the sunrise? It is amazing feeling. Do you take a tour?"

The pungent strong coffee fumes lifted straight into my nostrils while I mixed in the sugar, but I shook my head at his question.

"Nah, no tour. We just take a local tuk-tuk, not like those on the main road though. Do you know anybody who could take us?"

"Yes, they are taking the money from tourists. Wait second."

He already started to step away to serve more people but shouted over to a heavy-set man who had engulfed the stool he sat on. The guy shouted something back, looking in our direction, and nodded. Alex was too busy trying to get into her banana leaf to notice. Steam escaped before a mushy warm banana revealed itself. Since Vietnam, it had become her favourite breakfast and continued to be in Cambodia. The small man floated over once more and pointed back to the heavy-set man.

"My friend, he drive the tuk-tuk. He can take you for local price."

"You sure? We just need him to drop us off. We will make our way around and find our own way back."

"But very expensive there, much walking too, you need ride from each complex and there tourist price only and coming back expensive. My friend, he drive you there, take you to all temple, and bring back for local price only, but not tour guide."

I looked over to Alex and she nodded with a mouthful of mushy banana, agreeing with the coffee man. Although we knew what the local price range was, we still haggled a little more even though he was a local tuk-tuk driver. Once satisfied, we accepted. Haggling in Cambodia was a lot calmer and less stressful than in Vietnam. A love-hate relationship had grown with the region—certain areas I loved and felt connected to, but others I couldn't wait to see the back of.

We had also gone further behind the veil, there was more understanding of how things worked, the way tour companies would rip tourists off, and we saw more of the fake facades put in place to entice tourists. While looking from the outside in, there was a lot dressed up to look appealing and enticing to travellers and tourists, but what was shown was not always the reality. Over time, we had become numb to certain situations, used to the way of life, aware and wary of tourist traps. And through many experiences of being stung, we now saw scams a mile off. In saying that, though, we were far from perfect travellers, there had still been a trail of screw-ups behind us.

Unlike Vietnam, Cambodia had captured me and I'd found an unexpected connection with. It wasn't as strong as the one I'd felt in Laos, but it was there. And learning about its war-torn horrendous history had unexpectedly touched me emotionally. It was quite the education too about the disgusting evil former dictator, Pol Pot, and the genocide that was committed. It was a testament to Cambodians and just how friendly they are, even after going through such a turbulent and violent history. They had every right to be angry at the world turning a blind eye to things going on here, but they weren't.

There's a lesson of humility in that, and it put a lot into perspective. This region as a whole has helped strip away a lot of self-righteousness and arrogance I seemed to have carried when I arrived. All those times I had kicked up a fuss, moaned, and even got angry about simple things like Western food not being cooked properly or transport not being on time (or going missing), Wi-Fi connections being weak, accommodation not being up to standard—I had no right to complain or get angry about any of it. Even my own personal past pre-travelling, it was a walk in the park compared to what they have had to live through. It was very humbling.

"Shall we go? We should get there with plenty of time before the sunrise. We don't want to get stuck behind all the tourists." Alex broke my thoughts as she stood up, stretching.

The early morning warm air blustered through the tuk-tuk, nothing but open flat dried fields surrounded the dusty straight road, leaving the town in our wake. Well, nothing except for the hordes of other tuk-tuks, taxis, and buses all heading to the same destination as us. Angkor Wat wasn't officially one of the seven wonders of the world but was unofficially known as the eighth wonder. Cambodia's most famous crown jewel. The driver, being just that and not a tour guide, remained quiet, but the fat on the back of his head jiggled away, making us both smirk until he pulled up to what looked like a huge open car park with other tuk-tuks, buses, and taxis.

A ticket was required to enter the huge temple complex in the middle of the jungle, but our driver helped to get into the local line rather than pay the tourist prices. Another trick we'd learnt in Southeast Asia was there was almost always a tourist price and a local price.

Before long, we were back on the road for the last leg before he dropped us off at the entrance of the complex.

Darkness masked the most famous main central structure, and walking along the wide gravelled flat bridge felt like walking into history. Southeast Asia was full of temples, and although the architecture was incredible and intricate, after a while, they all looked the same. The novelty had well and truly worn off. However, this felt different. It was almost as if the breeze floating through was actually ghosts whispering stories of its history. Goosebumps started to pop all over the closer the structure became, although it remained hidden in the darkness. Voices and excited accents from all over the world became louder. Most people chose to get as close as possible, but Alex noticed an open spot—one perfect to capture the sunrise, but far enough away from the crowd. We both perched on to the steps along with a handful of others on this small open concrete bricked structure.

"Have you thought more? Before, at the cart, you were deep in thought… was it about your decision?" she asked as she sat a step lower but turned back towards me.

"I've not given it much thought at all to be honest—just thinking about what this place is going to be like… you know, the conspiracy theories."

"OK, well, you know what I think. But it will come to you, the right thing as always. Just do not force it, let it happen naturally and the right decision will come."

"Yeah, I know, I will do, but not today."

Alex untwisted, staring back out at the darkness as light excited voices lifted from the huge gathering crowd in front and the handful behind on the steps. Angkor Wat was one of the most famous ancient temple complexes in the world. It was up there with the pyramids of Egypt, and the Aztec and Mayan temples of Central America. But through ignorance, I had no knowledge of its significance or history other than knowing it was used in movies like *Indiana Jones and the Temple of Doom* and *Tomb Raider: The Last Revelation*. That was the main reason I wanted to visit it—to feel like Indiana Jones.

However, I had learnt it was the largest temple complex in the world, measuring 162 hectares, and was the capital for the Khmer Empire. It was originally built as a Hindu temple, but was later converted into a Buddhist temple. All of this was learnt through research over the past few nights. But more than its place in religion, which I had no interest in, it was its mythology that fascinated me. More so the amount of conspiracy theories surrounding Cambodia's most famous ancient complex.

Most conspiracy theories revolved around aliens, one even suggesting the whole complex was built in one day by a divine entity. I don't know if I believe in that, but from the pictures and videos—and even sitting here not being able to see it yet—there was a mystical feel to it.

A collective gasp replaced all the light chatter in the air. A violet beam shot and grew from the horizon, the tiniest glimmer of light peeked through in the far distance. It wasn't aliens coming to marvel at their own work, but morning was breaking. The violet beam grew bigger before turning into a lavender sheen, lifting like a curtain against the pitch-black sky. The defeated army of darkness started to retreat. Silhouettes of the surrounding jungle trees started to appear first before three large cones from the central structure made their presence known. Its appearance turned the gasps into cheers for the grandest of unveilings. The lavender sheen had taken over the immediate sky, but darkness lingered above in the distance.

The goosebumps started to pop again, covering every inch from my toes to the back of my neck. With daylight getting brighter by the second, the cones started to reveal they were, in fact, intricate carvings. A blazing orange tint replaced the lavender sheen, setting the sky on fire as a bright glowing dome caused sunglasses to drop over eyes as it peeked over the jungle canopy. Like stretching in the morning, rays burst out—the sun had woken up, raising the curtain further, turning the orange tint into a baby-blue sky. Pink brushstrokes laced through the morning sky, it was a natural masterpiece in front of thousands of eyes.

The giant ball of fire slowly kept rising, spreading its light over the surrounding jungle canopy. With every inch it lifted, the temperature turned up. Thousands of bodies were on the field. Most standing behind the moat, surrounding the incomparable main stone building and cheering on like they were at a music concert. The whole central structure came into view, it was even more impressive in real life than the videos and pictures.

Who built it though, primitive man or aliens? Look how detailed and huge it is, no may man made this. Like, did someone just walk into the middle of the jungle one day and be like, 'This is a great spot to build a massive fuck-off complex that will stand the test of time'. No way.

Alex jumped off the steps, bouncing around a little like an excited child wanting to explore. I nodded back but watched as the train of tour groups followed familiar flag-bearing tour leaders in the same direction.

"We should go the other way to the crowd, they all are going the same way," I suggested.

Once most were out of sight around the corner, we headed across the little bridge over the giant luscious green lily pads covering the moat.

Ain't there meant to be crocodiles in there?

My attention was switched straight away to the intricate carvings of deities, gods, and symbols etched into the dark stone walls. The precision was immaculate.

It would take lasers to create this much detail. Look at this, eyes, fingernails, feet... they're so detailed. No way ancient man could make this. Keep an eye out for spaceships and aliens in the carvings.

My inner voice was determined to find something to back up some of the conspiracy theories. It had a point though, how were these structures built without technology for everything to be so symmetrical and intricate? It was hard for most to draw a straight line without the use of a ruler. These were not just light etchings either—every inch was carved deep into the stone. Those alien theories didn't feel so farfetched seeing it up close and personal.

Alex was lost in the carvings too, pointing to one after the other, as was everybody else making their way around this side. There was definitely a mystique and wonder to the whole complex, built in the twelfth century with supposedly primitive tools and still standing today.

Instead of carrying on around the perimeter of the structure, taking the gravelled path through the jungle to the next one seemed a better option to avoid the hordes of tourist groups.

Trees and vegetation hung over, although the structures around the complex had been cleared to make getting from one to the other possible, it was still in the wild jungle, a dense one at that. It was the jungle where my eyes searched high and low, imagining what the French explorer who rediscovered it in the 1840s must have felt. The real Indiana Jones.

Birds in the canopy sang out sweet melodies. Beams of sunrays shot through openings in the luscious green thick vegetation. Even people walking around talked in a whisper almost to not disturb nature or the breathing jungle.

"Incredible, so beautiful and peaceful. Can you feel that... the peace?" Alex bounced on her toes, taking it all in.

"Yeah, I can. It's weird, isn't it? Like so many people here yet it's so calm. It's weird energy."

The jungle opened up to reveal the next structure, she was already floating up the steps into the long stone carved corridor. The stone felt grittier in this one, almost volcanic against my fingertips. Angkor Wat was originally built as a Hindu temple, which explained all the Indian gods. A lot of them were familiar from when I was forced into temples as a child and told to believe in gods with seven arms or three heads or half-monkey half-human, but it didn't wash.

Alex stopped for a moment—a little Hindu ceremony was taking place in front of one of the god statues.

"It's beautiful, isn't it? Shame you don't understand it or you could translate for me."

"Yeah, what a shame... Hey, I can translate, he's praying to a fictitious character because somebody else told him to?" I smirked while studying other carvings.

"Oh, come on, don't be a dickhead, have respect."

We carried on a little further past the ceremony as a monk appeared in the distance. The whole complex was turned into a Buddhist temple towards the end of the twelfth century and has been ever since. The monk was lighting incense sticks to one of the Buddha statues that had been placed in the temple, not carved like the Hindu ones. In seeing us, he asked if we would like to light one for good luck. Alex nodded and lit one and teased that I would need to light ten for some good luck. He told her where to place it but instantly demanded a donation, but Alex shook her head, saying she had no money, and quickly moved away. I couldn't help but laugh, the first person to try and scam us in Cambodia was a monk.

The laughter continued as we admired the detail, the eyes, clothing… it was more than what some artists can do on canvas let alone stone. Whoever carved these stones had some immense talent. Neither of us had stopped snapping away on both the little digital camera and Alex's smartphone.

Jungle noises surrounded the open air. Stepping through the next walkway, squeals could be heard in the distance from what animal was anybody's guess. The next set of stone structures opened up more like ruins, rooves caved in, fallen giant stones and a mini complex of its own. With the sun bearing down, they lit up like huge golden bricks. Sculptures and heads were carved into the tops of the small stone buildings.

"Hey, dickhead, up here," Alex's voice floated down.

"How the fuck you get up there? Wait… when did you get up there?"

"Magic… no, there are steps, come up, it's an amazing view."

It didn't take long for me to join her on top of the collapsed structure—she wasn't wrong. The whole complex could be seen, most of the structures poked out through the jungle canopy. The jungle itself went on as far as the horizon. We both sat there just taking it all in.

This is my life, I explore places like this when I want, sit in bars on beaches, living life to my own schedule. I am the architect of my own travel design.

So, why give it all up to go and be put back in the box I craved to escape from?

My inner voice was persuasive in the argument not to give this life up. Even with that giant ball of fire penetrating through my skin right now, how could I and why would I want to give up this life? This place might be the biggest tourist attraction in Cambodia, but being up here, staring out at the jungle and this ancient stone complex, it still felt like an adventure. Maybe I should stay.

But how long can I keep it up for? There's only so long I can keep doing this. I've been doing this for years now. There's nothing to prove to anyone now. I've proved I can do it and last. There is a point I have to grow up, and this job offer in the Czech Republic keeps me from having to return to England and gives me a career pathway. I need to start thinking about the future.

Oh, shut up. Look at this, no way I wanna give up this life.

"Amit, I thought you said no thinking about it today."

She could always tell when I went deep into my thoughts. I broke free of my inner voices and climbed back down to the ground, ready to explore the next set of structures, which meant another little trek through the jungle. She was right, no need to let it swim around in my head today.

The pathway opened a little, but a crowd had gathered, although there wasn't another structure in sight yet. My eyes bulged open, toes pushed off the ground, just like that, the adult suit was unzipped and the inner child burst out.

"MONKEYS!"

Instinct took over, my brain turned primitive at the sight of them and my legs started to move, but I didn't. The t-shirt nearly melted into my skin as Alex grabbed the back of it, holding me back like a naughty child.

"Dickhead, no… remember Thailand!" scoffed Alex.

Those words were all it took to for the adult to return. That was so long ago now, it had escaped my memory.

She let go of my t-shirt, laughing while stepping in front of me.

"I'm not leaving here to take you to the hospital today."

My eyes hadn't left the monkeys playing around on the edge of the jungle, performing to the crowd taking pictures of them.

"OK, no playing with monkeys, but I do wanna get a bit closer."

We had seen monkeys since the incident, but that inner child always wanted to burst out, forgetting what had happened. I was that child who burnt my hand on a hot stove and didn't learn from it the first time. The crowd gathered around maintained a good distance while cameras snapped away, the monkeys—the same type of macaque I'd been bitten by—were a lot calmer than the ones in Thailand. It was as if they were used to humans.

They're tamer, probably won't bite, get closer to them.

No, don't do it.

A foot left the ground, alarm bells rang, and alerts went off internally. My foot felt grass in the same spot, I didn't move. Finally, I may have learnt my lesson.

However, a Chinese woman was braver... her phone was out, taking selfies from a distance but creeping closer to them. With each step she took, she screamed like she wanted to interrupt the monkeys, but she kept getting closer, looking for the perfect picture. I was one to talk, but she was being stupid. Her screams were upsetting the monkeys, and one of them lunged at her—her scream turned into a high-pitched siren as she launched herself away. The monkey, however, gave chase, she ran in circles jumping away, the monkey must have thought she was playing games. She reached into her oversized handbag, throwing something at the monkey. It stopped but wasn't hurt. It was curious at what she had thrown, and so was everybody watching. An egg! She threw an egg at the monkey.

"What the fuck? She just threw an egg!" My face scrunched up as I looked at Alex.

Alex was as perplexed as anyone, shrugging back. Why would she throw an egg? It was bizarre, why was she carrying around a raw egg? It wasn't hard-boiled. Did she bring that with the intention of egging Angkor Wat or was this a pre-meditated attack to egg the monkey? It made no sense. The monkey, though, was enjoying it, and by the woman's look of fear and embarrassment, it seemed she was the one with egg on her face. I could easily remain in this spot for the rest of the day watching the monkeys, but there was more to explore. Only a few yards away from where the monkeys were, it opened up to a host of tuk-tuks lined up. Unlike in the early morning, none ignored us. We waved off each one despite their cries of a cheap ride. However, just like in Laos, one quick wave of the hand and they fell back. However, one called out louder… he didn't give up, there was a reason—he was our guy.

As we headed towards the next set of temples, elephants were marching towards us like a royal procession. All the tuk-tuks rolled to the side, switched off their engines, and stopped to give way. Some drivers even got out to give them a bow. None of them had any straps on, nor was there anybody leading—it was just the elephants.

Are they wild elephants? Is that why people are showing so much respect? If they're wild, where are they going? Should I bow too?

It was only once they were long gone that the driver started back up. We tried to ask if they were wild, but there was no answer. More from lack of understanding than just ignoring us.

He dropped us off right at the foot of the next set of temples, much deeper in the jungle. It felt denser immediately, but the structure was rubble.

The closer the ruins became, the more my eyes were on alert—not for any big jungle animals, but for the local little kids running around approaching tourists. People were getting sucked in by their innocent puppy-dog eyes, but all through Southeast Asia, we had got wise to their tricks. These little beggars were masters of their trade— many of them were not even homeless. We'd seen it all before.

"Don't make eye contact, just keep walking."

One pounced on us, and as much as we pushed him away, told him to leave while making sure the sneaky kid didn't steal my wallet, Alex caved.

"No, what are you doing?"

"It's OK, I have something for him," she whispered back.

Shaking my head, I moved away. He tried to say he needed money to get to school, he even had a book with him to show her. This kid was on his game, I'll give him that.

Alex, what are you doing, why are you entertaining this? You know better. Oh shit, why are you reaching in your bag for, you were strong with the monk earlier, why are you caving with this kid? OHH.

"This is all you get. If you are homeless, then you will be hungry?" she sniggered

"Why I want fucking apple. Stupid. Give me $50!" Just like that, the kid spoke perfect English.

"No, you get nothing from me."

The kid started swearing at her, trying to reach into her bag, I had to step back but she had already started to scare him off.

"See, why even entertain it?" I asked.

"Wanted to see what he do," she shrugged back, taking a bite of her apple.

It was the same everywhere throughout the region. There were some genuinely homeless people, especially here in Cambodia where many had lost limbs from surviving the evil Khmer Rouge regime. Many, though, were just out to scam foreign tourists. We had been burned a few times by them, and since then, all sympathy was gone. My attention was quickly snapped away by the sight in front of us. It wasn't monkeys or wild elephants, but the ruins were dwarfed and taken over by giant trees with their roots so thick, growing through and over the structure. They were like alien tentacles reaching down, sucking up the temples. These were no thin viny roots or ivy stuck to walls, the roots were thicker than most tree trunks. These roots had crushed some stone buildings like they were giant Lego and reached up into the heavens. It was such a surreal sight to see this clamour of trees taking back their part of the jungle, but it also gave a true sense of just how old these temples were. If we had seen nothing else but these trees and humungous roots, it would have been worth it.

The more we had seen throughout the day, the deeper into the jungle we had gone, it had been mind-blowing. The mystique had kept growing, we could feel the history throughout the complex—it felt inhuman. These trees topped it all off. The sheer size of them reaching high into the heavens. Every tourist tried to climb up it, including us. Just standing at the bottom of the root made me feel like an ant. Not a single person could get on to the root, let alone the trees.

What are these roots hiding under the rubble? I wonder what treasures are buried within these temples… there must be something here, even an alien aircraft buried underneath.

Alex had disappeared into one of the open brick structures, but I was mesmerised by the trees. The alien conspiracies came flooding back, and from what we had seen throughout the day, I was less convinced that this majestic ancient structure was built by man. There was a weird energy around the whole complex, which played into the thought too.

We had been roaming around for nearly eight hours but hadn't even explored all of the complex yet. It was no wonder some people take days to see and explore it.

She popped back out, beaming like she had discovered something.

"Find any buried treasure, Miss Indiana Jones?" I asked.

"No, but so incredible. I love it. We go to the next one?" Her smile widened.

"Yup, who knows what we'll find next."

The longer we had travelled through Southeast Asia, the fewer touristy attractions we had started to visit, due to reality generally not meeting up with expectations and most places being overpriced tourist traps now the more popular they had become. In fact, the last real touristy thing we had done was Ha Long Bay in Vietnam. It was a decent experience, but not mind-blowing, and the number of tourists there made it more difficult to enjoy. However, this was a different story, in avoiding the mass crowds, going at our own pace, exploring it for ourselves, the reality had more than matched expectation.

So much so, apart from a couple of instances, it had kept my mind preoccupied with what to do in the next stage of my life. I was at a crossroads, either to grow up and take the job offer in the Czech Republic or to continue travelling. I was getting older now, and money... well, it was practically gone. A decision was needed to be made soon.

Ghetto Snobbing

It had been like looking in the mirror. Every action, reaction, behaviour, and mood was virtually identical. Step by step, from landing into the chaos to the tension visibly lifting, aided by a tranquil tropical island. Just as I had felt when arriving in Bangkok to feeling the soft sand of Ko Phi Phi Don, Tom and Vicky had felt the same from arriving into the chaos of Bali, Indonesia, to sitting on beanbags on the tropical Island of Gili Air. It was the quietest of the three Gili Islands. These smaller islands lay just off the coast of the bigger island of Lombok, which was largely untouched by tourism, unlike its much more famous neighbour, Bali.

The ironic thing was, Bali was known to be the tranquil island, full of spiritualists, yoga lovers, and peace. In recent years, though, it was the latest Southeast Asian island to feel a surge of tourism, partly due to the famous book and movie, *Eat Pray Love,* and various digital nomads and expats settling there. The influx of travellers and Western expats to the southern part of the island had turned it into a mini Bangkok. The southern popular tourist spots of Legian, Seminyak, and especially Kuta were a barrage of traffic, mopeds, taxis, hawkers, scammers, and had become non-stop chaos.

People escaped the bigger Indonesian islands to relax on Bali, but those who called Bali home, as I did now, headed to the even smaller Gili Islands for an escape. That was exactly what we were doing for Christmas and New Year's Eve. My second Christmas and New Year in Southeast Asia, and this year, Tom and Vicky had come from Australia to join me.

Another two Bintang beers (the cheapest and most popular local beer for backpackers) arrived, along with my costly raspberry mojito. The cheeky boyish smile was back on Tom's face. We hadn't seen each other since the night before I left the land Down Under and headed over to New Zealand, but still kept in touch as travelling friends do. My back rolled into the sandy bean bag under the sun umbrella, while Vicky worked on her tan in the direct heat. Soft reggae music sang out through speakers fitted to the cluster of palm trees belonging to this small beach bar behind us.

"Feel better now? This more like what you expected?" I asked.

The soft waves rolled in and out in front, adding to the calmness of the island, and with the other two islands in eyeshot across the blue ocean.

"Yeah, this place is much better than Bali. This is what I thought Bali was going to be like. That place is crazy, geeza, how do you cope with it?" asked Tom.

Since we last saw each other, ginger fuzz had started to take over his face, which lifted to wait for my response.

"I'm just numb to it, mate. I've spent so much time in Southeast Asia now. Apart from the three months in the

Czech Republic, I've been in Bali six months now and nearly a year Southeast Asia beforehand."

The beanbag started to sink deeper into the soft sand. He shook his head, laughing before trying to lift a little more.

"I can't believe you're still living this travelling life after all these years. How many years has it been now? I wish I could still be doing it with ya. Come a long way from getting drunk in the Kings Cross and head-butting people."

"Yeah, I know, right? The Kings Cross is like another lifetime ago now. It started in 2010 and we're here about to see in 2015. It's gonna be the fifth year. But I wouldn't really consider myself a traveller right now, trying this expat life out."

"It's only temporary for a few months though, save some money and then you'll be flying off like the free bird you are? Dude, you're a full-on nomad... no fixed address, just going where you feel like it, stopping and moving on when you want! Living the dream, geeza. So feared!"

"I still can't believe you live in a three-bedroom villa with a private swimming pool. Beats hostel life, right? So awesome," said Vicky as she pushed herself up on her tanning elbows, smirking from behind her huge sunglasses.

"Yeah, right, been quite the turnaround this past year. Started the year deciding whether to quit the travelling and try adulthood. Against my better judgement, I went to the Czech Republic, started a career, was more broke than usual, hated it. A bit of luck and I end up in Bali as an expat, earning a shit ton of money being a ghetto snob. But, yeah, this ain't permanent, just save some cash and see where the wind takes me."

"Wait, so this will be your fifth Christmas and New Year's away from home? That's crazy, and what the fuck is ghetto snobbing?" He burst out laughing while finishing off a beer and calling for another.

More drinks arrived, the young waiter handed over their beers and my expensive mojito. Beers were dirt cheap, but spirits could turn out to be quite costly—but money wasn't an issue for once in my life, I had struck gold—well kinda.

"A ghetto snob is what I am. Somebody who never had any money, now rolling in it, living like a king, experiencing the high life. From the streets to having a shitload of money—a ghetto snob."

"That's why he can afford to drink raspberry mojitos, not cheap beer like us. You've changed," laughed Vicky.

"We all change, not the same guy I was in Australia anymore. I've grown and become sophisticated… nah, I've just drunk too much Bintang and I can't stomach it any more. Seriously, though, I know it's temporary. So,

I'm making the most of it before I go back to being a broke ass backpacker living the basic life."

We both cracked up—so much so that Tom rolled off his bean bag and on to the sand.

"You're still feared, bro."

"Have you not stopped saying that fucking word yet?"

He remained on the sand for a little while, shaking his head. It felt good to be back in their company. It was always good meeting up with old friends from Sydney, but I had spent so much time in Sydney with these two, it was like being around family again. Tom crawled back on to his bright-yellow bean bag, chugging back his beer before calling for another. It was going down like water.

"We're spending Christmas on a tropical island. I still remember your last New Year's in Sydney. You were such a mess, causing havoc all over Bondi and even on the beach for sunrise. So feared!" sniggered Tom.

"What did you expect? I had to leave when I wasn't ready to. I was trying to build a life and it got snatched away at the last minute. I was so fucked up at that point. But, honestly, it was a blessing in disguise. I've been able to experience so much over the past few years since leaving."

"And you're a ghetto snob," Vicky chimed in.

"Yeah, exactly. The thought has popped up a few times. If I had got sponsored, I wouldn't have had any of the experiences I've had over the past few years. I'd not be an expat, getting a taste of the high life. Sometimes you just gotta ride the wave and wait for the bigger picture to unravel."

Vicky turned back as I started to adjust the bean bag, getting right under the shade.

"Some things never change, though, still hiding under the shade," sniggered Tom once more.

"You damn right, this is the fucking equator—or as close as you can get to it. There have been days I've had to push my cigarette through the crack of the door to smoke. Like it can get stupid hot here."

"Feared, bro. But what about tomorrow though?"

"Yeah, are you going to actually do it tomorrow with us? That guy we met earlier said he would take us out on his boat in the morning," said Vicky.

"Yeah, of course. Oh yeah, you still remember Amit being scared to get in the sea. That's another thing that's changed, I'm starting to embrace and get to know the sea."

It was time for another mojito—the heat was helping them go down quickly as I nodded back.

"Bullshit. Don't fucking believe you one bit. You'll say yeah now, then tomorrow find excuses to back out like in the Great Barrier Reef," laughed Tom.

Both of them sprang up as I stood up from the moulded bean bag, placing my sunglasses down and stepped into the direct heat from the giant ball of fire in the sky.

"I need to take a picture of this… nobody will believe it if I don't have proof," yelped Tom.

The cool water was a welcome relief to my burning body, instantly cooling it down as the soft lapping waves wrapped around my ankles, then knees and waist. It cooled my organs as I finally stopped neck-deep. The two of them looked out in shock, but it was the palm trees behind them and the beach bar where my eyes rested. The palms waved from side to side like arms at a concert.

How good is it to have these two around and say what we want without risking upsetting the sensitive souls I live and work with?

There had been a generational shift while being in Bali. For the first time, I felt like and was the older guy. It was weird and, apparently, the younger generation have become quite sensitive. Words had to be chosen much more carefully at the risk of upsetting them. Everything seemed to be more politically correct. That old saying of sticks and stones had flipped on its head and words were now just as harmful. The new generation were a fragile bunch, but it was the way of the world and it was something new to adapt to.

The other two had got over their shock and were looking through the menu. They had started their journey for residency in Australia. My mind flicked to nine months ago when I made a last-minute decision to become an adult and tried to live a normal life. I took the job offer in the Czech Republic and it was the worst decision I'd made. Alex had returned to Germany and slipped back into her previous pre-travelling normal life, while I struggled adapting to being put back into a box. It was a waste of three months, dying a slow death, living a robotic life of work, eat, sleep, and repeat.

But luck came knocking in the form of an old friend I'd met in New Zealand. She had landed a job in Bali and offered me one too—it was a no-brainer… more money, no tax, American dollars, and a return to this region. It was like waking from the dead—and happiness returned to my empty body. In the space of three months, I had gone from living my version of hell to life being as perfect as it could possibly get, living like a king, spending how I want, and still able to save money for wherever this crazy journey of mine takes me.

Feeling my skin start to shrivel up, it was time to get back to the other two. They too had started on the cocktails.

"I can't believe what I saw, and not just a little dip, you stayed in there. Who are you? Where's Amit? That guy has no money and never gets in the sea," said Tom, lifting his gaze.

"I told you, I'm embracing the sea nowadays. It's all about opening the mind and not letting fear control it. I control the fear—mind over matter. It's all part of my development and evolution. Change is good, experience provides understanding."

The sun didn't take long to air-dry my skin before I dropped down to the bean bag and lit up a smoke.

"Now you're Buddha, spouting out wisdom too—feared. Seriously, who are you?"

"All part of the new me. Older and wiser. I'm hungry, you guys wanna get some food? I know a place that does an amazing seafood barbeque platter."

"Yup, let's do it." Tom sprang off his bean bag before his words were out.

"It's a bit pricey, but well worth it."

"Ghetto snob Amit taking us to fancy restaurants on the island. Old Amit would have just wanted chips." Vicky dragged herself up, wiping grains of sand off her body like it was glued on.

As the bill was settled, we weaved through the palm trees on this tip of the island and back on to the main stretch. It was a very small island—one that could be walked around, but most people rented bicycles to get around, which was the plan for the rest of our time here— along with skipping over to the more party-orientated island of Gili Trawangan in the evening.

There was no escaping the sand though, the rim of the island was sand and the interior was tropical vegetation. We headed down the main stretch, between the inland vegetation and the restaurants and bars lined up against the beachfront, until we found the seafood platter restaurant.

It wasn't a place backpackers would usually eat in. This was a little more upmarket, and while most of the people seated were dressed nicely in pristine white cotton and linen shirts, we rolled in looking the way we did. Tom in his vest top, looking like a typical Brit abroad with red-raw arms, Vicky in her denim shorts and rolled-up t-shirt, and me in an oversized airy American football jersey and swimming shorts. I loved doing that, rolling up to upmarket places dressed the way I was, but knowing I had the money to get into these types of places now.

A waiter arrived looking us up and down, but instantly, I asked for a beachfront table with an unobstructed view of the sunset. I knew those tables were placed specifically for certain types of people. He stuttered a little to ask if I was sure, but I nodded, handing him a healthy tip. As soon as he received the tip, his demeanour changed. With a smile, he proudly led us through the indoor marquee and past the normal tables and chairs to a fancy larger table with no obstruction. In turn, he quickly beckoned another waiter over, who arrived promptly in a crisp, ironed, white linen shirt with black trousers, and a notepad in hand. This table came with a personal waiter—no need to hang about for someone to become free, we had priority service. He took our drink orders and sped away as I leant back on the cushioned chair, smiling.

"See, ghetto snobbing."

The other two were gobsmacked, even Tom was lost for words. Slowly, he leant forwards, taking in the view, the cove curving beside us on this private beach. The sun turning a fiery red, ready to settle for the night.

"Geeza, this is the fucking life. When you start travelling again, you're gonna be a luxury traveller now? No more backpacking?"

"Nah, I'm living it large here while I'm working, but it will be back to tight budgets and living off the basics." A cigarette was pursed between my dry lips as I shook my head from side to side.

"How long do you think it will last for?"

"Not sure, bro. I'm throwing money around here, but already thinking of going to Hawaii or back to Queenstown for my birthday in a couple of months."

"That's crazy. Why back to New Zealand though? Still can't do Australia yet?"

"Nope, not yet, still another year on that. And New Zealand for two reasons—one is spite. And the other... I still have friends there who I wanna see."

"Spite? What do you mean? "

"The Lakeside Hotel, it wouldn't even let us backpackers in for a drink in the bar... well, I wanna go there, slap my card down, and ask to stay there—stick my fingers up at them for judging me."

"Amit with money is an asshole," sniggered Vicky.

"Nah, not really, just proving a point. You get dicked on without having money, but as soon as you do, people treat you differently. Look at this place, that waiter thought we were off the street, then give him a tip like I did and he's practically kissing our feet. So, while I can, I'm gonna enjoy it. I know it's not gonna last."

The waiter was back with our drinks, placing them carefully in front of us, and handed us the food menus, but instantly, I asked for the sharing seafood platter. Tom and Vicky had both wanted to try it and were happy with the choice. In fact, Vicky had left her seat to get a little closer to the sea and was taking snaps of the sun lowering inch by inch while spreading the golden glow further.

Since living in Bali, sunsets on the beach had become an everyday occurrence. As soon as we finished work, it was out to one of the resort beach bars in Jimbaran, which was very close to the airport. With drinks and food flowing, watching the non-stop train of planes landing and taking off, locals playing on the beach while the sun created a golden glow not only over the ocean but also the beach too. No matter how many times I saw it, it never got old, nor did it tonight.

A camping table was set up next to ours by one of the workers as a huge silver tray came out, along with the fries Vicky asked for on the side. Tom's eyes widened as the lid was lifted to reveal all kinds of sea creatures. Garlic muscles, soy oysters, giant crabs, chilli squid, whole barbequed lemon and herb fish, and garlic king prawns and lobsters were revealed.

"Tonight, we feast as kings and queen," I joked at the sheer amount of food laid out for us.

"Well, this makes a huge change from eating stew on the beach together. Remember the castaway trip—you two were so disappointed. And you, Amit, always with the mood swings," Vicky remembered.

"Yeah, at the time, I thought somebody was running around with my identity—fucking tax office... and that fucking pilot. I genuinely thought I was going to die during that plane ride over." I laughed.

All those memories of the east coast came flooding back while we gorged on the perfectly cooked food. Nothing was overcooked and it all melted in my mouth. I could see on their faces they were in seafood heaven. Tom picked up the crab and the nutcracker, not having a clue how to deshell it. To be honest, nor did I. Normally, I was with people who knew how. I left it to him to make a fool out of himself while more memories of Australia were re-lived.

* * *

The little, long wooden fishing boat rocked from side to side as Locks, the local we had got to know over the past few days, stopped the motor. He stood at the front, both bare feet on either side of the boat and thick locks flowing behind like a cape. His name wasn't actually Locks, we just called him that because of his thick dreadlocks. The three of us sat in the middle under a makeshift wooden roof.

"This is a great spot—we will see lots of them here. Away from the tourist boats. Out here nobody comes," announced Locks while studying the ocean.

We couldn't even see land anymore, none of the three Gili Islands, the larger island of Lombok, or Bali. We were just floating somewhere in the Bali sea with just a few gulls flying around and the giant ball of fire blazing down as it did every day. From the day Tom and Vicky had arrived, this was the number-one activity they wanted to do—so did I up until about an hour before I was sitting on the wooden slats of this boat. Since Thailand, I had been pushing myself and learning to stop fearing the ocean. I'd been in the sea more than I ever had in Australia or New Zealand. But that was getting in neck-deep, with the safety of the ocean bed at my feet and the shoreline in sight. This was like the Great Barrier Reef all over again. Out in the middle of the ocean and the seabed wasn't there as an immediate safety net.

Tom and Vicky had already wet their gear and put their flippers on, ready and eager. Tom laughed his head off at my expense, remembering how I struggled and was nearly dragged under the boat in the Great Barrier Reef. As I reached for my gear, fighting through the thoughts, one of my inner voices popped up. Fear and anxiety started to build.

Nah, fuck this, I don't wanna do it. Just say the seafood last night was dodgy and you can't do it.

No, fuck off, we're doing this. We have been doing great, this is just the next step. Think about how incredible it's going to be seeing them.

Both started going back and forth as my feet pushed into the flippers and I grabbed and wet my snorkelling gear. We were not just snorkelling in the shallow waters or on the surface… we were going under.

The wall of fear needed to be bulldozed down, it was not going to win today. Southeast Asia had all been about facing, embracing, and dealing with demons, fears, and insecurities. If that didn't work, it resorted to sticking a middle finger up and just doing it without overthinking. This latest one wasn't going to be any different.

"You're actually going to do it? You know you've already made me lose a bet." Tom smirked, looking back.

"Yup, he bet me you would already chicken out, make some excuse this morning, and even on the boat." Vicky nodded with glee.

"Drinks are on you later then? I ain't gonna lie, I did think about it, but I'm gonna do it. Not going to miss out on this. It's happening, let's get in there." I shrugged back as the little boat rocked a little.

The wall was getting knocked down until there was just a little fear left. It was good to have a little fear, it kept my alert levels high enough not to make mistakes. It was something that I'd learnt in Bali. There was a time I let go of all fear, and as a consequence, over-confidence took over and I took my eye off the ball. But that lesson had been learned. Not to have so much fear that it takes over, but not to get rid of it completely. The sea lapped around the boat—we were the only ones out here. It helps when you get to know locals. Locks had all his gear on, as did we all, and he jumped in first.

Don't do it, just sit back in the boat, say you got a stomach ache or something—the flipper was still the in the air. *Fuck this!*

Don't listen, don't overthink it, just do it. No thinking. Just do it—jump!

To Tom and Vicky's surprise, I followed them in. Coldness took over as if breaking through ice, my whole body submerged before I bobbed back up. My lips were welded to the snorkel mouthpiece, remembering to breathe in through my nose and out through my mouth. It took a few seconds to get my breathing to calm down and let my body temperature regulate to the water.

Locks had already started swimming around, diving under, and erupting out of the water like a shark. The three of us waded around waiting for Locks to re-emerge from under the surface once more.

That's it, control the breathing… the water isn't cold, it's warm, you are one with the sea, same temperature, and relaxed like the fishes down there. In through the nose, out through the mouth. That's it.

It was working, I could feel the heart slowing down—there wasn't any panic. Locks had appeared once more.

"Down here, spotted one but it's gone, but there will be more."

The surface had become the ceiling as we entered another world, a new dimension. The others had already started to swim away. Sea life approached—the smallest fishes curious to know what this brown object in their world was, it felt like a repeat of the Great Barrier Reef all those years ago, but today, there was no getting scared. It didn't take long to catch up to them, feeling like a fish for the first time in my life while swimming among them. The sun shone through, creating vivid and bright colours from the corals and multi-coloured fishes. Unlike the Great Barrier Reef, there were no sudden flinches or panic at every slight touch. It was a proud moment, a sense of accomplishment. I faced, embraced, and defeated another mental barrier and fear.

Just like with my second skydive in New Zealand, where I'd been told that because my adrenaline wasn't as high, more was being processed, it was the same here. The colours seemed much more vibrant—blue, red, orange corals and multi-coloured fishes stood out the deeper we sank. It was like watching in Ultra HD 4K high resolution. It was beautiful and so relaxing. More fishes approached calmly, none were panicked, some were a little more inquisitive while others carried on with their day like they were too busy to nose around. A soft undercurrent started to separate us, but all were in eyeshot. It didn't take much effort to float through, and the underwater calmness had slowed everything inside me down to nearly to a complete stop. While in the Great Barrier Reef, it felt like my heart would explode, but it couldn't be heard here.

Locks started swimming deeper, having lived most of his life around water, and mentioned how he preferred the sea to land. I had met quite a few people like that in Southeast Asia, even people who lived on the water. All attention was diverted though, water ran through my fingers a little quicker as a huge shadow appeared from above, and for once, it wasn't my dark cloud.

Keep breathing, nice and relaxed, slowly, this is why we're down here. It's fucking huge.

Locks appeared from beside me, smiling wide and showing the OK sign, which was reciprocated. The shadow grew larger like an alien mothership flying over. My heart started to thump, not in fear but because my adrenaline had kick-started.

Huge flipper-like arms and legs belonging to a soft yellowish spotty underbelly carrying a hard dome shell swam effortlessly overhead. My heart pumped faster, my eyes widened while trying to remain calm, my lips wanted to smile but remained welded to the snorkel. It was majestic and agile, switching from left to right, dropping down. Locks encouraged us to get closer and I duly obliged. Either it had no idea or didn't care if I was behind it, but it was nearly as big as me. The giant sea turtle glided majestically and effortlessly through the calm blue waters. It was like a cartoon—the colours were so bright and bold. This was its domain, and it swam around with the same swag I had on land from being a ghetto snob.

Locks swam closer, right up against it like they were friends—maybe they were. He encouraged me to do the same. Again, I didn't refuse, it was fast though, requiring some effort, but the hard granite rock-like shell came into contact with me. My mind started up the theme tune to one of my favourite cartoons and movies as a child.

Teenage Mutant Ninja Turtles, heroes in a half shell—turtle power!

It ran on a loop as the rock-like shell felt impenetrable. Here I was, a guy who, up to this point, was shit scared of being out in the sea, touching and swimming up alongside a giant sea turtle. Even when its pointy head looked back to mine, it wasn't bothered, I just wanted to smile.

Tom and Vicky soon swam up, both giving a thumbs up. Here we were, swimming with a local, not just seeing one but swimming alongside a giant sea turtle. My attention was diverted as another torpedoed through like a shooting star. It was a lot smaller, but there were more. In the excitement, my hand left the turtle's back, breathing in through my mouth and not nose, water entered the snorkel tube and into my mouth. I panicked, tasting the salty water and swallowing a little. But instantly, like the torpedo turtle, I shot up to the surface. The calm surface of the ocean erupted, and I spat out the snorkel while having a coughing fit. All composure was lost, breathing became hard to control and out of sync. My head was spinning.

Fear and anxiety pounced to take advantage as my eyes shot around, looking for the boat.

Where the fuck is it? There's just ocean, what the fuck? Get me out of here. I don't like it. I'm done.

Will you shut the fuck up and just breathe? I'm not done, I'm going back in. Slow the breathing down. Fuck off, fear, you're not winning. Deep fucking breath, out slow. Deep in, out slow. That's it and stop thinking.

Tom and Vicky popped up soon behind Locks, asking what was wrong. I explained water got in and I panicked, but that I was OK to go back in.

"Back in? You serious? Yeah, buddy! Dude, you have changed. You would have just quit before like you did in the Great Barrier Reef."

Tom was making a big deal out of it because it was a big deal—I'd had a genuine fear of the ocean, which I'd spent the past year and a half conquering. The fact I was willing to go back down after panicking like that only rubber-stamped it. With the snorkel clear of water and my lips welded around the mouthpiece, I was back into the vivid colours. Another level of calmness spread through me, like that little panic attack was needed to fully calm all nerves.

We followed Locks further down, swimming in his slipstream with not a single thought and my peripheral vision felt wider. Taking in more, processing more detail down to the bright scales on little fishes, but on the lookout for more turtles.

I started to play around with the fishes, the blue-and-yellow ones, the black-and-white polka-dot ones—all of them—even manoeuvring around, my body had just completely relaxed and there wasn't a stiff muscle. Another large rock-like shell came floating through from beneath. This time, I didn't need Locks' encouragement. I was down next to it, my hand sliding over the rock shell, even making eye contact with it, thankfully, it didn't try and bite though. Time had stopped down here, swimming around with the fishes and the incredible sea turtles, I was so lost in them that if a shark turned up, I probably wouldn't notice. OK, that's a lie… of course I would notice. Tom did appear though and pointed to the surface. I followed behind as all four of us floated back up. I'd spent most of my travelling life refusing to get in the water, and now I felt disappointed that we had to get out. As we popped our heads up and spat out our snorkels, the blue fishing boat was still out of sight.

"That was fucking amazing, I just swam with sea turtles and touched them. By the way, was anybody else singing the *Ninja Turtles* tune in their heads?" I gleefully asked.

Both of them agreed it was an amazing experience.

"I've seen them all my life but never got bored. Such amazing creatures. And so peaceful down there," Locks chimed in.

Vicky couldn't stop giggling, no doubt because of what she had just experienced.

"We can add sea turtles to the list. Fed dolphins, seen them in the sea, watched a humpback whale dive out of the water in front of us, seen one decomposing, seen sharks swim around, tried to take a tooth out of a dead one, stingrays, jellyfish, and now sea turtles."

"I've seen sea snakes too," I added to the list.

"Yeah, nobody likes a show-off."

Laughter erupted between us, but his list was what we had all seen and experienced up the east coast of Australia, and the three of us were lucky enough to experience giant sea turtles together. I was looking forward to spending Christmas and New Year's Eve with them.

The boat started to come into view. This was the end of the sea adventure for the day, but I was certain it wouldn't be the last.

Once back on the boat and out of the gear, we all sat on the deck, in no rush to get back but just staring out at the ocean. There really was another world down there… one I was beginning to want to explore as much as land.

"Next time I come to Bali, we have to try and get out to Komodo Island," implored Tom.

"Hundred percent, we will do a little island hop and chase Komodo dragons," I confirmed.

My eyes drifted back to the ocean as we returned to the island, feeling an inner warmth rush through with a sense of accomplishment. Who would have thought a few years ago I would have dared to go under the water swimming with giant sea turtles? Not me, that's for sure, but it just showed how I was changing as a person, willing to push my own boundaries, conquer fears, and gain confidence in going down there of my own accord. Now I needed a mojito.

Backpacker to Nomad

"Geeza, come back to reality." Tom laughed.

"Fuck, I drifted away with the waves there," I replied, stretching out on the padded luxury lounger.

"Another raspberry mojito, Amit?" asked the sandy-haired barman.

Tom ordered another beer. This was his second visit to Bali—six months after his first visit, this time he came alone. We had done nothing since returning from Ubud the day before where we had turned into monkey boys in the monkey forest, and not one of them bit me while climbing all over me.

However, the whole reason for his trip this time was to get out to Komodo Island but that turned out to be an epic fail—we didn't leave Bali. Not for the want of not trying, but the flight got cancelled at the last minute. It was life reminding me it could and will fuck with me at any given time it chooses to.

With the experience of his first visit, Tom was much more prepared for the chaos and was able to adapt better to it this time around. He, in fact, had started to embrace it, even teasing hawkers on the beach, especially those trying to sell him 'authentic' fake souvenirs.

The crashing of waves onto the beach front took my attention, although the giant ball of fire was out in force shining down brightly, the waves were furious today. White foam churned, rolling into a heavy ball before crashing down. Since being in Bali, I had started to get an appreciation for violent waves—they felt soothing and therapeutic. However, a group of lairy holiday makers being obnoxious ruined the moment.

For Australian travellers, it was what Magaluf or Benidorm was to the British, or Cancun was to Americans. It was their holiday dumping ground—arrive, cause carnage, and leave it in a mess. A chuckle escaped me, remembering what a local taxi driver once said. "There are two types of tourists that come to Bali, stupid tourists who get ripped off, and stupid drunk tourists who get ripped off even more." Those were his exact words and the way locals predominantly saw many tourists and foreigners on the island.

But for all the tourists piling in and out, it was also home to a number of spiritualists—who preferred Ubud in the centre of Bali—and to digital nomads and expats. And veganism was a growing trend here too. That is what I'd been over the past eight months—the expat, not the spiritualist vegan. Bali also had its own dark side. While I was here, the Bali Nine had been executed despite the wide pleas for their lives to be spared. The political fallout between Australia and Indonesia had come and gone. But I had seen and experienced how corrupt government officials and police officers were becoming.

It's funny the things you start to see the longer you are in a place. For many tourists who pass through, all they see is the beaches, how cheap things are, waterfalls, and temples, but they don't see what life is really like behind the veil, or as I was finding out, what was behind the facades.

I stretched out on the lounger, finishing my mojito to notice Tom wasn't there… he had wandered off somewhere, probably got distracted by something shiny like a magpie. The waiter came over once more.

"Just one more, Amit?"

"You know me too well." I smirked.

Tom had made his way back from his little wonder, red as a lobster as always—some things will never change. He finished his beer and called for the waiter before jumping back on his lounger.

"Geeza, do you realise, you're an actual nomad now? Like this is what you do, this is your normal life," Tom professed with a hint of envy in his voice.

My feet slipped off the lounger and dug into the cool shaded sand as I sat up. Finally, my eyes averted from the sea, looking towards him and nodded back.

"Yup. Forever roaming the world, mate. I don't think I can ever just go back to living in England like a normal person. People will think it's crazy, can't keep doing it, but I reckon I can. I've gone this long when nobody expected me to."

"Well, wherever you go, when I've got a holiday, I'll come and join ya. You excited to get back to backpacking life?"

"Kinda, gonna be weird, after living this life of luxury, back in hostels, sharing dorms on the move all the time, haggling, new currencies, oh… and fucking night busses. Bro, I've tasted the forbidden fruit, how am I going to go back to basic budget backpacker life?"

Tom couldn't stop laughing at my realisation, shaking his head but not leaving the sun lounger.

"I dunno, mate, you're gonna be feared. But do you even know where you're going yet?" He sat up as the waiter came back.

"Not a clue. Gonna go to England for a week, pick a place, book it, and go."

"Amit, I cannot believe you are actually leaving." He handed over my mojito and handed Tom his beer before taking his leave.

"Yup, this is the end of this road for me. But another journey begins. Don't know where, but let's see where it goes."

When this all started in 2010, nobody thought it would last longer than a few weeks. No one believed that I could make it last. To be honest, even I didn't think it would last that long—after all, I arrived in Australia insecure, with just £600, and no track record of seeing things through. But there was one thing that wasn't taken into consideration—determination. There was good reason for it too. I never really had it in my pre-travelling life, except for when I realised somebody like me, from the gutters of society, could actually travel the world.

It is remarkable just how far determination and desire can take you, no matter what the situation or circumstance.

The desire to stay away from my old life and dark reality in England had been the number-one reason to keep going. Of course, the love of experiencing and discovering new countries and cultures played its part too. But it didn't matter how broke I'd been at times, what life threw in my direction, or the mental and emotional anguish suffered, determination has never wavered.

But let's not kid anybody, not for a single moment did I think when leaving a freezing cold Heathrow Airport in 2010 bound for Australia that this journey would just keep going. Determination has opened doors I didn't think possible. Who could have ever guessed one year would turn into five via the brink of sponsorship in Australia, living out dreams, the unimaginable wonders in New Zealand, the highs and lows of Southeast Asia, the detour of trying to be an adult in Czech Republic, to ghetto snobbing in Bali. My travelling habits, perceptions, feeling more experienced, understanding of the travelling industry, and views towards the world may have changed, but my thirst for wanderlust and the determination hasn't dwindled.

I had turned from inexperienced naïve backpacker to nomad and ready for the next part of my journey, wherever it leads.

I hope you enjoyed reading about my journey, found it entertaining and got an insight into what my every day long-term travelling life was like during those first five years.

Before you click away or put the book down, it would mean the world to me if you could leave a review. Being an independent author, reviews help to get the book more exposure and get it into more hands, so it would be very much appreciated.

Your words can make the world of difference to the success of this book.

COMING SPRING 2023

Join Amit in Volume 2 as he continues on his journey of nomadic evolution, with many more twists and turns, adventures and misadventures and find out how the travel stories in this book relate, influence and shape the bigger story. Check out the sneak peek on the next page.

To keep up to date with Volume 2, sign up to Amit's monthly newsletter, and get a FREE photo album relating to all the stories you've just read.

Sign up for FREE right here: foreverroamingtheworld.com/travel-memoirs-amit-vaidya

Exclusive sneak peek for you

"There… Look, can you see it?" pointed Dennis.

Dennis was still learning his way, still advocating TripAdvisor, but agreed to explore the jungle and not just stick to the higher ground like most tourists did. A ghostly dark figure jumped from one branch to another, taunting us with its screams. Like a pinball machine, my eyes bounced, trying to follow it, but it was difficult in the thick canopy.

Come on, where are you, just wanna say hi, pleaded my inner voice.

More branches cracked, echoing through, wisps of wind pushed by like it was stalking me. But then, the ghostly shadow grew thicker, denser, nearly revealing itself.

"Gotcha!"

I locked eyes on the target. The chase was on, crunching footsteps over the soft jungle floor, instinct helped navigate me past exposed vines and rocks lodged into the earth while it crashed through the canopy above. Between the two of us we could have woken up everything in the jungle. It didn't take long for the little kid within me to burst out of the adult suit once more while I was in pursuit. The ruins, snakes, the most incredible waterfall flowing off rock formations, even the rope bridge took a back seat. With every step getting quicker, my foot sank deeper into the boggy dirt. All the bugs on the floor must have thought there was an earthquake as the chase went on.

How far are we willing to go and what are we going to do if we come face to face with it?

As far as it takes and don't know yet. Concentrate!

Squelches rose up from the ground as the pace quickened, did it know it was being followed? It stopped, waited and carried on after making eye contact.

It knows, it's taunting us, the cheeky fuck.

The chase continued, we crashed through foliage, pushed away, some snapped and others whipped back in descent. It stopped once more, but this time there was a clear opening and nowhere for it to go. Its haunting howl screeched loud, making even the leaves shudder in fear, but it was visible. Its oily thick black fur revealed itself, glistening from the beam of sunrays pushing through the canopy.

Climb up to it, see if it wants to play.

That thing was happening again, turning primitive with my cousin in sight and Alex wasn't here to stop me.

No, idiot, don't do it. Remember Thailand!

"Hey, what are you doing?" Dennis's voice carried through the trees, as he caught up.

"Shh, don't scare it off. Don't worry, I know what I'm doing."

"You, shouldn't, it's dangerous. You get crazier by the day, it's not safe."

The thick bark provided excellent grip. Lifting myself a little higher, ready to reach for my phone, another much sterner – in fact, angrier – voice cried out…

BACKPACKER TO NOMAD VOLUME 2: WATERFALLS, HANDCUFFS AND REVELATIONS!

SPRING 2023

Sign up for FREE right here:
foreverroamingtheworld.com/travel-memoirs-amit-vaidya

If you would like to connect with Amit online and would like to get to know him on a more personal level you can on the following sites:

Website: www.foreverroamingtheworld.com

Facebook: AmitVaidyaAuthor

Twitter: @av9901

Instagram: amit_foreverroamingtheworld

About the Author

For the best part of a decade Amit has got lost chasing waterfalls deep into jungles, been chased by wild animals (and locals), lounged on paradise Islands, and embraced cultures all over the world. He is now using his unique travel experience by writing books to bring joy to avid reading fans and inspire anybody who wishes to travel long term in the future

Printed in Great Britain
by Amazon

23588749R00320